SERGEI TRETYAKOV

a revolutionary writer in Stalin's Russia

BY
ROBERT LEACH

SERGEI TRETYAKOV
A Revolutionary Writer in Stalin's Russia

by Robert Leach

Proofreading by Richard Coombes

© 2021, Robert Leach

Book cover and interior book design by Max Mendor

Publishers
Maxim Hodak & Max Mendor

© 2021, Glagoslav Publications

www.glagoslav.com

ISBN: 978-1-914337-17-8
ISBN: 978-1-914337-18-5

First published in September 2021

A catalogue record for this book is available from the British Library.

This book is in copyright. No part of this publication may be reproduced, stored in a retrieval system or transmitted in any form or by any means without the prior permission in writing of the publisher, nor be otherwise circulated in any form of binding or cover other than that in which it is published without a similar condition, including this condition, being imposed on the subsequent purchaser.

SERGEI TRETYAKOV

A REVOLUTIONARY WRITER IN STALIN'S RUSSIA

BY
ROBERT LEACH

GLAGOSLAV PUBLICATIONS

CONTENTS

List of Illustrations 7
Introduction 9
Prologue: Death of a Poet 13
    Chapter 1. Childhood 15
    Chapter 2. Moscow – The Silver Age 29
    Chapter 3. Revolution 47
    Chapter 4. Moscow – A Golden Age 64
    Chapter 5. The Left Front of Art 89
    Chapter 6. Professor Te Ti-Ko 112
    Chapter 7. Roaring China 124
    Chapter 8. I Want a Baby 142
    Chapter 9. Factography 162
    Chapter 10. To the *Kolkhoz* 185
    Chapter 11. Sharing a Bonfire 205
    Chapter 12. 1935 223
    Chapter 13. At the Crossroads 238
    Chapter 14. And Afterwards 254
Epilogue. *Dustprints* by Robert Leach 261
Index 278

Sergei Tretyakov

1892 – 1937

LIST OF ILLUSTRATIONS

1. Tretyakov, left, aged about 12 19
2. Riga Gymnasium in 2019 22
3. Tretyakov aged about 18, with his younger brother, Lev . . 24
4. Tretyakov, right, with his father, bearded, centre 41
5. Tretyakov after the revolution 61
6. Tretyakov, about 1923 67
7. Poster for *Zemlya Dybom (The World Upside Down)* . . . 74
8. Outdoor setting for *The World Upside Down* 81
9. *A Wise Man* 85
10. Tretyakov photographed by Rodchenko 93
11. *Gas Masks* in Kursk Station gasworks 103
12. The cover of Tretyakov's poetry collection, *Itogo* . . . 107
13. Tretyakov in China, 1924 114
14. *Roar, China!*: Chi and Holey fight on the boat 128
15. Den Shi-hua 133
16. Milda: the Freedom Monument in Riga 146
17. Tretyakov by B.Antonov 153
18. Olga Viktorovna Tretyakova 159
19. 1928: Gorky returns 170
20. Tretyakov, a *kolkhoznik* 186
21. Tretyakov, about 1931 200
22. Friedrich Wolf, photographed by Tretyakov 204

23. Bertolt Brecht, from *People
    Who Shared a Bonfire* by Tretyakov 212
24. Mei Lan-fang 230
25. Mei Lan-fang with Tretyakov and Eisenstein 232
26. Mugshot of 'Tretyakov, S.M.' 244
27. Robert Leach with Tanya Tretyakova, 1991 260

INTRODUCTION

*'Human biographies, or parts of them,
make the most remarkable books.'*
— Sergei Tretyakov, 1934

Sergei Tretyakov collaborated closely with Sergei Eisenstein in both film and the theatre. He was one of the poet Vladimir Mayakovsky's most intimate associates. He was a crucial influence in the formulation of Vsevolod Meyerhold's biomechanics and of Bertolt Brecht's *Verfremdungseffekt*. He was a potent force behind Walter Benjamin's *The Work of Art in the Age of Mechanical Reproduction*. He was therefore absolutely at the heart of *avant-garde* modernism. Yet he seems curiously elusive. Who exactly was he? What did he do? A victim of Stalin's Great Terror, declared an 'enemy of the people', his works were 'disappeared' and his name forbidden to be mentioned.

The first aim of this biography, therefore, is to excavate Tretyakov's life, to give a more rounded, more detailed account of his work, and to indicate the vitality and continued relevance of his thought. A second aim is to humanize him. When he is mentioned in works on Russian Futurism or the *avant-garde* of the 1920s, he seems a distant, almost austere, figure. This book aims to show him as a warm, even charismatic person, an energetic youngster who became an affectionate and caring husband and a fun-loving father. He was kind, sociable and possessed a strong sense of humour and irony. He made rhymes and drawings of and about his siblings, his friends and acquaintances, and he was a gentle and tender-hearted nurse when any member of his family was sick. But he was also an unyielding writer-fighter, the implacable proponent of a happier, revolutionized future.

From his earliest years, expectations were placed on him. He was a leader of the games he played with his brothers and sisters when he was a child, and he turned into a brilliant student and a young poet of the highest promise. He was also interested in ideas. When he addressed a subject, he was determined to get to the bottom of it. He was argumentative and passionate in his belief in the need to drive his projects forward. To call Tretyakov a 'revolutionary writer' (as the subtitle of this book does) is actually to underestimate him. A poet and a playwright, he was in fact an artistic polymath, an intellectual and a formidable cultural theorist. He played the piano with skill, precision and feeling, he could draw cartoons good enough to be reproduced in newspapers, he became one of Russia's foremost radio broadcasters, and he was an outstanding photographer. He approached everything he did ambitiously and critically. He consciously strove to articulate the function of his art, to show how it could organise life, and he addressed these questions thoughtfully and productively.

He lived in a time of transition, when the world was just moving into the technological and informational age, and all this fired him. He worked on such a variety of projects simultaneously that the biographer is sometimes baffled by how to keep each strand of his life and work in balance and comprehensible. For instance, in 1928, Tretyakov was engaged with the theatre and the fate of his play *I Want a Baby*,[1] he was heavily involved with film-making in the Georgian Film Studios, he was editing the *avant-garde* journal *New LEF*, he was experimenting in depth with photo-journalism, he published a long book about China, and he was answering the call of the First Five Year Plan for writers and artists to go to the countryside and help with the collectivization of agriculture. For most people, one or two of these undertakings would have sufficed; for Tretyakov, they were not even all his activities in that one year. Consequently, in this book, the reader will find that the contents of many of the chapters overlap in terms of

---

1 A volume of Sergei Tretyakov's plays *I Want a Baby and Other Plays* was published by Glagoslav Publications in 2019, in my and Stephen Holland's translation into English.

the time they cover, as each one tends to follow only one or two strands of Tretyakov's work over a period of years.

In 1988 I met Tatyana Sergeyevna Gomolitskaya-Tretyakova, the adopted daughter of Sergei Tretyakov, who never had children of his own. She was known by the diminutive, 'Tanya', which is how she usually appears in this book. Her encouragement set me off on this project to make Tretyakov's life and work more accessible to the world. She was a beautiful person, beautiful in her appearance and in her soul. How she retained this intrinsic beauty after all she had been through, I am not qualified to explain. My personal tribute to her appears in the Epilogue to this book, which was originally published by Q.Q. Press in 2004.

Over a period of years I talked with her at length. She stayed at my house in England on more than one occasion, and I saw much of her in Moscow. I recorded some of our conversations, she wrote down for me some of her thoughts and memories, and she gave me copies of playscripts, articles, typescripts and books. These included the memoir, running to over twenty closely-typed pages, 'My Family', written by her aunt, Tretyakov's younger sister, Nina, when that lady was well into her eighties. These materials form a unique source for this book, but they are unpublished. Consequently, usually in the text, where I quote other writers, I have added footnotes to my published sources, but where there are no footnotes, the quotation is taken from one of the typescripts (or sometimes manuscripts) given to me by Tanya. All translations are mine unless otherwise stated.

* * * *

I wish to record my sincere thanks to many people who have helped to make this book possible.

First of these, of course, for the reasons given above, is Tanya Tretyakova, who committed suicide in 1996. Even after her death, she continued to motivate and inspire me.

I am also deeply grateful to Mark Rozovsky, who invited me to direct the first Russian production of Tretyakov's formerly-banned play, *I Want a Baby*, at his Teatr u Nikitskikh Vorot in Moscow. Thanks, too, to my assistant director, Svetlana Sergiyenko, to my translator and personal assistant, Angela Yermarkova, to Viktoria Zaslavskaya who played the part of Milda, and to the whole of the theatre company, actors and crew, who worked on that production.

I have directed this play twice in England, and I would like to thank all those who took part in those productions, too, especially Sarah Rose and Caroline Hadley, my two English Mildas. Thanks too to those who took part in my production of *Gas Masks* at the Midlands Arts Centre in 1989.

Many people have answered my queries, entered into correspondence with me, supplied me with information, or read various chapters of the book in draft form. I wish to thank all of them, including Janis Silavs who showed me round Riga Gymnasium (secondary school), John Biggart, Katerina Clark, Chris Creed, Eddi Ditschek, Mark Gamsa, Rod Griffiths, Tatjana Hofmann, Steve Holland, Jules Horne, Christina Lodder, Simon Nicholls, David Parker and Olga Taxidou. Any mistakes, omissions or misapprehensions in this book, however, are – needless to say – my responsibility.

To my wife, Joy Parker, a special thank you for reading drafts of the book, for reading the part of Milda in public and above all for living with Sergei Mikhailovich and all his works for so many years.

Finally I would like to record my gratitude to Ksenia Papazova of Glagoslav Publications for her enthusiasm, her efficiency and her support throughout my 'Tretyakov project'. She never thought when she took on the project that it would include playing a part in public readings in English of *I Want a Baby*, but even here she did not let me – or Tretyakov – down!

Robert Leach

PROLOGUE: DEATH OF A POET

At the end of March 1930, Sergei Tretyakov returned home to Moscow from the 'Communist Lighthouse' *kolkhoz* (collective farm) where he had been working as a cultural animateur.

A fortnight later, on the morning of 14 April, the phone rang in the Tretyakov flat. Olga Viktorovna, Tretyakov's wife, answered. She went pale, put the phone down. 'Volodya Mayakovsky has shot himself', she said. Their sixteen-year-old daughter, Tatyana, burst into tears, but it was as if Olga had been turned to stone. Tretyakov himself immediately left for Mayakovsky's flat, but the phone in their apartment kept ringing. Olga repeated to all the callers: 'Yes, it's true, this morning'. As her daughter explained, 'Everybody was ringing because if Olga Viktorovna said it, they knew it was true'.

Mayakovsky's body was moved that afternoon to his flat in Hendrikov Alley. The OGPU, the secret police, were in charge. That evening Olga and Tatyana went there, joining Sergei in the adjoining room. Mayakovsky 'lay on the couch in his own room, covered with a rug to his chest, and on his chest was a rose. It was only because of this that one could accept that he was dead. We sat in the next room, weighed down with immense grief. This was not only the shock and the bitterness at the loss of a great poet and a close friend, but a kind of inconceivable sense of the approach of something horrific', Tatyana wrote.

She had known Mayakovsky for almost a decade. Indeed on one occasion when she was a small girl, he had strapped her small body to his own and they had dangled together on a rope over the stage of the Meyerhold Theatre in Moscow while he declaimed his ferocious lines as 'The Person of the Future' in his play *Mystery Bouffe*. Tretyakov had known him for much longer. They had been bohemian Futurist poets together before the First World War, when Mayakovsky had had a brief love affair with one of Tretyakov's sisters. After the revolution they had stood shoulder to shoulder as revolutionary writers: they read their poems together at poetry recitals, they had worked on pro-Soviet advertising jingles and posters together, and they had co-edited the revolutionary *avant-garde* journal, *LEF*.

For three days, Mayakovsky's body lay in state at the Writers' Club with a changing guard of honour of poets and writers – Tretyakov, Nikolai Aseyev, Boris Pasternak, Viktor Shklovsky, the artist Alexander Rodchenko, the former Minister for Education and the Arts, Anatoly Lunacharsky, and others. There was a screen like a slanted black wall over the casket as endless crowds, probably at least 150,000 people, filed past.

The funeral was held at 3 o'clock on the afternoon of 18 April. The first speaker was Sergei Tretyakov. After other speeches, the coffin was draped in black and borne by Tretyakov, Aseyev, Osip Brik and others to the hearse. In the street, mounted police had to hold back the swarming crowds, who followed the procession past more crowds, including people hanging out of windows, up lamp posts and on roofs. At the crematorium the throng was so dense the cortege could hardly pass through. Only family and Mayakovsky's closest friends, including the Tretyakovs, were allowed in. They paid their last respects, the 'Internationale' was played, and the coffin disappeared from view.

Tatyana Tretyakova wrote: 'Then the end, and the terrible anguish. My father threw himself into work'. But something had changed.

CHAPTER 1.
CHILDHOOD

Sergei Mikhailovich Tretyakov was born in the small town of Kuldiga (then called Goldingen) in west Latvia on 21 June 1892.

The region was largely forested. In the summer there were berries to be picked and in the autumn mushrooms. Midsummer days had twenty hours of daylight; midwinter days were correspondingly short.

What is now the independent country of Latvia was then a province in the Russian Empire, though for much of its history it had been dominated by Sweden or Germany and the Lutheran Church. The struggle between Germanic and Russian influences, and the fact that both were in conflict with any independent Latvian aspirations, was the cause of ongoing social and indeed political tensions which simmered, not necessarily openly, all through Tretyakov's childhood. It may be illustrated by the existence and use of different languages in the country at the time – Russian, German and Latvian (also known as Lettish). Thus, Sergei Eisenstein, the future theatre and film director, who grew up in Latvia at the same time as Tretyakov, recorded that he spoke German first, and then Russian, whereas Tretyakov himself claimed that the language he spoke first was Latvian.

By the end of the eighteenth century, Latvia, which incorporated what had been Swedish Livonia and the independent Duchy of Courland, where Kuldiga was situated, had become part of the Russian empire, and in the following decades the tsars devoted considerable energy to Russifying the province. The abolition of serfdom throughout the Russian empire in 1861 was one step in this process, and from the 1880s Tsar Alexander III's policies overtly aimed at reducing the sway of the landholding Baltic German nobility. A primary battleground was over the language question. Alexander III ruled that Russian should become the official language, replacing the use of German – and incidentally Latvian – in educational establishments and in the conduct of official business. It was not a way to reduce tensions.

However, the Russian influence was not entirely baleful. Once serfdom was abolished, Latvia began to industrialise. Railways, factories and banks were opened, and cultural life – new schools, theatres, museums and public parks – began to flourish. In terms of industrial productivity, Riga became the third most productive city behind Moscow and St Petersburg in the Russian empire, and it was the empire's busiest port. Moreover, the long sandy beaches on the Gulf of Riga led to its development as a spa in the 1880s, and it became noted for nude bathing. By the 1890s, over ninety per cent of the Latvian population could read, and Riga's growing importance and prosperity led to the building of some of the most spectacular *art nouveau* buildings in the world. Typically, they were tall, decorative, and even palatial, and still today almost a third of the buildings in the centre of Riga are in this style. It is worth noting, too, that many of the most impressive were designed by Mikhail Osipovich Eisenstein, father of Sergei Eisenstein.

At the same time there was a slow national awakening in Latvia, with an emphasis, perhaps not surprisingly, on the Latvian language. Even as early as the 1850s the 'Young Latvian' movement was gaining adherents. A largely cultural campaign which excavated traditional folk arts, crafts, stories and legends, it was instrumental in planting the seeds of the idea of Latvian independence, and by the 1890s it had given way to the 'New Current', a much more political and aggressive nationalist organisation. It was led by two brothers-in-law, the poet Rainis (whose real name was Janis Plieksans) and Peteris Stucka, and found its voice in their newspaper, *Dienos Lapa*. Self-proclaimed Marxists, New Current was behind the founding of the Latvian Social Democratic Labour Party, and became most active in the 1905 Russian Revolution.

These developments were clearly observable in Kuldiga. With a population approaching 10,000 by 1900, this pleasant town stands at a crossroads between the waterway of the Venta River and the overland route between Riga and Prussia. With wide streets, slatted wooden houses and Lutheran, Catholic and Orthodox churches, Kuldiga is probably best known for the Rumba waterfall, which is reputed to be the widest in Europe at 250 metres. In the second half of the nineteenth century, small industrial enterprises sprang up, making needles, cloth, tobacco products, soap, and vodka and soft drinks. In 1868 the City Hall was erected, followed by a new bridge over the Venta, a new prison, and a German-language secondary school. Social civic societies were established, such as the German Society, the Muse Union and the Latvian Fellowship Union, a gym hall was built in 1877 where annual sporting festivals were held, and a Cyclists Union was formed in 1880. The first local newspaper, the German language *Goldingenscher Anzeiger*, began publishing in 1876, and the Baltic Teachers' Seminary, noted for its choral concerts, was founded here ten years later.

It was in this expanding town that Sergei Tretyakov's parents, Mikhail Konstantinovich Tretyakov and Elfrida Emmanuilovna Meller, met, fell in love and were married. They were an energetically happy couple, but there were skeletons in both their cupboards.

When they met, Elfrida was governess in a well-to-do Kuldiga family, but she had come there from Archangel in the far north of Russia, where her German-speaking, strict Lutheran family lived. Her father taught German in the Archangel secondary school. He was renowned for the flowers he grew in his garden, including, for example, pale blue and black tulips imported from the Netherlands, and his garden was a sight not to be missed by visitors to Archangel. Her mother was Dutch (née van Brinnen), and there were seven children in the family – five boys, none of whom survived into adulthood, and two girls, Elfrida and her sister Emma, a spinster who came to live near the Tretyakovs and who was adored by the Tretyakov children.

Mikhail Konstantinovich was born in Trubchevsk, Orlovsky Province, south west of Moscow. His grandfather was a self-made shoemaker and cobbler but his son, Konstantin, seems to have been something of a wastrel, overfond of alcohol. Mikhail, however, was a clever boy, especially good at Maths, and his teacher, a Mr Sokolov, spotted his potential. Weighing up the situation, Sokolov suggested to Mikhail's mother that the boy should live with him and his family, and this move probably ensured his successful school career. Mikhail graduated with a gold medal, which enabled him to be accepted as a student at the Teachers' Seminary in Moscow. From here he obtained his first job, teaching Maths in the gymnasium at Yelgava, then called

Mitau, before moving to the gymnasium in Kuldiga. His was a restless intelligence: for instance, in later life he taught himself to make shoes like his grandfather, and he also learned bookbinding, and though he remained a member of the Orthodox Church, he indefatigably upheld Tolstoy's social philosophy.

The marriage brought Elfrida and Mikhail into sharp conflict with her parents. Once they had decided to marry, Elfrida had to convert to Orthodoxy, at which point she took the name Yelizaveta. Her inflexible Lutheran father was furious, and refused to accept her. It cast a shadow over the otherwise gregarious Yelizaveta's life, and though she and her father were superficially reconciled some years later when Yelizaveta brought the five year old Sergei to visit her parents in Archangel, the *rapprochement* was partial at best.

Nevertheless she and her husband created a warm, affectionate family. They loved each other and rarely if ever quarrelled. Their shared liberal values meant that they never smacked the children, and if it was Mikhail who spoiled them and Yelizaveta who was the stricter of the two, they never disagreed about how the children should be brought up. Sergei ('Seryozha') was the eldest and there were four other boys – Vyacheslav ('Vava'), Valery ('Lyussik') who died at the time of the Bolshevik revolution, Oleg ('Olezhika' or 'Olka') and Lev ('Levushka') who succumbed to kidney disease in 1940. The three girls were Natalia ('Natasha'), Nina, and Yevgenia, the youngest child, born in 1903. Both Natasha and Nina became actresses: Natasha emigrated to Paris, but Nina, having trained in the Stanislavsky system, remained in Russia. She was reputedly the best looking of the girls.

All the children were gifted, especially in the arts, but probably Seryozha was the most talented. He quickly discovered his natural abilities in the arts, drawing cartoons of his family and friends, learning the piano and discovering he had perfect pitch, and writing little verses about his brothers and sisters. When he was three his father taught him to swim and he became an enthusiastic swimmer. He remembered at the age of four taking gigantic strides down the street in Kuldiga and hearing a voice shouting in Lettish: 'Pietur! Pietur! Pagaid bishkin!' ('Hold on! Hold on! Wait a bit!'). The rhythm of this echoed in his head, as did the cries of the street hawkers who plied their trades in the town. He attended church assiduously, and soon learned the service by heart. These were perhaps scraps which fed his nascent attraction to poetry.

Tretyakov, left, aged about 12.

Meanwhile as a small child he played outdoors by creating a feast of berries which he served to himself on a plate made of a maple leaf. His game of 'robbers' climaxed when he stabbed his 'victim' with a wooden sword, then robbed the body before performing a solemn funeral rite for him. Indoors, he remembered imagining the chair legs as trees and digging up imaginary mushrooms, only to discover that in reality mushrooms are not dug up but gathered. This realization made him furious with himself for what he described later as pandering to a non-realist illusion – an intellectual response which he claimed led to his later theoretical formulations about the arts.

When he was eight he encountered a 'real' poet for the first time in his life. This was Vsevolod Yefgrafovich Cheshikhin, translator of Wagner's *Tristan and Isolde*. 'He sat on the verandah of the *dacha* by the Riga seashore on a small chair with his back to the people passing by and wrote. It seemed to me that his ink flowed like water'. Here was perhaps a model to be followed.

In 1902 the family moved to Tartu in Estonia which, like Latvia, was within the Russian tsarist empire. Tartu was famed for its ancient University, and among young Estonians there was a strong movement, similar to the 'Young Latvian' movement, to rid the province of the longstanding oppressive German culture and landlordism. Like Latvia's 'New Current', the young Estonians claimed to be Marxist, and they, too, would support the 1905 revolution. The family lived in the centre of the city at 11 Myasnitskaya Street in a five-room, first floor flat across the main boulevard from the Emayogi River. It was here that Yevgenia was born, and the family hired a nanny to help them cope.

The Tretyakovs still found plenty of ways to amuse themselves. Mikhail, the father, kept bees in seven squat yellow hives in the garden of the school where he now taught, beside a pond alive with noisy frogs, fruit trees and flowers. Seryozha was his father's assistant in the bee-keeping project: they both wore black net masks making them resemble, as Nina Tretyakova put it, 'devils practising witchcraft over the little yellow dwellings'. Yelizaveta, the mother, followed her estranged father's hobby of cultivating exotic flowers, and the flat became known to their friends as the 'Botanical Gardens'. She even grew an Italian palm tree in a tub.

When Nina and Lyussik fell seriously ill with scarlet fever, their father was their chief nurse, fussing around them in a white lab coat, following the doctor's instructions. Seryozha was again his chief assistant, and he cared for the two younger children 'very tenderly'. One of his jobs was to feed them grapes, which he peeled, removing the pips before commanding the patient to open their mouth. Then he lobbed the fruit into the gaping maw. By this time he was wearing spectacles, but his sister remembered him as tall, handsome and very kind. He was also progressing with his piano playing: he was to become something of a virtuoso amateur musician, playing the piano for pleasure or relaxation for the rest of his life. His sister remembered how he would practice for hours works by Liszt, Skryabin, Chopin and others, and how the family would 'get cosy on the big sofa and listen to him play'.

In 1905 Seryozha was accepted as a pupil at the prestigious Riga Gymnasium, which had been founded as early as 1211 and so was one of the world's oldest educational establishments. The school's *alumnae* from this period included poets, architects, scientists (including a Nobel Prize winner for Chemistry) and politicians, one of whom was Peteris Stucka, co-founder of the New Current movement and later leader of the Bolshevik government of Latvia at the time of the Latvian war of independence in 1918. The school is still housed in the imposing, white-fronted building which Seryozha knew, with wide corridors and high ceilings, where footsteps echo on the uncarpeted floors and the classrooms still contain straight rows of old-fashioned school desks. The Gymnasium was funded by the state, not the city, and consequently accepted students from across the Baltic provinces.

Pupils were aged from 11 to 20, and the main teaching language was Russian. For students who did not speak Russian there were two years of preliminary classes which concentrated on teaching the language. The basic subjects taught, which Seryozha must have learned, were religious studies, Russian, Latin, mathematics, and sports. These subjects were compulsory throughout the student's life at the Gymnasium. In the earlier years, geography, art (mostly drawing) and handwriting were added to this basic curriculum, and these subjects were more or less replaced by Greek, physics, history, German and French from the second, third and fourth grades, while Logic and Cosmology were added in the final year. School started at 9 a.m. and continued until 3 p.m., and each class contained between 35 and 40 pupils. The best students graduated with gold medals, which gave them access to Universities such as Riga, Tartu, St Petersburg and Moscow.

Riga Gymnasium in 2019.

Two years after Seryozha had started his school career here, his father, Mikhail Konstantinovich, was appointed Inspector of National Schools in Latvia, and the family moved to Riga. They rented a cottage near the beach on the gulf of Riga, though Mikhail Konstantinovich also retained a *pied à terre* in Riga itself, where Seryozha stayed during the school term time. The boy's interests at this time ranged widely, from collecting stamps to spiritualism to archaeology and beyond. He read classical literature – 'Ovid's primitive hexameters' particularly appealed – and modern Russian authors such as Konstantin Balmont, Alexander Blok, Mikhail Kuzmin and even more controversial authors like Igor Severyanin, and continued to draw cartoons. In fact his sketch book, full of cartoons, fell into the hands of the headteacher, who easily recognized one caricature as being of himself. Instead of – as expected – flying into a rage at the boy's impertinence, he was delighted, and begged Seryozha to let him have it. When Seryozha gave it to him, he carefully preserved it.

As for poetry, his earliest work mixed Lettish and Russian more or less unintelligibly, but created interesting 'soundscapes':

>   Lyura – plyura
>   Noodle – poodle[2]

Of course he learned rude rhymes from other boys, which amused him, but he attempted to create more ambitious works of his own, including love poetry –

>   It was in the snow
>   That I saw her:
>   You appeared to me,
>   And wound round my heart.

He also made a bold attempt at writing an epic, which described the events of a single day. It opened:
>   The air is pure, the day clear
>   Under the limpid shade.

---

2   Kruchyonykh, A., *15 let russkogo futurizma, 1912-1927*, Moscow: Vserossiiskii soyuz poetov, 1928, p. 46.

Tretyakov aged about 18, with his younger brother, Lev.

It continued in a style which aimed to emulate Gorky's *Song of the Stormy Petrel* and *Song of the Falcon*, but he felt it became contaminated by echoes of Alexei Tolstoy as well as the children's author Sasha Chorny, and he left it unfinished. He was also the moving spirit behind a class-created 'civic poem' which was sent to the writer and human rights activist, Vladimir Korolenko, though no answer was received.

Seryozha was top of his class all through his years at the Gymnasium, and consequently was highly valued by his teachers, though by his own admission he never worked hard at his school books. Still, one teacher told his father that he had never had a student like him – the best pupil he had ever taught, he said. He made friends easily, and many of these visited the family home where they argued, laughed, and enjoyed themselves. Seryozha began to enjoy girls' company, too, laughing with them, making eyes at them and composing little poems for them. At home, he organised any of his contemporaries who visited into a sort of choir to sing favourite Latvian folk songs, or led them in traditional dance figures, perhaps indicating his own sympathies with the New Current movement. All this was watched over by his parents' benevolent eyes. Seryozha's relationship with his mother was particularly strong at this time. When he arrived from Riga at the cottage, he would spend time with her relating what had happened to him that day, perhaps sharing his troubles with her.

In the dark winter afternoons, Seryozha would arrive home, sometimes accompanied by his father in his long fur coat, the pockets of which contained little presents for the younger children. The big stove gave off a warm glow, the samovar was on the table, beside sweets and cakes. Sometimes the family would go skating as the light faded. In summer, long walks were more in order. In the evenings, the family would sit outside till late, talking, Seryozha telling jokes, making comedy out of the day's happenings or reading his latest comic poem about one or other of his siblings:

> Here along the edge of the wood,
> A hen strolls pensively.
> Olka the rascal shoos it along,
> His little freckles bursting with life,
> His nostrils forward-pointing like a cannon.

Or:

> Vava blooms like a spring flower.
> One day he will grow,
> But time stands still waiting for this
> And Vava stays the same.

In fact Vyacheslav grew to be taller than Seryozha. Favourite games were hoopla, 'Cossacks and brigands', and lapta (somewhat similar to cricket or baseball except that the bowler or pitcher had a bat, too, with which he or she hit the ball towards the striker).

They went out at daybreak with large baskets into the forest to find mushrooms, which grew there in wonderful abundance, as well as soft fruit, bilberries and wild raspberries. When they brought their harvest home, they formed a sort of factory chain on the terrace under the management of their mother – one washed the fruit, another dried them, one put them in the pot to boil, another pickled them. The mother was indeed the centre of the family, especially at this time. She not only played the piano well, she also made all the children's clothes. She insisted they all wrote diaries, and, being a native German speaker, she made them all learn German. She read them stories in German and one day each week only German was permitted to be spoken in the house.

The summer of 1909 was particularly remembered because the seventeen-year-old Seryozha organised his siblings to construct on the beach a huge labyrinth made of sand. It took them several days to create this masterpiece even though the sand was damp enough to make building with it comparatively easy. The labyrinth was made of trenches two metres deep and over twenty metres in extent. It had a sand-made flight of steps for people to enter it, and each of the children had a 'room' of their own, the finest being reserved for Seryozha. A flag was flown near the entrance, sacks of new-mown hay made cushions and mattresses, plates, dishes, knives and forks were requisitioned from the family kitchen, and flowers were brought in and arranged in Seryozha's retreat. This enormous enterprise attracted the attention of all sorts of holidaymakers and local people, who came from miles around to admire it. 'They ooh-ed and aah-ed and told of the glory of the Tretyakov labyrinth all down the coast', and it was literally months before all traces of it had been washed away.

Nina remembered one evening in 1912 near the seashore. The children were barefoot. Mikhail Konstantinovich sat on the little porch, his wife not far away, while Seryozha and Natasha sat on the step beside him, and Vava and Nina found room for themselves on the lower step. The night was warm and fragrant with jasmine and lilies, and they watched the stars gradually appear as the sky darkened. When the moon emerged, the scene was washed with a pale light. For a long time they sat silently, until the father began to speak of the stars. He knew the names of many of them, how far they were from earth, how the constellations had been formed and the cosmic history of the planets, the sun and the moon. Nina remembered: 'We sat spellbound, suppressing our breathing so as to hear papa the whole night through! He seemed like a magician!' And she added: 'Under the influence of things like that, our rare, wonderful Seryozha grew up and was formed'.

Yet beyond the peace and fun of this almost idyllic life, the forces of discontent were rising not just throughout the Baltic states, but through the whole Russian Empire, and this social and political unrest must also have impinged on Seryozha's consciousness. The world was entering the bloodiest century in human history, and Russia was at the start of fifty years of irreducible storm and stress. 1905, the year Seryozha went to Riga Gymnasium, was also the year of the 'first' Russian revolution. In Riga, when news of the shooting of peaceful demonstrators in St Petersburg on 9 January was received, a general strike was called. On 13 January the strikers were confronted by the tsarist police and soldiers, who opened fire: 73 were shot dead and more than two hundred wounded. Over the following months, many rose against the oppression of the tsarist regime and also against the privileged German nobility whose huge wealth and land holdings were a stark provocation to poor Latvian peasants and workers. New councils ('soviets') were formed, mostly in rural districts, to voice the people's discontent, and over four hundred estates were seized and often burned to the ground. Through the summer and autumn there were armed conflicts between the poor and their German landlords, notably in Courland around Kuldiga.

In August, martial law was declared by the tsar's pitiless Governor General, Baron A.N. Meller-Zakomelsky, and Cossack cavalry units were drafted in to protect German property holders. The reprisals were brutal: over two thousand Latvian people were executed without trial, teachers and intellectuals as well as peasants, and the military torched ordinary houses and some public buildings in their revenge. More than two and a half thousand Latvians were exiled to Siberia, and many more fled to become refugees in other parts of Europe. Though this dampened the fire of revolution, it failed to extinguish it, and dissent continued for years, marked by daring or insurrectionary acts. In January 1906 a band of revolutionaries raided the main police station in Riga and liberated their comrades held there, and over a period of years the struggle continued even beyond the bounds of Latvia. In the notorious Sidney Street siege in London, for instance, in January 1911, there was a shootout between Latvian revolutionaries on the one hand and on the other the Horse Guards and the Scots Artillery, overseen by Winston Churchill, then British Home Secretary. This smarting political bitterness festered like an inflamed sore through all Seryozha's formative years.

But in the summer of 1913, he graduated from Riga Gymnasium with a Gold Medal, and entered the Law Faculty of Moscow University.

CHAPTER 2.
MOSCOW – THE SILVER AGE

The Moscow to which Sergei Tretyakov came as a student in 1913 was a city in the throes of rapid change. St Petersburg was the capital of the tsarist empire, but Moscow was its engine. Though Russia was still an overwhelmingly rural country, the population of Moscow had now reached a million and a half, and there was an air of thrusting self-confidence in it. Moscow was brash where St Petersburg was effete, and the difference was crystallised in each city's favourite dramatists: where Moscow loved Chekhov and Gorky, St Petersburg preferred Blok and Andreyev. The poet and composer, Mikhail Kuzmin, wrote of

> The loud Moscow accent, the peculiar words, the way they clicked their heels as they walked along, the Tatar cheekbones and eyes, the moustaches twirled upwards, the shocking neckties, brightly-coloured waistcoats and jackets, the sheer bravado and implacability of their ideas and judgments.[3]

The leaders of the city were at this time demanding a much greater voice in the nation's affairs, one commensurate with what they deemed to be their economic and political significance: after all, Moscow had its own newspaper, its own political party, and a burgeoning civic magnificence, evident in new buildings such as the Metropole Hotel, the Trade and Construction Headquarters, and the Moscow Art Theatre.

---

3 Figes, Orlando, *Natasha's Dance*, London: Allen Lane, 2002, p. 211.

Russia was a society deeply divided, the classes rigidly stratified. At the top, of course, was the tsar. Deeply shaken by the revolutionary events of 1905, Nicholas II had with single-minded determination reasserted his authority, and now, in this year of 1913, his fight back climaxed with a series of events to commemorate the tercentenary of the Romanov dynasty, which had ascended the throne in 1613. He undertook a pilgrimage to various historic sites, a journey which ended in Moscow, where he prayed in the Cathedral of the Assumption. Beneath the royal family, but welded to it, was the Orthodox Church, whose ubiquity and power was seen in the ikons visible everywhere – in homes, businesses and shops, as well of course as in the magnificent glittering churches, of which there were so many.

The real power in the city, however, belonged to the 'merchants', the *bourgeois* businessmen, who demonstrated their importance when the tsar arrived in Moscow. Ordered to attend the emperor in the second reception room in the Kremlin when the nobility were to be received in the first, they refused, demanding equality with their supposed superiors – and attaining it. They were the Morozovs, the Shchukin brothers, the Alexeyev family (whose scion, known as Konstantin Stanislavsky, had founded the Moscow Art Theatre): their fortunes were immense, garnered from their huge enterprises – over half Moscow's businesses employed more than a thousand workers each, and industrial production doubled between the 'first' revolution in 1905 and the outbreak of world war in 1914.

But the workers rarely felt the benefit. Because of the fast-increasing demand for factory labour, many peasants flowed into Moscow, which had little by way of suitable accommodation. Many lived in dormitories or barracks which were insanitary and overcrowded. Their working day usually lasted for at least ten hours and wages were less than half of those paid to British workers in comparable positions at the time. No wonder there were strikes – over half a million Russian workers were involved in strike action in 1912, more in 1913. There was a sense that everything was provisional, that political instability – perhaps worse – was virtually inevitable.

And beside, but outside, this simmering volatility was the intelligentsia, the perhaps *déclassé* intellectual elite, cut off from *bourgeoisie* and worker alike, and consisting of writers, musicians, artists and, of course, students, now including Sergei Tretyakov.

Actually, the world of the University was not entirely beyond the political struggle. In 1905, over 3,000 students had demonstrated against the autocracy, burning a large portrait of the tsar and bedecking the University buildings with red flags; and in 1911, when the government moved to limit the University's autonomy, large numbers of the academic staff resigned in protest. The curriculum was still narrow and government-imposed, and a degree was seen as a stepping-stone to nothing much more than a career in the civil service. Tretyakov studied jurisprudence, and though the fees were very low, he earned extra money by tutoring young people, as did other students. But in his case at least, his devotion to his family remained strong, and he gave most of what he earned to his mother.

What really excited Tretyakov when he arrived in Moscow was what has come to be known as the 'Silver Age' of Russian arts and culture. It was a sudden unexpected blossoming which made Russian theatre, dance, and poetry newly admired in western Europe, where it became synonymous with everything modern and *chic*. St Petersburg was the centre of this upsurge, where the royal family marvelled at Fabergé's eggs and where daring night clubs were filled with animated punters. These years before the First World War marked the height of fashionable Symbolism, the ivory tower of Vyacheslav Ivanov, the less easily classified *avant-gardism* of Fyodor Sologub, Mikhail Kuzmin and Nikolai Yevreinov and the strange mysticism of Dmitry Merezhkovsky and Zinaida Gippius. Self-conscious self-doubt was the vogue, and was shared by other, greater poets – Alexander Blok, Andrei Bely, Konstantin Balmont. It was also, of course, the great age of Russian ballet, of the choreographer Mikhail Fokin, and dancers such as Vaslav Nijinsky, Anna Pavlova and Tamara Karsavina. In music, there was a new flowering in the work of composers such as Alexander Skryabin, Alexander Glazunov, Sergei Rachmaninov and others. In Moscow, the deep bass voice of Fyodor Chalyapin was heard, first at Mamontov's private opera, then at the Bolshoi. And these were the years when the Moscow Art Theatre of Konstantin Stanislavsky and Vladimir Nemirovich-Danchenko was at its most influential and popular, and the comedy of its offshoot, the Bat cabaret, under Nikita Balieff, was provoking howls of laughter. The most charismatic and brilliant name in the theatrical world, however, was Vsevolod Meyerhold, and Tretyakov recorded almost with awe two meetings with Meyerhold at this time.

The first took place on the beach at Riga in 1913. Meyerhold appeared, 'a Childe Harold figure in a Spanish cape'. Tretyakov did not dare to approach him, but he wrote a 'hyper-Kuzminish' poem in which he speaks of 'sighing' Meyerhold's name in a typical Silver Age image, 'an amber sigh'.[4] His second meeting was at a party he attended at the great director's flat in St Petersburg. The discussion was animated, much of it centring on contemporary poets and poetry. Meyerhold strongly advocated the work of the newest and youngest poets, not just well-known names like Severyanin, Burlyuk or Shershenevich, but a writer of whom Tretyakov had never even heard – Vasilisk Gnedov. Gnedov was a radical Futurist whose best known work, perhaps, was his poem 'The End', which consisted of the title followed by a blank page. Tretyakov had been a star in his own right in Riga; now his eyes were opening to a much wider, more astonishing cultural and aesthetic world.

The Futurists were the new force in the arts. Poets, playwrights, painters, musicians, they were dedicated to sweeping away the timid and inoffensive (as they saw them) Symbolists. But they went further than this, and swore they would throw the great Russian classical writers, Pushkin, Dostoyevsky and Tolstoy, 'overboard from the Ship of Modernity'.[5] This was from the aggressive and controversial manifesto, published in 1912 under the signatures of David Burlyuk, Alexander Kruchyonykh, Vladimir Mayakovsky and Viktor Khlebnikov, and called, provocatively enough, *A Slap in the Face of Public Taste*. Schismatic and cliquey, the Futurists' love affairs were often torrid but brief, and they formed and fractured artistic alliances with alarming frequency. Among the Futurist poets and other writers, for instance, there were the Moscow Hyleans who became Cubo-Futurists, who opposed the St Petersburg Ego-Futurists, who were allied with the Moscow Mezzanine of Poetry, many of whom were to dissolve into the Centrifuge group in 1914.

But 1913, the year Tretyakov arrived in Moscow, was the *annus mirabilis* of the Futurists, when they produced a wealth of pamphlet collections ('almanacs' they liked to call them), and staged their first

---

4   Tret'yakov, Sergei, *Slyshish' Moskva?!*, Moscow: Iskusstvo, 1966, p. 162.
5   Lawton, Anna (ed), *Russian Futurism Through Its Manifestoes, 1912-1928*, Ithaca: Cornell University Press, 1988, p. 51.

theatre presentations: Mayakovsky's *Vladimir Mayakovsky, a Tragedy* and the opera *Victory Over the Sun* by Khlebnikov, Kruchyonykh and Mikhail Matyushin. They also made a notorious film, inspired by the artists Mikhail Larionov and Natalia Goncharova, *Drama in the Futurists' Cabaret No. 13*, which was released in January 1914. In the visual arts there were Rayonnists, Suprematists, and Non-Sense Realists, who formed groups like the Jack of Diamonds and the Donkey's Tail, and exhibited, including in the notorious 'Target' exhibition in Moscow. The founder of Suprematism, Kazimir Malevich, designed the extraordinary and original costumes and backcloths for *Victory over the Sun*. The Futurists were noisy and iconoclastic, they painted their faces and wore extravagant costumes, and caused mayhem and outrage by their performances in cabarets and on the streets. Two of their most prominent artists, Vladimir Tatlin and Malevich, actually came to blows at the provocatively-titled exhibition 'The Last Exhibition of Futurist Painting' in St Petersburg in 1915.

This was the dazzling, dynamic world which appeared before Tretyakov when he arrived in Moscow. His first ambition was to be a poet. Besides those schoolboy attempts already noticed, he had tried more public poems, such as patriotic verses about the Russo-Japanese War of 1904-5, and he estimated that he had written over 1,500 poems by this time. But he admitted later that most of them were as detached from life 'as the ocean bottom is from a shellfish in the shallows'. He was scared out of his wits by 'real' writers like Sergei Yablonovsky, an art critic who was to disparage Futurist art so brutally that Aristarkh Lentulov, one of the Moscow-based 'Jack of Diamonds' painters, was constrained to squeeze a tube of yellow paint onto a square of cardboard and exhibit it as 'Sergei Yablonovsky's Brain'. But Tretyakov was excited, eager to take part in the ferment, and, as Viktor Shklovsky put it, 'Never was poetry more open to invasion'.[6] And only the poet, according to Ivan Ignatiev in this year of 1913, 'holds in his power the keys to the gates of the Future'. Tretyakov's own efforts were excitable, even grotesque:

> The switch hiccoughed
> And the room gaped white.

---

6   Shklovsky, Viktor, *Mayakovsky and His Circle*, London: Pluto Press, 1974, p. 27.

> So they were already in print?
> Ah, this is poetry?
> > Well, where are you!
> Eat better water melons.
> > Isn't it true?
> > On approval.
> Don't say a word – muse ...[7]

As good fortune would have it, another Moscow University Law student, a year ahead of Tretyakov, was equally enthralled by Futurist poetry. He was Boris Lavrenov, a Ukrainian who had published his first verses in 1911. Tretyakov, with encouragement from a friend, took a 'madrigal-style' poem of his to Lavrenov, who was active in the newly-forming Mezzanine of Poetry group centred around Vadim Shershenevich. Though Lavrenov's contributions to the new group's first 'almanac', *Vernissazh*, are poems described by one of Futurism's most discerning critics, Vladimir Markov, as 'exaggeratedly foppish',[8] he was obviously a well-practiced networker: he also appeared in the film, *Drama in the Futurists' Cabaret No. 13*. Later he became known as a novelist, and he was to help formulate the theory of 'drama without conflict' in the 1930s and win a Stalin Prize in 1946 and again in 1950.

Shershenevich was a prolific poet, dramatist and theorist who was busily buzzing with his project to create the new Mezzanine of Poetry. He was the son of a Professor in the Faculty of Law in which Tretyakov was studying, but his writings, as one critic noted, 'express a fundamentally *avant-gardist* rebellion: he is alienated, bitter, aggressively hostile, but at the same time witty, ironic and humorous'.[9] The group met at Lavrenov's lodging, and consisted usually of Lev Zak, the artist also known as Khrisanf, Konstantin Bolshakov, Rurik Ivnev, as well as Lavrenov himself, Shershenevich and Tretyakov, with David Burlyuk and Alexei Kruchyonykh also in attendance occasionally. Zak

---

7   Kruchyonykh, A., *15 let russkogo futurizma, 1912-1927*, Moscow: Vserossiiskii soyuz poetov, 1928, pp. 53-4.
8   Markov, Vladimir, *Russian Futurism: A History*, Washington D.C.: New Academia, 2006, p. 101.
9   Bristol Evelyn, 'Turn of the Century: 1895-1925', in Moser, Charles A., *The Cambridge History of Russian Literature*, Cambridge: Cambridge University Press, 1989, p. 446.

proclaimed from their inception that these Futurists were 'all a little crazy', but the group – and Shershenevich in particular – was extremely important to Tretyakov, whose poetry now appeared in the group's first almanac, *Vernissazh*, published in the autumn of 1913. Shershenevich's fundamental argument was that 'our era has changed human sensibility too much for my verses to be similar to the works of past years', and he proposed a completely new subject matter: the city, the machine, urban life. But formally he also contended that 'poetry is the art of combining self-sufficient words, word-images. The poetic text is an uninterrupted series of images'. These images should be based on 'exceptional novelty', he said, and should be 'fast as a bullet',[10] and their purpose was to rejuvenate the subject. Shklovsky famously suggested that a stone's 'stoniness' should re-emerge because of the power of the poetic image, though this was not perhaps as original an idea as it seemed to many at the time. Shelley, for instance, had argued a hundred years earlier that poetry 'purges from our inward sight the film of familiarity which obscures from us the wonder of being'. Nevertheless, all this, which seemed so new, was absorbed by Tretyakov, pushing his work towards quintessential Futurism. Shershenevich and Tretyakov became fast friends, and despite the vicissitudes and quarrels among the individuals and the groups forming the Futurist movement, the two remained close at least until the revolution: when Shershenevich published his major theoretical treatise, *Green Street*, in 1916, he dedicated it to Tretyakov.

But the Mezzanine of Poetry was not Tretyakov's only contact with prominent Futurist writers. In 1913, perhaps through Shershenevich, who had a foot in most Futurist camps, he also met the boldest, most brilliant and most conspicuous Futurist poet in Russia, Vladimir Mayakovsky, who was to play an altogether more central role, not only artistically but also politically and socially, in Tretyakov's life. Tretyakov's early attempts at Futurist verse had been comparatively crude. When he went with Bolshakov to hear Mayakovsky read at a Symbolist literary salon, he was amazed and awed at the way Mayakovsky was able to shock and dumbfound his audience by his stormy reading from his just-published first slim volume of poems, called unashamedly *I*:

---

10   Lawton, Anna (ed), *op. cit.*, pp. 148, 150, 151.

> On the trampled pavements
> 		of my soul
> 		the footsteps of madmen bang
> hard phrases of heels
>   where
> 		cities
>   are hanged
> and in cloud-nooses congeal
> 		towers' illucid
>   flight –
> I alone go to shriek that on cross-
> 						roads
> 		policemen
> 		are cruci-
> 				fied.[11]

Mayakovsky's explosive presentation as much as the work itself intimidated and amazed his hearers, and that evening Tretyakov did not dare to read: he had nothing explosive enough.

But perhaps Tretyakov's reluctance stemmed also from the fact that he hardly knew what to write about, he suffered from 'a lack of themes'. He wrote later: 'I am bewildered when I recollect how, in my student years long before the revolution, there were times when I did not know what to write about, that I suffered from the disease of "subjectlessness".'[12] Despite this, he determinedly followed his urge, and soon became one of the more prolific of the Futurist poets. Markov sums up his achievement in these years thus:

> In 1913 Tretyakov wrote urbanist poetry, which, in true Mezzanine fashion, showed the modern city both from outside and inside. In one poem the poet feels a gay desire to approach a female passer-by; in another an automobile ride to the beach is described in all its futurist beauty of speed; in a poem filled

---

11   Marshall, Herbert (trans. and ed.), *Mayakovsky*, London: Denis Dobson, 1965, p. 95.
12   *Literature of the Peoples of the U.S.S.R.*, Moscow: VOKS illustrated almanac, No. 7, 1934, p. 117.

with images of steel, factories, railroads, and construction, a paean to the strong is sung and new music is heard in the clanking of metal.

Markov adds that 'in this characteristic, Tretyakov strikes an original note … anticipating much of the early Soviet poetry, both futurist and non-futurist', and continues with an evaluation of Tretyakov's 'inside' urbanist poetry: 'It is a true poetry of the interior, concentrating on little objects in a city apartment, while the city outside the walls is not forgotten'. He quotes 'A Blotter':

> A rocking-chair of a pampered lady.
> A sole has stepped on my poetry.
> And everything is in reverse.
> Ha, Ha! It rocks to the left, to the right.
> Is it not the drunken pendulum of a sober clock?[13]

The poems are often in free verse, though sometimes Tretyakov employs more formal metre, and sometimes these features are combined imaginatively, as in 'The Lift', with its alternating long and short lines. Deft and mischievous, this poem records a fleeting but common experience:

> In the lift, you're reading, like a cat,
> The dimming print.
> Straight up – that's our common path
> In the singing lift.
> We two are here in a moving cupboard.
> Let's play flirting!
> Don't brush off with that reproachful look
> My offering of myrtle.
> I mean, you know, children play at love!
> Ah, my god!
> I completely forgot, this is your floor – the third.
> Mine is – the eighth.

---

13   Markov, Vladimir, *op. cit.*, pp. 112, 113.

Other poems are even more adventurous formally: 'The Fan' uses double columns, folding and unfolding like its subject in what is perhaps a very early example of concrete poetry.

His longer poems tend to be less experimental formally, relying on a kind of impressionism to make their effect, while maintaining the futurist stance, as in 'The Fireman':

> Smoke twists like a blue pretzel.
> The iron flanks sweat oil.
> Gleams from the lamp kiss the engine tender
> Dressed in its anthracite bonnet.
> An iron pause.
> Then the cockerel bell crows,
> The brakes draw breath,
> Over the funnel a fluff cloud rises.
> I listen for the squawk of the wheels,
> The cheeping of the piston in its cylinder.
> I'm heady with the sparks, the clanking
> Raising wind like a propeller.
> Under the rods, the splashboards bang,
> Spinning, plunging, squealing through the aperture.
> I grease the rust spots with lamp-black,
> With a red rag on the blue footplate,
> And below me the system guffaws,
> Gargling the oil in its belly.
> We move forward … Nerves black …
> Strung rails … Faster … Tack – tack – tack …
>
> And further.
> And further.
> In the boiler the atmosphere strains
> Every sinew.
> The pressure gauge advances towards danger.
> Anthracite blazes
> In the firebox mouth.
> It's grouching. Get it belching!
> What if a tooth is shattered,
> If buffers crash into buffers?

Get on! Get on! Get on!
Get on with a stump of a spoke.

Crunch. Jolt. More jolts. In the iron cell
I screw up my mug, grab the poker.
Rake the fire to its furthest corner.
Just a drop of squeezed-out oil.
Just drops from the light of my eye.

Cut the distance, cut the plains, cut the mountains.
Serene, smooth to the touch of the hand
The greased metal of tap and grooves.
Stand back!
The smeared sleekness of the gleaming engine
Flashes by.

Foo, it's hot. Foo, foo!
The signal drops its iron hand –
Under its arch cleanly, mettlesome, whistling.

Grit your teeth.
Don't breathe.
Stop, and freeze the iron orchestra.

Kettledrum – buffers.
Tympany – wheels.
French horn – hooter.
First violins – springs.
Flutes – pistons.

The rhythm is stuttering, sharper, shorter.
I'm in a turbulence of levers,
Teeth deflating the noise of the crank handles.

I'm nearer … getting nearer …
Sounds getting quieter … jingling deadening …

It fades in the ears,
Smooths the soul
Of the fireman.

'The Fireman' exhibits all the features of Futurist poetry which Shershenevich sought: the subject matter is typically 'urbanist', exulting in the beauty of speed, the power of the machine, the technical detail of the engine itself; and the images flash past, yet are unpredictable, startling (the blue smoke twisting like a pretzel, the bell like a cock's crow, the piston cheeping, the whole system guffawing). Typically Futurist, too, is the use of free verse, and the impressionistic fervour of the whole.

Thus in Russia's 'Silver Age', Tretyakov had found a distinctive voice. After *Vernissazh* his work was widely published. In 1915 he was well enough known to be included in the Odessa Futurist group's almanac, *Auto in Clouds*, and he made his first collection, to be called *Gamma Rays*, which however was never published, perhaps because of the war.

By 1914 the state of affairs in Russia was becoming seriously revolutionary, yet that summer was for Tretyakov extraordinarily happy and fulfilling. This was not simply because he was gaining a reputation, but because early that year his family moved to a temporary lodging in Moscow. This was ostensibly because the Baltic climate was undermining the health of Yelizaveta Tretyakova, Tretyakov's mother, but perhaps also the political situation played its part, as well as their wish to be closer to their beloved eldest son. Mikhail Tretyakov, the father, as has already been noted, was extremely close to Sergei, and even though they frequently disagreed, they talked and argued energetically and even their disagreements seemed to help cement their closeness to one another.

Then in the summer, Mikhail Tretyakov rented a *dacha*, a country cottage in the village of Pavshchina just out of Moscow on the Riga road. Soon after they had settled in, Yelizaveta was looking out of the window, expecting Sergei. She saw two people approaching – Sergei and another man, even taller than her own tall son. It was Vladimir Mayakovsky. With a cigarette in his mouth and a heavy walking-stick in one hand, he clutched a package in the other hand which he held out to the hostess. 'Something for tea', he said. The rest of the family

Tretyakov, right, with his father, bearded, centre.

had gone boating on the nearby river, and the two poets went to join them. He was to become their most frequent visitor that summer. All the family took to him, and he became 'Uncle Volodya' to the younger children. Despite being told not to, he almost always brought presents of sweets, knick-knacks or treats for them, and cakes or pastries to eat. They were amused and amazed by the way he could flip a cigarette up and catch it in his mouth, and they noticed he was very clean, always washing his hands, sometimes even in the bucket outside when there was no water available indoors. He rarely laughed out loud, but would grunt and curl his lips upwards, and he was always witty and fun.

Perhaps the only cause for disharmony was Mayakovsky's addiction to gambling. Sergei Tretyakov was always adamantly opposed to playing at anything for money. They argued. Mayakovsky continued to gamble. They remained fast friends. And an extra reason for his continuing frequent appearances was the presence there of Natasha, the eldest girl in the family, with whom he conducted a fairly discreet, but unmissable *affaire du coeur*. How serious this was is not clear. Natasha was certainly not the only young woman to catch Mayakovsky's eye at this period of his life, and this was probably not a *grande passion*, much as Natasha's siblings were excited by it.

And so the last summer before the world war passed in a sort of idyll – or so it was remembered by this family, as by so many families across the world. But this empyrean was not to last. At the beginning of August, suddenly Russia was at war with Germany. The Tretyakov family were caught unawares. After considering their options, they left for Moscow. They now moved into a flat at 7 Molochny Lane, which included a terrace and a fruit orchard, and Natasha began training to be a nurse with the Sisters of Mercy. Her romance with Mayakovsky was over.

But Mayakovsky remained Sergei's friend, and still visited the flat in Molochny Lane very often. He was not the only one. Many of Sergei's Moscow friends and colleagues called on the family, and stayed to tea or supper and into the evening. The autumn was mild, and the family and their visitors gathered on the terrace outside for tea while the weather lasted. They included Vadim Shershenevich, of course, leader of the Mezzanine of Poetry; Nikolai Aseyev, a poet with whom Tretyakov remained friends for the rest of his life, and who became something of a grand old man of Soviet letters after the death of Stalin in 1953; and the Formalist critic and writer, Viktor Shklovsky. There was much banter between these young men at the start of their careers – witty remarks, clever observations, learned arguments and much good-hearted laughter. Yelizaveta, their hostess, was constantly amazed by how much they knew, considering that they were only in their very early twenties. On some evenings, as it grew dark, Sergei played the piano. Everyone listened in silence. At other times, at the invitation of their hostess, the poets read their works, and then the literary discussion and argument lasted beyond midnight.

One evening Yelizaveta prepared a special dish of jellied fish. She was talking animatedly in one corner of the dining-room with Viktor Shklovsky, her daughter Natasha and others while Sergei sat at the piano, fingering out a melody which gave an aura of lightness and warmth to the gathering. The table was laid. It was time to be seated, but Yelizaveta wished to make some slight rearrangement. She put the circular dish with the jellied fish on a chair. A moment later, Shklovsky moved away to catch someone else's attention, and flopped down into the chair where the fish had been placed. A howl went up. For a moment Shklovsky was rooted to the chair, then he sprang up in horror. Realizing what he had done, he burst out into a guffaw which turned into a shriek. And with that, after a moment of puzzled silence, everybody else – nearly twenty people – was screaming with laughter and delight. 'We laughed till we cried', Nina Tretyakova remembered. Yelizaveta was more concerned that Shklovsky should not have hurt himself than with the fate of the jellied fish, which lay in two squashed pieces on the plate. And Shklovsky himself could barely stop laughing, if somewhat guiltily, as Sergei took him to his room to clean him up.

On another day that autumn, the guest was Alexander Nikolayevich Skryabin. The first time Tretyakov brought him home, his mother was in the house. She immediately recognized the composer, having been an admirer of his since attending concerts where he had played. When she offered him tea, he refused, saying he wasn't awake enough yet. But he was interested in what she was doing, and watched her attentively and encouragingly. She told him how her son played his twelfth étude, which she loved particularly, whereupon Skryabin turned to Tretyakov, saying: 'My dear Sergei Mikhailovich, I would be very happy if you would indulge me by playing my twelfth étude, which gives your mother great pleasure.' Tretyakov willingly obliged, and when he had finished Skryabin and Yelizaveta clapped. Then Skryabin went to the piano and improvised for perhaps five minutes. Shutting the lid, he stood up and expressed his admiration of the instrument – 'light touch keyboard and a beautiful sound'. The Skryabin scholar, Simon Nicholls, confirms that this response is not surprising: 'he would have loved an instrument with a light touch, as he himself was a pianist with not much physical strength but an exquisite range of tone colours'. Nicholls, assuming correctly that Tretyakov was not a professional pianist but a very talented amateur, further notes that 'there may have been something not stereotypical in the playing, a touch of imagination and originality which Skryabin enjoyed, and maybe not such a massive sound production as one would expect with a professional Russian pianist'.[14] The two men continued friends, and soon Skryabin would get Tretyakov to play early drafts of his late piano sonatas, which they would then discuss and Skryabin would amend and improve for Tretyakov to play again.

Another musical connection was with Alexander Nikolayevich Vertinsky, a Ukrainian singer and actor who had come to Moscow in the hope of joining the Art Theatre company. When that failed, he trained as a male nurse and met Natasha Tretyakova, and they served together on a hospital train tending the wounded who were being brought home from the front. As their relationship blossomed, Vertinsky became a regular guest at the Tretyakov flat, and stayed there when in Moscow for some days. He clearly respected and trusted both Sergei Mikhailovich and his mother, and confided his feelings to them both. Tretyakov also worked with him on his songs, sitting at the piano and harmonising the music while Vertinsky hummed the melody. In 1916 Vertinsky left the hospital service to concentrate on his performing career. He created a Russian Pierrot character, and quickly became immensely popular. On one occasion that winter Natasha took her younger sister Nina to the Little Petrov Theatre to one of his concerts. 'We arrived. It was impossible to fight one's way to the entrance! The hullaballoo was unbelievable! I had not seen such a stylish audience for a long time. Ladies in fur coats, jewels sparkling. The men were all in beaver fur. It was the winter of 1916, and no-one, obviously, had the slightest idea that this was the last winter when

---

14   Private communication, March 2020.

they would be able to be so ostentatious in their magnificence!' After the war both Natasha and Vertinsky moved to Paris, but by then their relationship was over.

Tretyakov shone not merely in music. His cartoons were reproduced in a number of papers and journals, and he also practiced poker work. He drew on a piece of wood, and he – and sometimes his mother – then went over the lines of the drawing with a red hot poker. The resulting burned impression was then varnished and polished to make a kind of traditional Russian folk artwork in its own right.

And meanwhile the war rumbled on, with Russia trying to keep pace with the other belligerent powers. The first battles, at Tanenburg and the Masurian Lakes, had seen heavy Russian defeats. By the end of 1914 at least a million Russian soldiers had been killed, wounded or captured. And the next year saw more defeats, climaxing in the 'great retreat' of the summer when the Russian army fell back over 300 miles after losing the Battle of Gorlice-Tarnow. In Moscow, German shops and offices were looted and set ablaze, and there were even demonstrations against the tsarina, Nicholas II's wife, who was of German origin. The following year matters degenerated further, despite the pyrrhic victories of the 'Brusilov Offensive' in the summer. There were dire shortages of bread and fuel, and inflation was rampant. At the front the soldiers were ever more likely to refuse to fight – 'Give us boots first!' was their cry, while a Moscow joke had it that the English were happy to fight to the last drop ... of Russian blood! Deserters were everywhere. The shambolic Duma, dissolved, then recalled, was unable to intervene in the tsar's incompetent autocracy which was in charge of the fighting. By 1916, hopelessness had set in, an acknowledgement that Russia could not continue.

That was the year Tretyakov graduated from Moscow University with a first class degree. Although he himself said that he 'lived like a marmot', that is, he kept his head down, during his University career, he also admitted that he never worked hard at his academic studies, which surely must be true of his years at the University since he spent so much time and energy on his poetry. Now he went to work for the city's civil service, and lent his support to the Social Revolutionary Party, though it is doubtful that he ever became a paid-up member of the party. Tatyana, his stepdaughter, said that he was never a member of any political party, though under interrogation after his arrest in 1937, he said he was a member of the SRs from 1915. This may be doubted.

The Social Revolutionaries aimed to unite the intelligentsia with the peasantry, and also with the working class, especially those many workers who had recently been drawn into the cities from the countryside. The basis of their appeal was their belief in and work for a democratic revolution, which many felt was the only possible way of saving war-ravaged Russia. The party had been established in 1901 under the Moscow University law graduate, Viktor Chernov, a well-read radical who liked to lard his speeches with slightly abstruse quotations while he 'minced and rolled his eyes' dramatically.[15] Even as a student leader he had been imprisoned for his political actions, and he was in exile in Paris in 1917 when the second revolution broke out and the tsar was overthrown. The Social Revolutionaries looked for inspiration to two veterans of the democratic struggle in Russia: the renowned anarchist, Pyotr Kropotkin, who also returned in 1917 after no less than forty years in exile, and Yekaterina Breshko-Breshkovskaya, who had spent almost as long in prison or in Siberian exile. Their most charismatic leader, though in 1916 he was barely known, was Alexander Kerensky. He and Chernov cordially detested one another, but Chernov was to serve in Kerensky's short-lived Provisional Government in the summer of 1917, as indeed was Breshko-Breshkovskaya. Their drive towards democracy was widely supported in 1916, even if their libertarianism, radicalism and anarchism, however appealing, remained very ill-defined. And this vacuity was soon to be found out.

But at that time, towards the end of 1916, Tretyakov was not the only person who saw hope in the Social Revolutionaries. It was only in the furnace of the coming revolution that this vague optimism faded away.

---

15   Trotsky, Leon, *The History of the Russian Revolution*, London: Pluto Press, 1979, p. 247.

CHAPTER 3.
REVOLUTION

1917 – the year of revolution – began with a profound, irresistible rumbling through all Russia. Strikes, marches, demonstrations, and suddenly the people were rising up and the hollowness of the empire, and the nakedness of the emperor, were exposed. They hurled the tsar from his throne, and there was an amazed awakening. 'The revolution was a great and joyous surprise for us', said one Social Revolutionary.[16]

But, though the tsar had gone, the people were still hungry, they were still shattered by the relentlessness of the war, still yearning for a better world, a happier society. Peace, land, bread. To overthrow the tsar was not enough. More juddering convulsions were to come. A Provisional Government under Prince Lvov was established. It crumbled to nothing within less than three months. Alexander Kerensky, a Social Revolutionary, formed a new Provisional Government.

Sergei Tretyakov supported the Social Revolutionaries, though how ardently may be questioned. Growing out of the old *narodniks*, they had been an integral part of the 1905 revolution, and still aimed to bind the intelligentsia with the peasantry and, as far as possible, with the industrial working class, too. Their proposed land reforms were highly popular, and they rode a wave of support in the summer of 1917, but the peasantry were too fractured – rich peasants, middle peasants, poor peasants – and their aspirations too varied, and barely ever chiming with those of the SR intellectuals, so that it

---

16   Faulkner, Neil, *A People's History of the Russian Revolution*, London: Pluto Press, 2017, p. 112.

was no surprise when the party split into opposing groupings, 'Left' and 'Right'. Chernov and Kerensky had both been part of Lvov's Government. Now, just as his party was breaking apart, Kerensky rose to the top. But his principles or policies were obscure, and the agonising situation only served to obfuscate them further. Kerensky liked power, rather than what good he could do with power.

Kerensky's Government failed to answer the call: peace, land, bread. The peasants, the disenchanted soldiers, the furious proletariat had found a partial answer in their own Soviets (councils), which were established not only in the big cities but in many agrarian parts as well, and quickly became parallel if centrifugal powers in the land. Their affairs were often conducted rowdily, often anarchically, but they were the closest thing to democracy Russia had ever seen, and it was here that the Bolsheviks concentrated their energies. In a further spasm in October, they, the Bolsheviks, seized the central power of government. They proclaimed a Union of Soviets.

Most of this was centred on Petrograd, the newly-Russified name of the capital. In Moscow, where Tretyakov and his family were living, the opening shots in this revolutionary year had started on 27 February, a week later than in Petrograd. Disorder, vandalism and sporadic looting took place over the next months, and by September the Bolshevik majority in the city Soviet were demanding an immediate insurrection. In October, Petrograd revolted, and Moscow immediately followed suit. The Red forces bombarded the Kremlin, St Basil's Cathedral and other treasured buildings with a ferocity which brought even Anatoly Lunacharsky, a lifelong Bolshevik in Lenin's inner circle, to tears and the brink of resignation. John Reed, the American reporter, after some difficulty, found a cab driver who told him:

> It takes a good deal of courage to drive a sleigh [around Moscow] nowadays ... Driving along, or waiting for a fare on the corner, all of a sudden *pooff!* a canon ball exploding here, *ratt-tatt!* a machine-gun ... I gallop, the devils shooting all around. I get to a nice quiet street, and stop, doze a little, *pooff!* another canon ball, *ratt-tatt* ... Devils! Devils! Devils! B-r-r-r![17]

---

17   Reed, John, *Ten Days That Shook the World*, Harmondsworth: Penguin, 1977, p. 223.

Shop windows were smashed, shell holes pitted the streets, pavements were torn up. Banks, offices and restaurants were in ruins, and Reed heard how children had played a particularly dangerous form of 'Chicken' – they waited in doorways till the firing slackened, and then tried to cross the street without being shot. A Moscow joke told of a doctor, an engineer and a revolutionary each claiming that their ancestor had begun the world. 'Nobody could have been brought into the world without me', said the doctor. 'But without me,' said the engineer, 'the world couldn't have been created from chaos'. 'And who d'you think created chaos?' asked the revolutionary.

These were dangerous times for the Tretyakovs, living amidst this mayhem in their comfortable apartment with its terrace and fruit orchard. Sergei's attitude to the revolution at this moment in its stormy history is difficult to gauge, but it is clear that he was not much in sympathy with it. Unlike his friend, Vladimir Mayakovsky, or the highly-regarded theatre director, Vsevolod Meyerhold, he did not declare for the Bolsheviks as soon as they took power. The fact that there seem to be no records of Tretyakov's stance is typical for those who were not actively supporting the Bolsheviks at the time. Opposition to the revolution was not something to be spoken of after the revolution had happened. Moreover, to add to his difficulties, his mother's health was deteriorating. It seems that at some point in the early part of 1918, the family decided to decamp south. They reached the town of Nikolayevsk, found a suitable property, and waited. Interestingly, Nikolayevsk became Pugachyov that year, substituting the name of the leader of a famous peasant revolt for that of the abominated tsar.

Pugachyov, over 400 miles south east of Moscow, was on the edge of the Samara Province. The Bolsheviks had seized control here at the end of 1917, but by early 1918 they were losing their grip. The defence of Samara was left to a small force comprised mainly of Latvian volunteers. They were assailed by one of the marauding Czech Legions, who by the summer of 1918 had ousted them and installed a Social Revolutionary authority. Did either of these facts – the Latvian Red defenders or government by the Social Revolutionary party – have a bearing on the Tretyakovs' decision to move here? Under interrogation after his arrest in 1937, Tretyakov said he went to Samara after being asked to do so by prominent SRs in Moscow, and asserted that he worked for the Ministry of Internal Affairs of the Samara Government. It is impossible to tell what truth, if any, there is in this, since when he said it his life was at stake, and he was engaged in cobbling together a complex series of assertions and half-truths which might save him. Whatever was the case, Sergei himself was in Pugachyov for less than a year, though the rest of the family stayed longer.

Pugachyov, and the Samara Province, were actually trapped, caught between crossfires, as it were, though the situation was still so fluid this was barely discernible. It was a strategic pivot in the nascent civil war. White armies were threatening from the south and the east, while the Reds were regrouping to the north. The Social Revolutionary administration, which was actually only to last until October, called itself the Committee of Members of the Constituent Assembly ('Komuch'), with pretensions to all-Russian government. The Constituent Assembly had been disbanded in Petrograd by the Bolsheviks after a single sitting. Now any available members, mostly 'Right' Social Revolutionaries, but at its height numbering more than a hundred, joined it, including their leader, Viktor Chernov, as well as the 'grandmother of the revolution', Yekaterina Breshko-Breshkovskaya. Their aim was to restore parliamentary democracy, and perhaps to reinstate the government of Alexander Kerensky, although by now he had fled the country. Thus, it saw itself as temporary, a stepping-stone towards a restoration of what had been swept away.

The Komuch proudly proclaimed a new freedom, but was immediately found to be expanding the numbers of political prisoners, mostly Bolsheviks, until at least 4,000 were in gaol. They attempted to restore the old *zemstvos* (local councils) and return factories and land to their former owners, dispossessed by the revolution. But they were fatally lacking in genuine support: the middle classes were actually looking to the Whites for their salvation, while the workers and peasants had their own soviets which ignored many of the Komuch's rulings. Meanwhile food shortages continued and inflation climbed. In the Province's elections in August, nearly two-thirds of those eligible failed to cast a ballot, and the Komuch received the backing of only fifteen per cent of the voters. Furthermore, by this time, the Czech Legion which had protected them was disintegrating, so that Komuch was forced to try to create an army of its own. But the peasants refused to enlist, and even when Komuch introduced conscription, few were recruited. September was harvest time – the peasants had better things to do. The Komuch set up courts, sent Cossack mercenaries on punitive expeditions to villages, burned houses and flogged and hanged those still recalcitrant. In reply, many towns and villages, including Pugachyov, formed their own militias and joined the Reds. On 7 October the Reds re-took Samara. Most of the Social Revolutionaries and supporters of the Komuch fled east to join the White forces. Further chaos ensued: as Trotsky recalled, 'the civil war raged with especial fury in the south and was accompanied by constant changes of government'.[18]

And it was not just the south which was a cauldron of despair and rage. East Russia, too, was beset with warlords, gangsters and desperadoes, Red militias, White counter-revolutionaries, peasants trying and sometimes succeeding in organising more or less autonomous communes, and foreign invaders – Japanese, British, Italians, Americans and French. Most dangerous of all were the six invading Czech legions, whose power grew as they conquered and held the Trans-Siberian railway, the spine of all eastern Russia, its crucial communications and supply line.

There had been a muddled standoff between the Komuch and the White forces to the east. Now many from Samara Province drifted to the White would-be state centred on the city of Omsk and largely defended by yet more Czech legions. A 'Directory' was established which took over the Komuch's claim to represent the whole of Russia, though its headquarters seem to have been, literally as well as perhaps symbolically, a disused railway carriage shunted into a siding beyond the city's boundary. After several complex manoeuvrings, plots and intrigues, in November 1918 the leadership was assumed by Admiral Alexander Kolchak. A hot-tempered martinet with an exaggerated sense of his own substance, Kolchak was soon having his apparent Social Revolutionary 'allies' arrested, imprisoned, deported or simply murdered, thereby destroying any possibility of a compromise between Reds and Whites. His aim was to march on Moscow, despite continuing inflation, rampant corruption among his followers, and banditry and peasant opposition, often violent, in the area he purported to

---

18   Trotsky, Leon, *My Life*, Harmondsworth: Penguin, 1975, p. 20.

control. His forces were reinforced by conscription, but undermined by desertions. He was undeterred, and pressed forward westwards.

From January to April 1919, Kolchak's armies advanced on several fronts. However, they failed to reach Samara, one of their first objectives, even though they came close to Pugachyov. Then the Red Fifth Army counter-attacked. The White army was no match for them. They began an increasingly disorganised retreat, pursued by the Red Army as well as uncoordinated Red militias, and harried by unscrupulous outlaws and by rebellions in the cities and the countryside they thought they controlled. The Reds took Omsk in November, a year after Kolchak had assumed the title of 'Supreme Ruler' of Russia in that city, and his army ran ever faster as the cruel winter closed in. Kolchak's train broke down. The Czechs in control of the Trans-Siberian railway refused him assistance. He was stranded. Many of his soldiers, their families and camp followers were forced into the so-called Great Siberian Ice March, when up to 30,000 people attempted to cross the frozen emptiness of Lake Baikal and very many perished in temperatures as low as or lower than -40°. The Czechs handed Kolchak over to the Social Revolutionary authorities in Irkutsk and he was executed in February 1920.

By this time, Sergei Tretyakov was in Vladivostok. How he had reached this far eastern city from Pugachyov through all this lawlessness and disorder is impossible to say. Perhaps he had joined the Reds, possibly the Pugachyov Red Partisans, opposing the Komuch, and then fought against Kolchak's Whites, helping to drive them back and reaching Vladivostok towards the end of 1919, though the fact that he never claimed the kind of heroic status joining such an action might have merited in Soviet Russia makes this unlikely. It is also possible that he joined with the supporters of the Social Revolutionary Komuch, or perhaps was conscripted by them, and moved to Kolchak's Omsk province with them. When questioned after his arrest in 1937, in his account of his life, he mentioned Kolchak, but ambiguously, and it is impossible to draw any conclusions from this. He also said that it was the chairman of the Central Union of the Kolchak government who suggested he go to Vladivostok, but again it is hard to set much store by this. He could have joined the Whites, or been conscripted by them when they approached Pugachyov, though this seems highly doubtful as they never reached the town. The problem is not simplified by Katherine Eaton's assertion that 'During the Civil War, he first fought with the Whites but later joined the Bolsheviks', made without acknowledgement to any source.[19] But if he was in Kolchak's province in the summer of 1919, for whatever reason and however he had come there, he could have been caught up in the chaotic retreat eastwards, perhaps deserting the Whites, perhaps having fallen in with some of those harassing Kolchak's army. But perhaps he managed to make his own way as an independent traveller, yet still blown by the irresistible winds of civil war towards Vladivostok. In fact this seems most likely because he probably arrived earlier than the ragtag remnants of Kolchak's army, though it does not explain why he left his family at this most dangerous time. On the other hand, he himself confessed later that when the revolution broke out he was 'an intellectual', and disapproved of, and indeed was hostile towards, what had happened; it was only in the Far East, he said, in the revolutionary city of Vladivostok, that he changed his view and embraced the revolution.

Vladivostok itself of course was also caught up in the madly swinging contortions of the Civil War. After the Bolshevik seizure of power in Petrograd in 1917, the city had briefly fallen under their sway. But they were unable to hold onto power, and by May 1918 they had been ousted by the Czech Legions. The Czechs enabled the port to be used for landings by the forces of foreign powers intent on stamping out the revolution, and Vladivostok became an 'Allied Protectorate'. When Tretyakov arrived here, probably in the late autumn of 1919, the Reds were conducting an urban guerrilla struggle against this anti-Bolshevik alliance. Tretyakov joined the Red Partisans. Now he was certainly on the side of the revolution. And typically, once he joined the revolution, he threw himself energetically into it.

One of the Reds' leaders was Nikolai Chuzhak, an old Bolshevik since before the turn of the century (though this did not save him from Stalin's executioners in 1937). He was a journalist with a keen interest in contemporary literary practice, insisting that Futurism was the art of the revolution. Tretyakov was obviously influenced by this idea, and he quickly struck up a friendship with him which was to last for years.

---

19   Eaton, Katherine, 'Brecht's Contacts with the Theater of Meyerhold', *Comparative Drama*, Vol. 11, No. 1, Spring 1977, p. 10.

Chuzhak and Tretyakov enthusiastically joined the Vladivostok Futurist group 'Creation' ('*Tvorchestvo*') which had been established in 1918 by David Burlyuk – who gained a certain notoriety here by wearing trousers with legs of different colours – along with others who found themselves in the city at the time, including Nikolai Aseyev, Pyotr Neznamov and Sergei Alymov, as well as the visual artists Viktor Palmov, Mikhail Avetov, and others. Tretyakov took some classes at the Vladivostok Proletkult, but it was probably through Creation that he met Olga Viktorovna Gomolitskaya, who was to become his wife.

Olga was the twenty-three year old daughter of Viktor Petrovich Gomolitsky, who worked for the Chinese Eastern Railway. She had a six-year-old daughter, Tatyana, who was always called 'Tanya' and who was presumably the result of a teenage *amour*. Tanya never knew her father. Olga was a warm, intelligent and talented woman, who seems to have been captivated by the tall young poet, his energy, his good-humoured friendliness and his determination. According to her daughter, she never loved anyone else after meeting Sergei Mikhailovich. In Vladivostok, she was friendly with Vera and Boris Shtempel, a brother and sister who were probably also on the fringes of Creation. Their mother was a practicing midwife, who was able to provide Tretyakov, Olga and Tanya with the accommodation they needed, and they all three moved to her house, though Sergei and Olga were not married yet. There was a piano in the house which Tretyakov played, and Tanya was to recall years later how he accompanied Olga as she sang the romantic song, 'I kissed you under the stars, with only the stars to see'.

Sometimes the Futurist group met at this house, though more usually they gathered at the Café Balaganchik or the cabaret Bi-Ba-Bo in the city, where they argued, planned and put on readings of their poems and occasionally lectures. Nikolai Aseyev remembered the café as the Golden Horn. The restaurant was on the upper floor, the ground floor had a large hall for public meetings, and the basement was where the group usually met, and which they converted for the presentation of stage works. They published their own review, *Creation*, which carried writing from Moscow as well as from their own members. It proved remarkably popular, and was printed in editions of 7,000 copies at a time when the most the local daily newspapers could manage was

5,000 copies. On 1 February 1920 they published a *Manifesto of the Far Eastern Futurists* which was signed by David Burlyuk, Aseyev, Tretyakov, Viktor Palmov and others.

Tretyakov was soon also writing for the Bolshevik paper, *The Red Banner*, as well as non-Bolshevik papers such as *Far Eastern Review*, *Far Eastern Telegraph* and others, often using pseudonyms such as 'Zhen-Shen' (ginseng) and 'Tyutyun'. His acceptance of the revolution gave his work a sharper bite as he focused his satirical darts on the Whites and the Japanese invaders. He also managed to publish his first poetry collection, now called *The Iron Pause*, which included not only many of his Moscow poems, but also new ones from his new experiences. According to B. Rostotsky, his writing became 'inspired by the ideas of the revolution and a profound feeling for the responsibilities of the writer to the people, and to the demands of the times'.[20] At this time, it took the form of an adamantine determination, as in his poem, 'Young Guards', written in Vladivostok:

> With iron resolve
> We're sprouting up everywhere.
> We curse, but we will be the first
> In the regime, in the fight, in the work.

This poem was soon to be set to music in Moscow, and the revolutionary guards marched to its beat. There is still a certain crudeness about some of this work, as can be seen in another poem when he describes a young peasant who had been turned into an atheist by the revolution: 'God infects a fellow's stride'.[21]

The Creation group's New Year's Eve fling at the end of 1919 was the ambitious staging of a play based on the rape of the Sabine women, probably the version written just before the outbreak of the world war by Leonid Andreyev. Almost all the Futurists took part in the presentation, including Olga Gomolitskaya and Aseyev's wife, Oksana. Olga's daughter, Tanya, recalled her mother as one of the women 'in a low-cut evening dress of Japanese material, with two coloured panels, the first of waving sea plants blending into the second, black panel,

---

20 Tret'yakov, Sergei, *Slyshish', Moskva?!*, Moscow: Iskusstvo, 1966, p. 209.
21 Tret'yakov, Sergei, *Den Shi-hua*, Moscow: Sovetskii pisatel', 1962, p. 21.

with shoulder straps decorated with chalk-blue fishes. On her upper arms, David Burlyuk painted gold fishes'.[22]

On 31 January, the Red Partisans and guerrilla fighters, under their leader, the 25-year-old Sergei Lazo, and dressed in their goats' hair coats and tall fur hats decorated with fluttering red ribbons, came down from the hills and out from the woods, and marched in columns into the cobbled streets of Vladivostok. Citizens locked their front doors and drew their curtains, as foreign interventionists, White-supporting Russians and other anti-Bolshevik elements, fled for their lives. Only the Japanese – many of them civilians, shopkeepers, small traders and so on – remained, their presence ironically turning some remaining White Russians into Reds.

It was a bloodless takeover, and for the remaining Russians, freed from foreign domination, the city sprang back to life, even as a new danger approached: Spanish flu. Many people wore white muslin face masks against the spread of the disease, but it hardly stopped them from enjoying the new social easing. Red power quickly spread to nearby villages, there were political rallies, and a Military Committee was formed under Lazo's chairmanship. They began to organise food distribution, billets for soldiers, and even made a start on opening schools. But the Japanese were still in Vladivostok, their women in embroidered kimonos, the consular officials smiling in their green and yellow uniforms with epaulettes, and the Japanese tea gardens still provided geisha entertainments in the evenings. Then they were seen to be digging trenches, snooping on the Red emplacements, setting up sandbagged posts. Yet many, including the Reds, thought they were preparing to depart: their battleships and armoured cruisers waited in Golden Horn Bay, apparently ready to evacuate them.

It was not to be. On the evening of 4 April, the Japanese attacked the city from two sides with machine-guns and artillery. They bombarded the Red barracks and administrative offices for hours in the night. Some Partisans managed to flee back to the hills; others, along with many citizens, were captured, and taken to the waiting ships in the harbour, or tortured and executed. Sergei Lazo himself was caught and burned to death in the firebox of a steam railway engine, or so the heroic legend has it.

---

22 Tret'yakov, Sergei, *Strana-Perekrestok*, Moscow: Sovetskii pisatel', 1991, p. 554.

What could the Red Futurist do? On the evening of 5 April, Tretyakov took a new poem he had written that day to the local newspaper office, and it was printed in the next day's paper. It told of the Vladivostok workers whose curses, muttered through clenched teeth, made most swear words smell like lilies of the valley. It likened the machine guns of the Japanese to sewing machines, making red jerkins for Japanese revolutionaries of the future. And it vowed to change the sharpness of the pain burning in the eyes of the defeated Reds into the sharp points of bayonets. It was the poem which, Tretyakov claimed, signalled his arrival as a revolutionary writer.

And now the hunt was on for supporters of the Reds. Tretyakov was a marked man. Less than a month previously he had published in *The Red Banner* (under his pseudonym Tyutyun) a poem, 'The Tank', which employed Japanese poetic forms to ridicule the Japanese occupiers. The latest edition of *Creation* had contained poems, articles, and satirical pieces of an anti-Japanese nature. Tretyakov was the editor, as well as one of the authors represented. He spent several weeks in hiding before finding a friendly ship's captain whose steamer plied between Vladivostok and China. Leaving Tanya with her grandfather, Viktor Petrovich Gomolitsky, he and Olga were smuggled aboard the steamer as it was due to leave. They escaped, and a few days later landed in the city of Tianjin.

Tianjin was a somewhat dour seaport, but it was a place safe from Japanese soldiers. In 1907 it had become the first Chinese city to hold open elections for a City Council, and had thus had been able to modernise to some extent, but it was still overseen by a large garrison of western forces from several countries, including Britain and the USA. But it was here that Sergei Tretyakov began seriously to study Marxism, and when he decided to study a subject, he worked at it till he was convinced he understood it. By the end of his time in China, Tretyakov was fully conversant with even the minutiae of Marxism.

After Sergei and Olga had been in Tianjin for a month, the seven-year-old Tanya was able to join them, and the three lived there as a family until early 1921. Thus began Tretyakov's fascination with China, its people, its way of life and the struggles of its lower classes to free themselves from oppression. It was to provide him with much material for his writings, and all three of them would return to China for a longer period in a few years. This stay, however, was not easy. Sergei wrote for several journals, including *Shanghai Life* and other Chinese periodicals as well as for papers published in Vladivostok, Harbin and further afield. He also published a brief study of Mayakovsky's poetry, *The Poet on a Rostrum: On the Latest Poetry of Mayakovsky*, noting that the poetry was received in the far east 'cautiously' but 'with genuine interest'. He declared his intention to give readings of the poems, and of Mayakovsky's drama, *Mystery Bouffe*, when he returned to Vladivostok – which he never did. But all this did not generate sufficient income for the family to be able to live on, and Olga took a job as a sales person in a fancy goods store. He looked after Tanya. She remembered how when she fell ill, he entertained her by making paper birds with great enthusiasm. And Tretyakov himself recalled the odd feeling of celebrating New Year in the traditional Russian manner out there in the Chinese Far East.

In the spring of 1921, they decided it was time to move on. They travelled first to Beijing, where Tretyakov described the night:

> Green stars, thousand-pointed,
> In hieroglyphs of mythic velvet.[23]

But the family did not stay long in Beijing. Sometime in the spring of 1921 they moved north-west to Harbin, the city to which Olga's father had just moved. Viktor Petrovich Gomolitsky was not a supporter of the Communists: he had become a White refugee, but was still working for the railway company there. Perhaps partly because of his father-in-law's sympathies, Tretyakov found Harbin to be a nest of reactionary White Russians. His impression, however, was only partially justified. The city had grown up very recently as the centre for the Russian construction of the Chinese Eastern Railway, an extension of the Trans-Siberian Railway, linking Vladivostok with Chita. The project had been financed by the Russian Empire, and many Russians had come to the city as employees and contractors for its building. Their numbers had been further considerably swollen by a large influx of fleeing White Russians, including Olga's father. But Harbin was more than this. The Russians accounted for perhaps half the city's population of around 100,000, but besides them there were of course Chinese, as well as Poles,

---

23   Tret'yakov, Sergei, *Itogo*, Moscow, 1924, p. 41.

Ukrainians, Danes and other nationalities, so that it had something of a cosmopolitan character. Tretyakov noticed some of these, often not without a humorous twinkle, such as the couple who

> wore glasses as big as bicycles, their heads harnessed into these glasses by horn shafts, holding pipes between their teeth, wearing waisted jackets – well, imagine two Pilnyaks, that's how English their faces looked![24]

(Boris Pilnyak was a young novelist, rapidly making a name for himself at this time, but well known as a non-Communist.) Tretyakov wrote articles for the pro-Soviet Harbin paper, *The Tribune*, but he seems never to have felt at home there, despite – or perhaps because of – the presence of Olga's father. It was not long before he, his wife and her daughter crossed the border back into Russia, to the city of Chita.

Chita was the capital of the somewhat anomalous Far Eastern Republic, a sort of half-Bolshevised buffer state between Red Russia and the Japanese enclave centred on Vladivostok. It had been established by Alexander Krasnoshchyokov, a veteran Bolshevik who had spent years in exile in America, returning at the time of the revolution, when he landed in Vladivostok. Lenin had entrusted him with setting up the Far Eastern Republic as a nominally neutral state, and its existence allowed the trapped foreign interventionist forces to withdraw to Vladivostok unharassed. Krasnoshchyokov became Chairman of the Ministers of this state until 1921. In the next years, he was to pursue a chequered and colourful career, which included a love affair with Lilya Brik, Mayakovsky's beloved muse, as well as being imprisoned for corruption, and though he was rehabilitated and given responsible posts again, he fell finally, and fatally, a victim of Stalin's Terror, and was executed in 1937.

Tretyakov was not the only Vladivostok Futurist to appear in Chita at this time. Chuzhak, Aseyev, Palmov and others also arrived. Only David Burlyuk was missing: he moved to Japan and then to the USA. *Creation* resumed publication, and obtained support from Moscow. Tretyakov, Aseyev and Palmov also published briefly a satirical review called

---

24   Hofmann, Tatjana, 'Theatrical Observation in Sergei M. Tret'iakov's *Chzhungo*', *Russian Literature*, Vol. 103-105, 2019, p. 164.

Dubolom ('Stupid But Strong'). But Mayakovsky was their hero. Poems by Mayakovsky and essays about his work were published in *Creation*; on 18 and 26 May Aseyev and Tretyakov presented readings from his recent poetry, including *150,000,000* and *Man*; and on 31 May they presented their readings in the regional Soviet workers club. According to Tretyakov, 'we read at these workers' meetings, in the club and in the open air. The poetry woke them up and the high pathos pleased the audience, and won them over'.[25] And in December 1921 the group decided to mount a public reading of his early play, *Vladimir Mayakovsky, a Tragedy* with settings designed by Palmov and with Tretyakov himself reading the central part and directing the performance.

That autumn there was also a significant series of meetings, lectures and workshops in which the Far Eastern Futurists not only showed off their wares but began to develop a critical vocabulary with which to articulate their aesthetic. The thrust of the programme was an attempt to align Futurism with Bolshevism. This revolved essentially around the ideas, first, that Futurism was the voice of progressive thought, and, second, that they were the only group able to take art forward into the revolutionary era. Thus, at the end of September, Tretyakov lectured on 'Incomprehensibility in Art'; on 10 October he was joined by Aseyev to present an evening entitled 'Theatre and Revolution'; towards the end of the month, Tretyakov spoke on 'Tendencies in Futurism', while Aseyev offered 'Watchwords of Futurism'; and finally, on 21 November, the two again joined forces to present 'Futurism and Proletarian Art'. But the Futurism which Tretyakov and Aseyev were by now promulgating did not meet with the Party's approval: it was too refined and claimed too much for itself, while the proletariat were – according to Party critics – conspicuous by their absence from the Futurists' formulations. Chuzhak publicly rejected this and began to develop the conception of 'production art', which would be amplified in the coming years, and to which the proletariat were central. It was an early skirmish in a battle which would continue. Tretyakov was to recall: 'It was annoying and painful to fight for aesthetic radicalism when the enemy turned out to be communist'.[26]

---

25 Cheryomin, G.C., *V. V. Mayakovskii v literaturnoi kritike, 1917-1925*, Leningrad: Nauka, 1985, p. 110.
26 *Ibid.*, p. 112.

Tretyakov after the revolution.

The explosion of cultural and artistic work in Chita, stimulating and fulfilling as it was for Tretyakov, was not all that claimed his attention. Besides his energetic championing of Futurism and clarifying what it meant in the new society, he obtained a post at the Ministry for Education for the region, and he also worked for the state publishing enterprise, where he was responsible for bringing out a regular children's newspaper. He was deeply involved in establishing the Far Eastern Workshop for the Construction of Art, he wrote for the local *Far Eastern Way*, and he also published two collections of his own new, post-revolution poems, *Yasnich* and *The Pass* (referring to a 'pass' in the sense of 'authorisation') in 1922. His energy and commitment were truly remarkable: they were traits which were to be typical throughout his career.

The connection with Moscow and the Futurists there was important, and Tretyakov was anxious to cement it. In the late summer of 1921 he went to Moscow, where he resumed his friendship with Mayakovsky and had a meeting with Anatoly Lunacharsky, the Minister for Education and the Arts in Lenin's Bolshevik government. He also met Vsevolod Meyerhold again by chance on a suburban train. Meyerhold, in the red fez he affected at that time, failed to recognize him initially, but he soon established who Tretyakov was and they chatted. When the latter returned to Chita, he organised the production of a series of 'ROSTA windows' along the lines of what Mayakovsky was doing in Moscow – colourful cartoons with rhyming slogans or exhortations to be posted in windows for public consumption. He wrote the verses and Viktor Palmov painted bold, colourful pictures to go with the rhymes.

Palmov had become Director of the School for Industry and the Arts, and the Tretyakov family – Sergei, Olga and Tanya – lived in a flat with him and his wife. Besides the kitchen, there were three rooms, in one of which the Palmovs lived, with the Tretyakovs in the other two. They ate together, with the two wives sharing the cooking duties. Tanya had a black cat called Kyopka whose chief characteristic seemed to be an insatiable hunger. He would put his paws on the table when the meal was being eaten, and would gobble up any scraps he could get, even including bread with mustard. Tretyakov made up one of his comic verses about Kyopka who 'snuggled up and purred' and wanted to know whether on holidays anyone would remember to give him a fish dinner – or would they pull his tail? Tretyakov still composed these comic *feuilletons* but now for Tanya, not for his siblings. Often in the evening he and Palmov would play chess, but Palmov was much better than Tretyakov, who felt he was lucky if he could get away with stalemate. When he lost, which he usually did, he could become quite gloomy. If Olga asked him why he was sad, he would reply with some kind of joke, such as 'The chimney needs sweeping!'

Then came the day when Tretyakov's father arrived from Pugachyov, bringing with him his youngest son, Lev. By now the family was terribly depleted. Three sons, Vyacheslav, Valery and Oleg, had all died, and in 1919 typhus had claimed Tretyakov's mother. When Mikhail Konstantinovich and Lev Mikhailovich arrived, Tanya was in hospital with scarlet fever. She survived, and very quickly she and her mother, Olga, made firm friends with these members of Sergei Mikhailovich's family. Tretyakov and his father were, of course, as close as father and son could be, and Lev and Tanya soon became close companions, too. Though he was her uncle, he was only four years older than she was. While she was still in hospital, Lev made paper cutouts of characters from Kornei Chukovsky's popular children's poem, *The Crocodile*, painted them and stuck them on cardboard backing. He sent them to her to play with as she recovered: she never forgot his kindness, and when she came home again, she and Lev became inseparable. It was a happy time. The relationship between Tretyakov and his father resumed from more or less where it had been before the revolution: they argued, and still felt deeply attached to each other, like best friends. There was laughter and fun, and soon Olga, and then Tanya, were calling Mikhail Konstantinovich 'papa'. And at the end of 1921 there was another memorable New Year's Eve, when Nikolai and Oksana Aseyev joined the party.

In October 1922 the Far Eastern republic captured Vladivostok. It was perhaps the last act of the Civil War, and on 15 November the newly-expanded Republic, including Vladivostok, was incorporated into the Bolshevik state. The 'Creation' Futurists – Tretyakov, Aseyev, Chuzhak, Palmov and all – moved to Moscow.

CHAPTER 4.
MOSCOW – A GOLDEN AGE

The Moscow to which Tretyakov returned after four and a half years away had changed markedly. When he left, the city had been shattered and battered by years of war and revolution, and had an air of desperation and perhaps hopelessness. Now it was springing up a different city, buoyant with youthful hope. It seemed to be the dawn of a new golden age, when all life could and would be made afresh. How to do it? When to do it? Where to do it? Artists, playwrights, poets, musicians – these were the visionaries who would hammer out paths to the brighter, happier future which the 1917 revolution had promised. Nothing was impossible.

In 1921 Lenin had introduced a New Economic Policy – 'NEP' – which seemed to open up the world again after the clamped-down misery of world war, revolution and civil war. It was an attempt to reset the economy, to enable the new Soviet Republic to take breath. Though it probably did help to give ordinary working people some respite, it also allowed new entrepreneurs, capitalists and rich peasants to flourish, and showed those bureaucrats running the new state enterprises how to make money for themselves. Those on the left, who considered themselves uncompromising 'Reds' – and their number included most *avant-garde* artists and writers – did not approve, because the out-and-out communism of the first phase of Bolshevik power was more to their ideological taste. It seemed purer, more true to the new spirit. But the unexpected freedoms NEP brought with it were also exhilarating, and after all it did provide them with some juicy objects for satire and caricature. However, they yearned for what they thought of as unadulterated communism, even while they revelled in this wishy-washy halfway house. One writer described the NEP period as 'not red but dyed a carroty henna colour'.[27] But it was a kind of golden age for the most progressive and innovative artists of the time, and Tretyakov was at the centre of almost all their most intriguing and challenging activities. Of all the artists, writers, theatre practitioners and commentators in the swirling dynamism of 1920s *avant-garde* Moscow, Sergei Tretyakov was perhaps the most forward-looking, versatile, energetic, and original.

He travelled from the Far East with Olga and Tanya, and they were accompanied by Nikolai Aseyev and his wife, Oksana. When they arrived in Moscow, the Tretyakovs had at first nowhere to live, but Sergei's old friend, the poet Vladimir Mayakovsky, rescued them, and made room for all three of them in his work room in Serov Passage. They stayed there for a few months, during which time Sergei and Olga were married, and Sergei adopted Tanya legally. The relations between all three were always extremely close: Olga consistently helped Sergei with his work, both intellectually and practically, sometimes acting almost as an unpaid secretary; and Tanya's relationship with Sergei was exceptionally fruitful and warm. She always called him 'Papa', and they played games together, shared jokes, and she listened intently to his talk. 'When he got interested in anything, he always wanted to get right to the bottom of it', she commented. 'That was why his conversation was so fascinating'. Their return was also excitedly welcomed by the remaining members of the Tretyakov family already in Moscow: Mikhail Konstantinovich, the girls, Nina and Yevgenia, and the youngest boy, Lev, were all now living in the former Lubyansky Hotel.

These were heady days. In Vsevolod Meyerhold's production of *Mystery Bouffe* by Vladimir Mayakovsky, the proletariat conquered the earth, then harrowed hell and went on to harrow heaven, too. In the final triumphant act, the new Soviet regime brought electric light to the people. In some performances, Mayakovsky himself played the Person of the Future, flying in from above, held by a cord, and declaimed his lines suspended above the stage. At one performance the mischievous Mayakovsky persuaded eight-year-old Tanya Tretyakova to be buckled to him, and she flew in, too, strapped to the poet: the child was symbol

---

27   Smeliansky, Anatoly, *Is Comrade Bulgakov Dead?*, London: Methuen, 1993, p. 25.

of the future – at least that is what she remembered decades later, though it is hard to fix a date for this spectacular happening.

Sergei Tretyakov plunged headlong into Moscow's *avant-garde* artistic and intellectual circles. He was tall, thin, clean-shaven and wore wire-rimmed spectacles. He could seem severe, even forbidding, though he never lost his sense of humour, and he always kept one foot in the family. But now his energy, his creative temperament and his quick responses to events as they happened marked him as a significant force in the wider world of culture as Moscow awoke and stretched itself. He lectured, taught and read his poetry to factory groups and military units, and he was also involved with Vkhutemas, the new School of Applied Arts established in 1920.

More significantly, he joined the Proletkult, the organisation for proletarian culture, whose work Chuzhak had applauded in the last number of the Far Eastern Futurist journal, *Creation*. Tretyakov, perhaps picking up from the Proletkult work he had done in Vladivostok, soon became a member of the Proletkult's Central Committee. Dedicated to the opening up of the arts to working people, it became immensely popular immediately after the revolution, and by 1920 there were over 300 Proletkult groups across Soviet Russia. It was ambitious, too, but not all its leaders agreed on the way forward. At this point, the most energetic proponent of Proletkult was probably the young artist and theorist, Boris Arvatov, also active in Vkhutemas, who was joined by Tretyakov and Sergei Eisenstein to propose an Experimental Laboratory of Kinetic Constructions under Proletkult supervision. This was to embrace 'conferences, banquets, tribunals, assemblies, meetings, audience spaces, sports events and competitions, club evenings, foyers, public canteens, mass celebrations, processions, carnivals, funerals, parades, demonstrations, flying assemblies, company work and election campaigns'—about as comprehensive a list as could be imagined. What exactly the processing of all this would lead to was not clear, but it is typical of the Utopianism which so many young revolutionaries believed in: artists, involved in the world, making a new culture for new times. As it was, Proletkult still provided classes and specialist workshops in all the arts – writing, painting, dance, theatre and more. Tretyakov taught classes in reading, journalism and poetry, and took over the writing classes for all Moscow, soon becoming the Head of the Literary Department.

Tretyakov, about 1923.

Proletkult had been assigned the empty and dispossessed mansion of the former Moscow millionaire, Savva Morozov, 'a gorgeous imitation Spanish palace ... Its capacious and luxurious ballroom was converted into a theatre interior',[28] and it was within this complex that the Tretyakovs finally found a home. The rooms were somewhat cramped in an outbuilding on the corner of Vozhdvizhenka Street (later changed to Kalinin Prospekt) and Nizhny-Kislovsky Lane. It had been converted into a communal house where most of the Proletkult artists and workers lived, a little like those other idealised artistic communes created in the artists' colony at Abramtsevo in the later nineteenth century, or the cultural experiment carried on at Dartington Hall in England from the 1930s.

The most popular of Proletkult's activities was its theatre programme, and Tretyakov was soon actively participating in this, too. Proletkult had set up dramatic circles and theatre clubs across the country, mounting lectures, demonstrations, practical classes in improvisation, the Stanislavsky system and so on, as well as staging play productions, 'trials' of enemies of the revolution, and 'living newspapers'. It had in fact become a central motor of the so-called 'theatre epidemic' which swept Russia after the revolution. And according to Valentin Smyshlyayev, a former actor at the Moscow Arts Theatre and by 1920 the head of the Moscow Proletkult theatre division, 'Theatre activities were the first to start in the Moscow organisation and they remained the most popular studio in the Proletkult. By 1919 there were nineteen Proletkult theatre studios in Moscow, drawing participants from all parts of the wage-earning population'.[29] By 1922 the rage for theatrical activity was dying down, and indeed Proletkult overall was losing members fast, not least because the Party found its popularity alarming, if not threatening. In October 1922, its state subsidy was removed, and its two central professional theatre groups, the touring company directed by Sergei Eisenstein, and the First Workers Theatre under Nikolai Beresnev, were in the process of amalgamating. Eisenstein became the overall artistic director. When

---

28   Carter, Huntly, *The New Spirit in the Russian Theatre, 1917-28*, London: Brentano's, 1929, p. 128.
29   Smyshlyayev, V., 'Deyatel'nost' teatral'nogo otdela Moskovskogo Proletkul'ta', *Vestnik Teatra*, No. 35, 1921, p. 4.

Tretyakov joined, therefore, it was to work with Eisenstein, like him also called Sergei Mikhailovich and also like him brought up in Latvia.

However, almost before the work with Eisenstein could begin, Tretyakov encountered Vsevolod Meyerhold, the dynamic and charismatic theatre director, whose acquaintance he had made earlier. Meyerhold recognized that the ideological skirmishes which had engaged Tretyakov in the Far East were part of the larger cultural wars whose central battlefield was Moscow. Meyerhold was himself one of the leading warriors fighting for the new art. Now he wasted no time. He immediately invited Tretyakov to work with him, and Tretyakov accepted.

It was autumn 1922. The theatre world – like so much else in revolutionary Moscow – was in turmoil. Meyerhold had his own acting company based in the old Zon Theatre on Triumphal Square. It was here that he staged one of the most famous and controversial productions even of his stormy career – *The Magnanimous Cuckold*, adapted from *The Magnificent Cuckold* by Fernand Crommelynck. It was the first production by Meyerhold to rely on his evolving system known as 'biomechanics' for its dynamism, and it employed a fantastic arrangement of platforms, stairways and moving wheels in a stage design by Lyubov Popova which was as startling and revolutionary as anything in that startling and revolutionary time and place. Tretyakov saw the performance when he returned from the Far East and warmly applauded it. In particular he liked the production's provisional feel, that it was acted not in a carefully true-to-life set, but among Popova's scaffolding-like construction. He also liked the costumes, based on working clothes, which denied the idiosyncrasies of naturalistic costuming, and the athletic acting work from Igor Ilinsky and Boris Zaichikov. All this 'de-psychologised' the play, giving it a bracing anti-realism which chimed with much *avant-garde* thinking.

Alongside his Actors' Theatre, Meyerhold had also been head of the State Theatre Workshop, which had been established in January 1922 only to be dissolved in July. In September, up to ten of the semi-autonomous theatre workshops and schools, including the Meyerhold Workshop, had been invited to amalgamate to form the new State Institute of Theatrical Art (known as 'GITIS'). Here he mounted a second 'biomechanical' production, this time of the nineteenth century Russian classic, *The Death of Tarelkin* by Alexander Sukhovo-Kobylin, with Sergei Eisenstein as his assistant director. The play premiered on 24 November that year, but by now the tensions inherent in the very conception of GITIS had become unbearable, and the Meyerhold Workshop found independent premises on Novinsky Boulevard, while the newly-named Meyerhold Theatre continued at the Zon. Alexander Fevralsky, a student at the Meyerhold Workshop, takes up the story:

> Into our midst came Sergei Mikhailovich Tretyakov, a thirty-year-old poet, who had just arrived from the Far East. He energetically entered into the turbulent life of the theatre and the workshop, and helped in much of the organising and planning. Tretyakov quickly became a valuable person for the Meyerholdites, and won solid prestige by his firm adherence to principle, his broad knowledge, his frank confidence in his own powers, his inexhaustible energy, his ability to organise work and a mode of life, and his genuinely comradely attitude to the students and actors.[30]

The Meyerhold Workshop was part laboratory, part acting school. Erast Garin, one of Meyerhold's most successful protégés, described how the student began 'as a listener, and soon inevitably (became) a participant, in the lectures, demonstrations and disputes, which were unusually interesting because Meyerhold invited prominent public figures, literary people, artists and musicians to speak'. The work, Garin continued, was aimed at 'the realization of each component of the creative process'. This demanded 'the dismembering of each of them down to its primordial state, and then the gradual building up of all the creative processes as a whole'. A ferment of ideas, experiments, arguments and practical research characterised the institution. As Garin summarised: 'Everyone learned – students and teachers alike. It was a laboratory for working through the foundations of a new aesthetic',[31] and Tretyakov was at the heart of it.

Tretyakov's main responsibilities lay in the exploration of speech, language and text. Fevralsky's notes give a flavour of some of this work:

---

30   Fevral'skii, A., 'S.M. Tret'yakov v teatre Meierkhol'da', in S. Tret'yakov, *Slyshish', Moskva?!*, Moscow: Iskusstvo, 1966, p. 187.
31   Garin, Erast, *S Meierkhol'dom*, Moscow: Iskusstvo, 1974, pp. 33, 44.

he introduced his listeners to the various problems which arose in the process of studying language; he dwelt on phonetic expressiveness, and spoke about the ancient roots of words and the 'adoption' into one language of words from another. Characterising intonation as a sequence of tones inherent in any speech, he touched on the question of intonation in different languages and outlined diverse professional and social intonations.[32]

He made strong play of the differentiation between 'depersonalised' and 'poetic' speech, laying emphasis on the former. Garin quotes an example of practical work on a speech from Shakespeare's *Julius Caesar*:

> Conducting with the hands to the count of 'four', the pupil simultaneously articulated the speech:
> 'Romans' – one, pause – two.
> 'Countrymen' – three, pause – four.
> 'Lovers' – one, pause – two, three, four. Etcetera.[33]

Tretyakov described the problem as being 'to teach the actor-worker not to converse and not to declaim, but to *speak*'. This he attempted to do by shifting the emphasis, firstly, away from the melodic elements of the spoken language, mostly the vowels, onto what he called the 'articulatory-onomatopoeic', by which he meant the hard consonants; and, secondly, away from the conventionally conversational (since real conversation generally involves the insertion of unnecessary words, such as 'um' and 'ah', hiccoughs, clearings of the throat and so on) into rhythmical configurations. These could often be crystallised from examples of common phraseology. Speech would thus take on the quality of 'verbal gesture', which enabled the actor to create a 'verbal mask' similar to the *commedia dell'arte* actor's mask, or, in Meyerhold's terms, his 'set role'. He argued that this technique enabled the actor to switch comfortably between the expressive mode and something more utilitarian. This was to bear noticeable

---

32 Fevral'skii, A., *op. cit.*, p. 195.
33 Garin, Erast, *op. cit.*, p. 28.

fruit in the production in March 1923 of his play, *The World Upside Down*.

He joined Meyerhold in teaching the key course in the Workshop, which was called 'Text-Movement'. As Meyerhold developed his system of biomechanics, it was clear that he needed to incorporate speech into the work, and this was what Tretyakov was able to supply. Tretyakov was also crucial to the creation of a theoretical base for biomechanics, and, as Meyerhold himself admitted, he 'more than anyone else' helped in the evolution of the system. It was again Fevralsky who summed this up most succinctly:

> In their artistic plan they drew together in their tireless search for precise expressiveness in stage movement and stage speech ... Under him (Tretyakov), Meyerhold's actors studied that magnificent possession, the Russian language, they grasped the characteristic possibilities of dialogue, freed themselves from verbal dross, and always spoke purposefully.[34]

The ongoing work was first demonstrated at the Zon Theatre on 22 January 1923 when the students presented a varied programme of short pieces designed to show off their technique. These included an excerpt from Ivan Aksyonov's adaptation of works by the French Symbolist writer, Paul Claudel, Act Three of *Nora Helman*, Meyerhold's adaptation of Ibsen's *A Doll's House*, performed in a Constructivist setting, and scenes from *Mr Troplong's Wooden Leg* by Sergei Bobrov. The students also performed biomechanical 'études' and read poems by Aseyev, Mayakovsky and Tretyakov. A second evening of demonstrations was held on 18 March when the students performed a piece they had created themselves called *The Paris Commune*, scenes from Mirbeau's *The Epidemic*, notable here for its linguistic demands, especially as translated into Russian, and finally Tretyakov's own mini-drama, *Immaconcep* (a typically Bolshevist contraction of 'Immaculate Conception').

Tretyakov wrote two such squibs, his first ventures into playwrighting. In December 1922 he made the scenario for a review to be called *Verturnaf*, which was an acronym for *The Versailles Tourists*

---

34   Fevral'skii, A., *op. cit.*, p. 206.

Who Bumped Into a Landmine, but which could be translated as *Spinball*. It was a kind of review, the basic structure and specific items of which were worked out by Tretyakov before he was joined in the actual writing by Nikolai Aseyev and Sergei Gorodetsky, so that the authors too became an acronym – 'AsGoTret'. Meyerhold began rehearsing this piece for presentation at the Theatre of the Revolution, but his production got no further than a truncated version which toured clubs and factories. The second, *Immaconcep*, was directed by Ksenia Goltseva and performed as part of the student-actors' demonstration on 18 March 1923. It was an anti-religious piece adapted from Pushkin's blasphemous poetic sequence, *The Gabrieliad*, but the miraculous birth is here that of the Komsomol, the Communist youth organisation. It was produced in the style of a clown show, as presented in a fairground booth, with a ringmaster, a parade of the characters and a good deal of topical satire, mostly expressed in short, sharp dialogue.

At the beginning of 1923, several international Communist congresses were held in Moscow. On 13 January Tretyakov invited congress delegates to the Meyerhold Workshop to meet the student-actors, during which he read some of his own poems. Two days later there was a meeting at the Zon Theatre of what was billed as an 'Art International'. The event was introduced by Tretyakov, who also made the final speech, and one of its highlights was his reading of his translations of poems by the young Turkish revolutionary poet then domiciled in Moscow, Nazim Hikmet.

On 28 March it was announced that Meyerhold was to be granted the title 'People's Artist of the USSR', the first theatre worker to be so honoured, and only the sixth artist in all. This was in recognition of his twenty-five years in the professional theatre, and his twenty years as a director. A committee had been formed to organise a jubilee celebration under the chairmanship of Olga Kameneva, Trotsky's sister, with Tretyakov, a member of the committee, busily engaged with the arrangements. The Jubilee was held on 2 April 1923 at the Bolshoi Theatre, perhaps a strange choice of venue for such an iconoclastic director. Tretyakov commented that it was 'like the daring boarding of an old barge, the Bolshoi Theatre, by a detachment of revolutionary guerrillas of art'.[35] The mighty theatre's regular patrons either stayed

---

35   *LEF*, No. 2, April-May 1923, p. 168.

Poster for *Zemlya Dybom* (*The World Upside Down*).

away or vented their disapproval in the stalls and boxes, as on stage were presented work from the Meyerhold Workshop itself and from Nikolai Foregger's Workshop, scenes from the Theatre of the Revolution's current repertoire, an excerpt from Eisenstein's circus-style production of Tretyakov's adaptation of Ostrovsky, now called *A Wise Man*, and demonstrations of biomechanics. Nazim Hikmet read his poems in Turkish, which Tretyakov then read in translation:

> The Bolshoi Theatre –
> Magnificent elevator of rust:
> The cracks in the decorations
> Are blots on the skirts of peasant wenches!

At this point an armed platoon of Red Army soldiers marched into the theatre and up onto the stage, where they halted. Their commander presented a red flag to the assembled members of the company, and then announced that Meyerhold had been invested with honorary membership of the Red Army. Hikmet read his poem:

> Meyerhold –
> Banner of unceasing insurrection
> In the hullaballoo of art!

And the event was over. But soon Tretyakov edited a collection of tributes to Meyerhold, which included this poem, as well as Tretyakov's own account of his first four meetings with 'The Master'.

The climax of Tretyakov's work with Meyerhold's theatre came in March 1923, when his play, *The World Upside Down* (*Zemlya Dybom*), was presented at the Zon Theatre. The title of this play has caused translators hair-tearing problems: it has been rendered *The Earth in Turmoil*, *Earth Rampant*, *The Earth Rebellious* and more.[36] Derived from a contemporary French play, *La Nuit* by Marcel Martinet, it was commended initially in Russia by Leon Trotsky, who had known Martinet in Paris during his exile before the Bolshevik revolution. He gave his reason for his enthusiasm in *Literature and Revolution*:

---

36 For a full translation of this play, see Tretyakov, Sergei, *I Want a Baby and Other Plays*, Glagoslav Publications, 2019, from which all quotations are taken.

> If an artist, looking at life from the peasant, or more often from the intelligentsia and peasant point of view, is struck with the idea that a union of the peasants and the workers is necessary and vital, then his artistic work, given the necessary conditions, will be historically progressive.[37]

This is precisely the author's thinking behind this play. It was translated into Russian by Sergei Gorodetsky and presented at the Theatre of the Revolution, Moscow, on 29 October 1922, directed by Alexander Velizhev. Gorodetsky's translation was published with an Introduction by Trotsky, who hailed it as 'a landmark play' and called it 'undoubtedly a noble work of art'. It was probably this encomium which prompted Lunacharsky, the Minister for the Arts, to suggest to Meyerhold that he should produce it. But Meyerhold detested the play. He found it long-winded, vague, monotonous. For him to direct it, he needed it completely re-made into a form which he could work with. He entrusted the re-making to his collaborator, Sergei Tretyakov.

The result was *Zemlya Dybom*, a title, by the way, which was only hit upon late in rehearsals, and insisted on by the author-adapter in spite of Meyerhold's preference for the original title. It was perhaps the least of the changes. The problems with the text in Meyerhold and Tretyakov's eyes were too many soliloquies 'in the pathetic French manner', generally monotonous rhythms and, in the text, too many 'petty subsidiary words and particles', even in the Russian version. Their aim was immediacy, a drama which would stir its spectators in the here-and-now. The performance was therefore to be agitational: they sought to transform the individual spectator into part of a wider collective. This intention was immediately evident in the cuts which Tretyakov made to the original script, especially in the monologues; in the excision of 'insignificant episodes'; in the reconfiguring of the rhythmic structure, both in individual lines and in the overall patterning of the action; in clarifying and simplifying the relationships in the play so that, for instance, the hero, Ledrux, is made the son of the old lady, Mariette, whose house is the central location of the action; in the creation of a language much closer to the audience's everyday way

---

37   Trotsky, Leon, *Literature and Revolution*, Ann Arbor: University of Michigan Press, 1971, pp. 222-3.

of speaking; and in reminding the audience explicitly of events from the Russian revolution. All this was intended to arouse the audience.

In January, six weeks before the premiere of the play, Tretyakov explained:

> In the use of words, the element of rhythm is important. Appropriate rhythms have been sought out in accordance with a speech's significance, and even when not sought out, the rhythms have become clear through the patterns which are formed by the spoken word.
> Tempo is also utilized as an expressive principle. The sound colouration of the words(particularly expressive or onomatopoeic words) has been tempered especially by the stresses.
> A staccato rhythm is built into places of dramatic tension, while the abatement of an impulse or an insinuating 'treatment for the nerves' … is signalled by a legato rhythm. Rhythm, melodics and pronunciation all lend intimations of the grotesque to the characterisations …
> Shock moments are marked by especially accentuated rhythmic effects.
> Thus, speech, besides its functions of communicating and explaining, also helps to make the play more trenchant, using sharp changes in the quality of the rhythms, melodies and tempo to create sound gestures. Traditional heroic melodies are gone. Speech is treated with special attention to the diction so that the whole text reaches the audience without any distractions.[38]

Thus, in place of the lyrically decorative original, Tretyakov created a script which was linguistically sharp, and instead of Martinet's flowing tale, it was rhythmically jagged, episodic, disruptive. It became an 'action construction' which turned on the incidents in the story: in other words, where Martinet's play focussed on the reactions to the events, Tretyakov's focusses on the events themselves. To emphasize this, the individual episodes were, in Tretyakov's words, 'marked by

---

38   Trabskii, A.Ya., *Russkii sovetskii teatr 1921-1926*, Iskusstvo: Leningrad, 1975, p. 203.

cinema-like captions with the aim of creating agit collisions': slogans and comments were projected onto screens above the stage. 'The largely figurative poetic phraseology was simplified', he added, and 'the re-formed action complied with the principles of montage'.[39]

To take a single example from the final text of *The World Upside Down*, in Episode 3 ('The Truth of the Trenches'), Goutaudier speaks to the crowd. In Martinet's original, he begins:

> Comrades!
> It is not any one of us in particular, as you know,
> Whose thought it was that we should meet here.
> No need for that! The idea, as you know,
> Had been, so to say, alive in us for a long, long time.
> For a long time, if we had dared to look within,
> Long, long ago, we should have said to ourselves:
> Here we are, countless in numbers; the masses, armed;
> 'None can stand against us if we have but the will.
> 'Why should we endure this dreadful trade, this daily martyrdom? ...

and so on for no fewer than 58 long lines, ending with:

> And if anyone has ever known what it is to have brothers,
> I think that we have seen and done enough together
> To say that what we have to do now is to join hands and to love one another like brothers.
> That is what I wanted to say to you, comrades, and you must all have understood me.[40]

In Tretyakov's version, Goutaudier simply says:

> Comrades,
> We've got our guns,

---

39   Tret'yakov, S., '"Zemlya dybom": Tekst i rechemontazh', *Zrelishcha*, No. 27, March 1923, pp. 6-7.
40   Martinet, Marcel, *Night*, trans Eden and Cedar Paul, London: C.W. Daniel, 1927, from which all quotations are taken.

> Now we want our share of the power.
> Murder and torture have gone on day after day.
> But we can stop all that if we're united.
> We've got to decide
> What we're doing here, why we've come together.
> Isn't it true for us,
> Comrades,
> That we've seen so much, and we've lived through so much,
> That it's time we stood together, time
> We lived like brothers?
> That's all, comrades.

The difference in the rhythms of these speeches is startling. The play becomes episodic rather than flowing: it jolts the audience into a response, and leads to an open ending. Under the projected slogan, 'The young take the place of the old', Mariette speaks the last lines of the play:

> When they're stirred up next time
> And the workers turn the world upside down,
> Please – be fresh, be upright, be ruthless.
> Tomorrow is your day.
> You're young.
> You'll be victorious.

The 'Futurist' orientation which Tretyakov thus gives his play is also a rousing cry to the young to fight for the revolution. As Tretyakov trenchantly remarked: 'The theatre show is to be replaced by the theatre blow'.[41]

The first showing of *The World Upside Down* was on 23 February 1923, the fifth anniversary of the establishment of the Red Army, when extracts were performed for the Moscow garrison. The official premiere was 4 March, the same day on which Tretyakov published his exegesis of his work on the language of the play in the magazine, *Zrelishche* ('The Show') under the title 'Speech and Text Montage'. The

---

41 Tret'yakov, S., 'Teatr attraktsionov', *Oktyabr' Mysli*, No. 1, 1924, p. 54.

production was dedicated to the Red Army and the First Red Soldier of the R.F.S.F.R., Leon Trotsky.

To further the 'theatrical blow' Meyerhold staged the play with an unusual reliance on 'real' (as opposed to 'theatrical') properties and stage furniture. Lorries, cars and motor-bikes were employed, and the 'props' included field telephones, a camp bed, typewriters and so on, though the real crane which he wanted proved too heavy for the stage to bear. 'No decorative embellishments, no theatrical tricks', Meyerhold insisted.[42] This consideration was also behind the use of projections, perhaps the first time such projections had been used in live theatre. Visual slogans, designed (as was the setting) by Lyubov Popova, connected the action to industrial, military and social reality, as well as to the Russian revolution. Besides being stirring and agitational, the projections were also sometimes used ironically, as when the priest begins to speak and the slogan 'Religion is the opium of the people' is projected in huge letters behind him. The lighting was by military searchlights.

How did all this appear to the spectator? Here is one description of the opening of the play:

> On a perfectly bare stage nothing was to be seen at first but a few constructions of wood and iron, several guns, a field-kitchen, and an aeroplane. After a bugle had sounded for the play to begin some automobiles drove right through the auditorium over a bridge connecting it with the stage, and were followed by a number of cyclists in uniform.[43]

The World Upside Down is difficult to categorize as a play. It veers unexpectedly between high farce, sharp satire and deep pathos. The farce was typified by the clownish cook, who, knife in hand, attempted to slaughter a live cockerel. He stumbled, the cockerel flew away but – usually – blinded by the stage lights, soon came to rest on stage. The cook chased it and the mad pursuit as the cockerel fluttered about helplessly had the audience guffawing. Sometimes,

---

42 Meyerhold, Vsevolod, *Stat'i, pis'ma, rechi, besedy*, Moscow, Vol. 2, 1968, p. 52.
43 Fülöp-Miller, René, and Gregor, Joseph, *The Russian Theatre*, London: Harrop, 1930, pp. 67-8.

Outdoor setting for *The World Upside Down*.
Note the screen for projections, right.

indeed, it flew into the auditorium, when either the cook jumped into the hall after it or a vigilant spectator caught it and handed it to the bemused cook. The satire was at its keenest when the Emperor, frightened by news of the revolt, was caught short: he demanded a chamber pot, which was brought on. As the Emperor relieved himself, the band played 'God Save the Tsar', and then a lackey removed the pot, emblazoned with the Romanov coat of arms, holding his nose as he minced his way out. The pathos was most powerful when the hero's body was brought back to his home.

> Slowly, to the steady sound of a motor, a lorry drives onto the stage. A pause. The close friends bid farewell to the body of the deceased; the coffin is loaded onto the lorry. The motor runs softly during the pause, as if to replace the funeral march with its humble sound. The final farewell. The lorry slowly begins to move, the motor's rhythm changes, and the lorry disappears from the stage with a roar of the motor that continues to be heard in the distance off-stage. Those attending the coffin freeze in place ... The hypnotic sound of the motor lingers in the ears of the spectators gripped by the scene's dramatic effect.[44]

The real things, the real lorry, the real cockerel, contributed to the overwhelming impression which this play made on its audiences. It was an enormous popular success. One newspaper recorded the 'delirious ovations from the public',[45] another described how 'with a stream of revolutionary slogans, and finely honed daring, Meyerhold's work bursts onto the stage ... Actor and theatre are united with everything which expresses the new social attitudes'.[46] Vasily Fyodorov declared that 'the importance of the formal and social elements of the performance made it the greatest achievement of the current season and the first major achievement in the sphere of revolutionary theatre'.[47] One evening Trotsky himself was in the audience. Half way through the performance, he strode onto the

---

44 Il'inskii, I., *Sam o sebe*, Moscow: Iskusstvo, 1984, p. 182.
45 *Rabochaya Gazeta*, 8 March 1923.
46 *Kommunist*, 27 May 1923.
47 *LEF*, No. 2, April-May 1923, p. 172.

stage. The actors paused. Trotsky made a short speech about the Red Army and, after a thunderous round of applause, he resumed his seat and the performance continued. At the one hundredth performance of the play on 23 December 1923, Tretyakov spoke before the play began. He suggested that *The World Upside Down* was a significant contribution in the struggle for a new revolutionary art, and asserted that the theatre had a crucial role in the restructuring of society. And it was performed outdoors on several occasions, at Neskuchny Park in Moscow in September before a crowd of 10,000 and later in Kazan before 12,000. On 29 June 1924 it was reworked for presentation on the Sparrow Hills to the delegates of the Comintern Congress, then meeting in Moscow. Somewhat adapted to make the references to the Bolshevik Revolution clearer, it employed for this performance no fewer than 1,500 participants and was watched by 25,000 spectators, who showed 'great enthusiasm' in spite of pouring rain.

While working at Meyerhold's theatre, Tretyakov had simultaneously been deeply engaged with Sergei Eisenstein and his First Workers' Theatre of the Proletkult, based in the mansion in whose grounds Tretyakov and his family were living. In October 1922 they had begun work on *A Wise Man*, Tretyakov's radical re-making of a classic nineteenth century Russian drama by Alexander Ostrovsky with another untranslatable title: it has been rendered in English as *Even a Wise Man Stumbles*, *Even the Wise Can Err*, *There's Enough Stupidity in Every Wise Man* and even *Too Clever By Half*. But before the writer's work-in-progress could be finished and presented to the public, the Proletkult actors had to be trained in the new system which Eisenstein and Tretyakov were then working out. Both had worked closely with Meyerhold, and both were influenced by him, but they felt themselves to be more radical than Meyerhold, and wanted to go further in their experiments and training methods. What they devised came to be known as 'Expressive Acting'.

> In the first place, it is a physical training, embracing sport, boxing, light athletics, collective games, fencing and biomechanics. Next it includes special voice training, and beyond this there is education in the history of the class

struggle. Training is carried on from ten in the morning till nine at night.[48]

The mornings were devoted to physical training, with classes in gymnastics, boxing, fencing and circus work, as well as biomechanics. This included famous Meyerholdian études like 'The Slap in the Face' and 'The Stab with the Dagger' but also exercises such as that involving pairs of actors, one on all fours, the other standing on his or her back. Then the pairs would race each other across the hall. Students were also encouraged to go horse riding and, indeed, to learn to perform acrobatics on horseback, as well as rowing, swimming and diving. In the afternoon there were team games, such as volleyball, with the teams captained by Tretyakov and Eisenstein, and a good deal of shouting, laughter and energetic attempts to win the game. Passers-by often watched the games, and sometimes fellow *avant-garde* intellectuals like Mayakovsky and Osip Brik came to view the spectacle. In the evenings, the work was focused on *A Wise Man*.

Influenced by Rudolf Bode, the German author of *Expressive Gymnastics*, the system was rooted in the idea that movement should be organic, rather than anatomical or physiological, concentrated in particular muscles. To balance a billiard cue on your nose, as Eisenstein pointed out, required effort and concentration throughout the whole body; beginning pianists play only with their fingers, whereas a maestro plays with the whole body, as anyone watching a concert pianist will notice. This required students to be aware of their centre of gravity, and to attain what Eisenstein and Tretyakov call the 'mastery of form' – that is, a mastery both of movement which is consciously controlled by the will and of reflex movement. They were aiming for something between the control of the dancer and the spontaneity of the sports person.

The key to *stage* movement, however, was then to distort it. Watching someone walking down a road is not interesting, Eisenstein suggested, but if the person walking has a limp, the walking begins to provoke curiosity. This idea is to be transferred to performance. And beyond this, the movement must then be 'sold' to the audience. For the tightrope walker in the circus, it is not enough merely to walk

---

48   *Rabochaya Gazeta*, 22 April 1923.

A Wise Man.

the tightrope, the walking must be 'presented' to the spectator. This is related to Meyerhold's concept of the 'emploi', that characterisation resides in specific physical forms – Pierrot's movements are 'closed' whereas Arlecchino's are 'open', for example. The aim for the actor is not to *feel* emotion, but to *communicate* it. Tretyakov and Eisenstein isolated three types of movement: the representational, such as pointing with the finger at the subject under discussion; the symbolic, such as clenching the fist to threaten someone; and the mechanical, like the orator's hand gestures (banging the table, wagging the finger) while speaking. But expressive movement, rather than being merely an imitation of 'real life', is an organic representation of the subject so that the audience will grasp not simply the fact of it, but what it signifies. Surprise, for instance, is now not merely registered by the actor's hand coming to the mouth: now the arms are flung wide and the body falls over backwards. This theatre is therefore audience-focused rather than actor- (or director-) focused. Proletkult had from its very beginnings attempted to be 'a laboratory' or 'factory for the new man, intellectually and physically',[49] that is, its aim was to mould the audience, to shape each individual spectator's response. The *audience* became the material purpose of the performance.

All this lay behind the production of *A Wise Man*, which premiered on 26 April 1923, less than two months after *The World Upside Down*, at the former Morozov mansion. The hall was quite small for a theatre, but had a high ceiling. The acting area was circular, like a circus or riding ring, covered with a green carpet, while the audience was accommodated on steeply banked seating which took up almost threequarters of the circumference of the stage space. At the rear of the 'stage' was a platform about eight feet high with ramps up to it and a curtain hanging from the front to create a 'discovery' space somewhat akin to that in the Elizabethan theatre. Ropes, rings, trapezes and ladders hung from the ceiling or were strewn about the acting area. As Maxim Shtraukh, one of the actors, wrote later, 'Those who came to see a play by Ostrovsky were in for a disappointment'.[50] What they were to witness was a political review-cum-buffoonade stretched on the barest

---

49 Margolin, S., *Pervyi rabochii teatr Proletkul'ta*, Moscow: TeaKinoPechat', 1930, p. 4.
50 Tret'yakov, Sergei, *Slyshish', Moskva?!*, Moscow: Iskusstvo, 1966, p. 179.

bones of the nineteenth century classic. Boris Arvatov remarked that Ostrovsky, 'the writer of the bourgeois way of life, a fetish of bourgeois art, (was chosen) because he was always presented traditionally. And this Ostrovsky was turned upside down. To bourgeois art a shattering blow was delivered, and bourgeois aesthetics were given a slap in the face'.[51]

There was a sense in which the play combined 'high' and 'low' art. The characters functioned simultaneously on three levels: Glumov, the scheming protagonist, was also the White Clown of the circus and a NEPman on the make; Gorodulin was also a juggler and a satirical representation of the newly installed Italian Fascist dictator, Mussolini; and Golutvin, the mysterious stranger, was also Harry Piel, the silent movie detective and a double-dealing NEPman. It sounds – and was – extremely complicated, but it did permit the satire and parody which takes aim at religion, politics and the whole New Economic Policy in what Eisenstein was to call an 'Aristophanean-Rabelaisian' spirit.[52]

In performance it was a 'very witty and gay' riot of tricks, gags and circus-like turns, which 'went at great speed, almost too quick for some spectators ... Perhaps the most amazing thing was the vitality of the players', as one English visitor recorded.[53] The kaleidoscope of stunts, derived from circus, *commedia dell'arte*, vaudeville, silent cinema and more, included Kurchyayev sketching a satirical cartoon of Mamayev on paper stretched over a hoop. When Mamayev saw it, he was insulted, furious, and in his fury he somersaulted through the hoop, ripping the paper in the process. Turusina wore a flimsy skirt and a top which consisted of two inverted lampshades: when she was excited, they flashed on and off. And Golutvin returned to Russia at the end of the play, taking as his route a tightrope stretched over the heads of the audience. Eisenstein recalled one particularly hair-raising performance:

> On the upper wire-rope, balancing an orange parasol, in top hat and frock coat, to the accompaniment of music – moves Grisha Alexandrov.

---

51 Trabskii, A.Ya., *op. cit.*, 1975, p. 275.
52 Eisenstein, Sergei, *Immoral Memories*, London: Peter Owen, 1985, p. 47.
53 Carter, Huntly, *The New Theatre and Cinema of Soviet Russia*, London: Chapman and Dodd, 1924, p. 93.

Without a safety net.
And there was an instance when machine oil was found on the upper part of the cable.
Grisha sweats, puffs, pants. His feet, shod in soft, shiny-soled slippers, although he is gripping the wire with his big toes, begin mercilessly to skid backward.
Zyama Kitayev, our pianist, begins to repeat the music.
His feet slip.
Grisha won't make it.
Finally, someone, realizing what is happening, holds out a pole to him from the balcony.
And Grisha arrives safely on the balcony.[54]

The show included two short films, the first ever made by Sergei Eisenstein. The final scene has the Red Clown left all alone. 'Everybody's gone, but they've forgotten somebody', he says, parodying Firs at the end of Chekhov's *The Cherry Orchard*. But Glumov's servant swoops in, sliding down the tightrope, holding onto a pulley by his teeth. The two clowns have a water fight, the Red Clown turns to the audience: 'The end!' Fireworks explode under the seats of the spectators.

The whole was a helter-skelter collage which moved so rapidly from one stunt to the next that audiences found it hard to follow just what was going on as far as any plot was concerned. Some spectators walked out, even though a synopsis was printed on the back of the programme, and indeed before some performances Tretyakov himself, or some other member of the company, explained the story to the audience. It was 'sensational and scandalous' and 'acquired great notoriety', yet was 'one of the sharpest in the history of Soviet theatre or film', according to Rostotsky.[55] It was what Eisenstein was to call a 'montage of attractions'.

---

54 Eisenstein, Sergei, *op. cit.*, p. 48.
55 Tret'yakov, Sergei, *Slyshish', Moskva?!*, pp. 213, 214.

CHAPTER 5.
THE LEFT FRONT OF ART

'The Montage of Attractions' was an essay by Eisenstein published in June 1923 in *LEF* magazine in which he theorised the new methodology of playmaking inherent in the script and the production of *A Wise Man*. *LEF* had asked for an article about the play, and Eisenstein wrote this without consulting Tretyakov, who only found out about it when it was published. He was offended, not least perhaps because it was he who had introduced the term 'montage' in reference to *The World Upside Down*. Eisenstein began by contrasting the 'figurative-narrative' theatre, which he characterised as 'static' and domestic, with the way he and Tretyakov had created *A Wise Man*, which was 'agitational', 'dynamic' and 'eccentric'. This, he claimed, was 'a new method of structuring a show'. The theatre's basic material, Eisenstein argued, derived from the audience, and the theatre-maker's task was to mould the audience in a desired direction through the deployment of attractions. 'An attraction', he explained, was 'any aggressive moment in theatre', one that 'subjects the audience to emotional or psychological influence'. Examples were the tricks and stunts enumerated in the previous chapter, the jump through the paper hoop, the flashing bra, the tightrope walking. These attractions were independent, primary elements, but each was relative to the others and to the responses of the audience. A show should therefore be structured as 'a free montage of ... independent ... effects (attractions) ... with the precise aim of a specific thematic effect'. Every theatre in the past had employed attractions – an effective entrance, a clever bit of 'business' – but now these were to be planned in such a way as to generate a cumulative response.

Eisenstein exemplified this by describing the sequence of attractions at the very end of *A Wise Man*.[56]

The attraction was thus the basic building block in the construction of the new drama. Its function as a structuring device was of more importance than any overt meaning the attraction might seem to embody in itself. The presentation of a series of diverse, self-contained attractions one after another clarified the theme at the expense of more traditional focuses of audience interest, such as the central character or indeed the story line itself, and thus became the centre of the audience's intellectual and emotional attention. Moreover, the series of attractions was constructed in such a way that the theme was not simply revealed gradually but had within itself a dynamism which moved the argument on, thereby confronting the spectator dialectically with a line of challenges. The play became a process of deepening perception achieved through the montage, or arrangement, of the attractions. In this way, it operated perhaps a little like photomontage, with the focus on action, not on discussion of, or reflection on, action. But Tretyakov added a cautionary note: 'Attractions must be checked in relation to the specific audience, otherwise the effect will be false and disparate'.[57]

Eisenstein's essay was published in *LEF*, and in the operation and writing of this magazine the tireless and tenacious Sergei Mikhailovich Tretyakov was central. In this 'golden age' of the Soviet *avant-garde*, it was the third of his full-time activities, besides teaching speech, text and writing, and creating his own plays: any one of these would have been enough for most writers or thinkers. But it was essential to a mind as thorough as Tretyakov's that he work out theoretically the implications of his work as playwright and poet, and this was for him perhaps the supreme reason for joining the editorial team at the new journal.

LEF stood for the 'left front of the arts'. It was only one of several new literary and cultural journals such as *Krasnaya Nov* ('Red Virgin Soil'), established in 1921, and *Novy Mir* ('New World') established in

---

56 All quotations from 'The Montage of Attractions' are taken from Taylor, Richard, *S.M.Eisenstein: Selected Works*, Vol. 1, 'Writings, 1922-34', London: BFI Publishing, 1988, pp. 33-6.
57 Tret'yakov, S., 'Teatr attraktsionov', Oktyabr' Mysli, No. 1, 1924, p. 55.

1925, that opened at this time. Literary and artistic groups proliferated. The Communist Party attempted to retain ideological control of the arts and culture: it had powers of censorship and could enforce restrictions on the private presses. But for many there was a restless seeking after a different kind of culture, and with no State-sponsored 'correct' way with literature or the arts, urgent questions abounded: how could literature relate to the revolution? Did the political revolution need a parallel artistic revolution? Single-mindedly seeking answers to these questions, besides the *avant-garde*, were the independent 'fellow-travellers', and the proponents of 'proletarian art'. Under NEP, private publishing was allowed, but because much of what the private publishers produced was either cheap and trashy or anti-Soviet, the government intervened in the market by subsidising pro-Bolshevik writers and groups. It was such a government subsidy which enabled *LEF* to exist.

This was partly because the *avant-garde* group whom the magazine brought together saw itself as a significant ally of the Bolsheviks. The members shared the Bolshevik aim of creating the 'new man' for new times, though since many were actually pre-revolutionary Futurists, they were regarded as unreliable, bohemian and decadent by some of their would-be political allies. The central figures establishing the magazine were Vladimir Mayakovsky, the greatest poet of revolutionary Russia and the figurehead of the group; Osip Brik, a key theoretician and organiser; two other progressive literary and artistic critics, Boris Arvatov and Boris Kushner; and the three members of the Far Eastern 'Creation' group, all now in Moscow: the poet Nikolai Aseyev, the Marxist Nikolai Chuzhak, and Sergei Tretyakov. Other *avant-garde* writers and artists more or less closely associated with *LEF* included the writers Vasily Kamensky, Alexei Kruchyonykh and Boris Pasternak, the visual artists Gustav Klutsis, Anton Lavinsky, Varvara Stepanova and Alexander Rodchenko, the critic Viktor Shklovsky, who had known Tretyakov and his family for a decade or so, and the film and theatre makers, Sergei Eisenstein, Vsevolod Meyerhold, Lev Kuleshov and Dziga Vertov.

They were a feisty faction, imaginative, impatient, hardworking and often dogmatic. The group's greatest weakness was its overwhelmingly male composition. Boris Arvatov was probably the chief theorist. He worked closely with Tretyakov and had a foot in most *avant-garde* institutions, INKhUK (Institute for Artistic Culture), Proletkult and so on. He had fought in the Red Army in the civil war and joined the Bolshevik Party in 1919. But he suffered from post-traumatic stress disorder and his mental health broke down in 1923. He recovered to do some of his best work in the next few years, but in 1930 he broke down completely and spent the next ten years in mental sanatoria, dying in somewhat obscure circumstances in 1940.

Gustav Gustavovich Klutsis, like Tretyakov, was Latvian. Three years younger than Tretyakov, he fought with the Latvian infantry in the civil war and, like Arvatov, joined INKhUK as well as teaching at Vkhutemas. He was best known at this time for his delicate Constructivist 'radio orators', one of which was installed on Tverskoi Boulevard in 1922 outside the hotel where the delegates to the Comintern were staying. These and other kiosks and street furniture are some of the earliest – and best – examples of Productivist art. Dziga Vertov was the pseudonym of Denis Kaufman. The first of his remarkable films, *Kino-Eye*, released in October 1924, still has the power to shock and surprise, and his work clearly influenced Tretyakov's thinking.

LEF was therefore wide-ranging in its artistic scope and coverage; it also aimed to be a mouthpiece for the international *avant-garde*, an intention it was not able to realize, though it was one Tretyakov was to carry forward in the future. All those associated with *LEF* were fundamentally opposed to realism, the imitation of life in art, *belles-lettres* and easel painting. They were in favour of applied art, utilitarianism and the aesthetic construction of life. Trotsky summed up their position surprisingly sharply in *Literature and Revolution*. They were, he wrote,

> against mysticism, against the passive deification of nature, against the aristocratic and every other kind of laziness, against dreaminess, and against lachrymosity – and … for technique, for scientific organisation, for the machine, for planfulness, for will power, for courage, for speed, for precision, and for the new man, who is armed with all these things.[58]

---

58   Trotsky, Leon, *Literature and Revolution*, Ann Arbor: University of Michigan Press, 1971, p. 145.

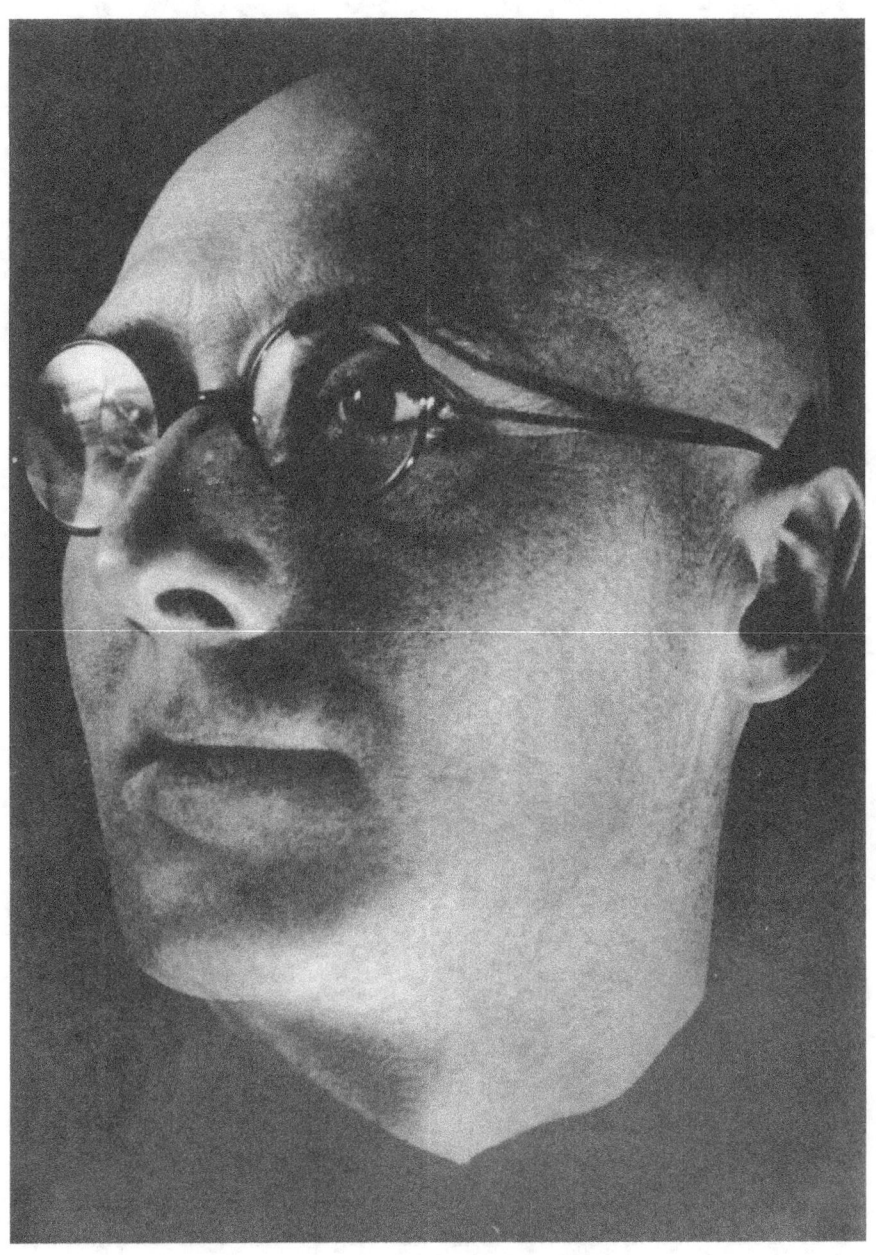
Tretyakov photographed by Rodchenko.

They were committed to rethinking the function of art in society and to defining a specifically Marxist approach to art. Tretyakov, once he had become convinced in 1919 of the integrity and necessity of the revolution, had studied Marxist philosophy intensely; now he applied it with the ferocity of the convert, and became perhaps the group's foremost spokesperson in formulating their priorities, both theoretical and practical. He was no longer the genial son in a happy family setting or the somewhat starry-eyed young poet before the glittering Silver Age. Fully conscious of his artistic and ideological stance, he became the unbending upholder of uncompromising Futurist Marxism.

He saw that *LEF*'s position was exposed, and in a powerful metaphor declared that he and his colleagues were 'in the trenches' and that

> the enemy's muzzles are in front of them (the *avant-garde*). Even when they grow potatoes around this trench and stretch out their hammocks beneath the ramparts, they never allow themselves the illusion that the trench is not a trench but a *dacha* ... or their enemies are simply the neighbours in the *dacha* next door.[59]

Private concerns (potatoes, hammocks, the *dacha* next door) must be subsumed in public responsibilities, imaged as the trenches facing the 'enemy's muzzles'. The tone is polemical, the feeling resolute. Tretyakov was working towards a definition of how an artwork operates, jettisoning the old dichotomy of form and content, the usual idea that form is determined by content, and substituting a tripartite formulation. He said that the operation of the new art should depend on the material (instead of content), the construction or the montage of attractions (instead of form), and added a key new element – the function. He suggested that these three interacted dialectically, that is, that the material depended on the function, the function depended on the construction, but the construction depended on the material, or rather, that each depended on the others. He also differentiated between two types of function – informational and agitational. But he insisted that the function should always be the advancement of the

---

59   Tret'yakov, S., 'LEF I NEP', *LEF* 2, May 1923, p. 72.

collective and the forming of the new man. Shklovsky's stone must now not only be stony, it must be seen as part of a potential barricade, or as a weapon to be hurled at the oppressors, or perhaps it should be seen as an integral part of a new house, or community centre, or even of a theatre. Its function gave it its power.

Tretyakov rapidly gained a reputation among his *LEF* companions for arguing. Viktor Pertsov recalled that though 'in the literary fight Tretyakov invested his whole passion as a Soviet writer ... in disputes on literary themes, (he) was sometimes too inflexible',[60] and his colleagues on occasion certainly found him difficult. Rodchenko recorded:

> It was in (Osip Brik's) room that the plan for *LEF* was put together, its visual components invented, and in the dining room Volodya (Mayakovsky) argued with Tretyakov and Chuzhak – they always argued. Volodya would get nervous and raise his voice such that the dishes rang in the cabinet.
> But anyone who knows Tretyakov won't be surprised. He is so argumentative and such a Talmudist that he could torture just about anyone.[61]

Rodchenko's wife, the artist Varvara Stepanova, referred to Tretyakov 'bawling like Chamberlain!'.[62] But Boris Pasternak, in a rather cynical description of the personalities associated with *LEF*, opined that 'the only consistent and honest man in this group of negationists was Sergei Tretyakov'.[63] And Tretyakov was not always serious: he carried over his *penchant* for amusing sobriquets, for instance, even to *LEF*. Thus, he dubbed Kruchyonykh 'the supernatural rowdy' and Pasternak 'a specialist in running out of the room'.

Nevertheless, Tretyakov in his theoretical work sounds sometimes more Marxist than the Marxists who had seized control of the country. It may seem surprising, therefore, that Lenin had condemned the

---

60 Tret'yakov, S., *Den Shi-hua*, Moscow: Sovetskii pisatel', 1962.
61 Lavrentiev, Alexander N., *Aleksandr Rodchenko*, New York: The Museum of Modern Art, 2005, p. 249.
62 Ibid., p. 265.
63 Pasternak, Boris, *I Remember*, New York: Pantheon Books, 1959, p. 98.

Futurists as early as 1919 and in 1923 Anatoly Lunacharsky, Minister for Education and the Arts, 'called for a return to the artistic traditions of the nineteenth century'.[64] But most of the Bolshevik leaders were notoriously conservative in their literary and artistic tastes; consequently, the cultural administration of the Communist Party always rejected *LEF*'s claims to be Marxist. Lenin, Lunacharsky, Bukharin and others believed that any concept of a new culture must be focussed on new content, not new forms, whereas Tretyakov believed that the use of old forms for agitational purposes was acceptable only insofar as it was seen as a stage in moving to the necessary new art forms.

The position of Trotsky, the most literate and imaginative of the Bolshevik leaders, was more perceptive and more nuanced. He believed in experimentation and in the freedom of expression, though this did not exclude his acceptance of the need for light-touch censorship. He agreed that *LEF* was raising important questions and asserted that art was 'not a mirror but a hammer: it does not reflect, it shapes'. But he added that '*at present* even the handling of a hammer is taught with the help of a mirror (emphasis added)'.[65] *LEF*'s position was articulated in its fourth number by Nikolai Gorlov:

> The politician organises the masses for direct action. It is important for him always to have a stout rope to hand, so that he can haul those who have fallen behind up to those who are in the lead. Tradition serves as just such a strong rope for him. The politician must be *understandable* to the masses in *elementary terms*. In order to make the present more understandable, he naturally compares it with the past. But the organisational task of the artist is quite different: it is not the use of the existent psyche of the masses, but the formation of a new psyche, not the hauling on an old rope, but the replacement of the old rope by a new one, not the grasping of tradition, but the rejection of it. For the artist the traditional image is already a worn-out and dead image.[66]

---

64   Stephan, Halima, *'LEF' and the Left Front of the Arts*, Munich: Verlag Otto Sagner, 1981, p. xii.
65   Trotsky, Leon, *op. cit.*, p. 137.
66   Gorlov, Nicholas, 'On Futurisms and Futurism', in Pike, Christopher (ed.),

However, Trotsky may have been correct to argue that *LEF* was mistaken in seeing the 1917 revolution as a break with the past when in fact it was an organic historical development.

The idea for *LEF* had been born while Tretyakov was still in Chita. Mayakovsky and his Moscow friends were initially seeking a supportive publisher for their works, especially after Lenin read Mayakovsky's poem, 'Lost in Conference', which satirized the burgeoning bureaucracy of the young state, and commended its sentiments as 'absolutely correct'. When Tretyakov returned to Moscow, the group had become known as the 'Left Front of the Arts' and it was only a matter of weeks before Tretyakov became its secretary. In January and February the state publishing house, Gosizdat, was wavering over whether to publish for the *LEF* group, first, a journal which they would produce, and second, a series of books which they would write. In March, although they rejected books by Mayakovsky, Brik, Arvatov and Chuzhak, they agreed to publish the journal. The first edition of *LEF* appeared on 5 April 1923.

It opened with three militant statements of its intentions: 'What Does *LEF* Fight For?', 'Who Does *LEF* Wrangle With?' and 'Whom Does *LEF* Warn?', signed by all seven members of its editorial board, Aseyev, Arvatov, Brik, Kushner, Mayakovsky, Tretyakov and Chuzhak. The most significant article in the first issue was by Tretyakov, entitled 'From Where to Where?'. In this, he traced the development of Futurism from before the revolution until 1923, suggesting that the new Futurism (embodied in *LEF*) would be functional, its aim to organise emotion. Analysis of form and content was to be replaced by an examination of how the *material* of the work was treated by the *devices* to fulfil the all-important *function*, thereby enabling art to expose the 'everyday-life quagmire' dialectically. Art was process, artists no longer 'owned' their work, and the future lay in 'production art'. The new journal's tone was starkly combative.

But Mayakovsky and Tretyakov complained to Gosizdat about the appearance of the journal. They argued that the price was too high for its intended audience. They urged again that Gosizdat should publish books by *LEF* authors and that the profits from these books should be

---

The Futurists, the Formalists, and the Marxist Critique, London: Ink Links, 1979, p. 175.

used to subsidise the journal. Actually Gosizdat wanted to step back from publishing it, and allow *LEF* to be its own publishing company.

The second issue, still overseen by Gosizdat, was intended for publication on the first of May, but it was delayed by several weeks. In it, the *LEF* poets set themselves a kind of challenge – to write a poem about May Day. Tretyakov's brief as a poet had already been outlined in the first issue: it was to experiment with march-like rhythms and structures and thereby bring order to the ferment of revolutionary times. Now he wrote 'First of May', an agitational piece in four-line stanzas, using slogans, colloquialisms, repetition and exclamations. Rhythmically, the lines had four strong beats to imitate a march. One stanza, concerning the union of the urban and rural worlds, is given here. This version attempts to convey the buoyant, inspirational feeling of the poem rather than to convey its precise meaning:

> The worker's the bridegroom, the village his bride,
> May Day's standing in for the father-in-law.
> Step up, all you youngsters, it's here and it's now,
> There's bread to be eaten and clothes by the score.

In the third issue, which appeared later in the summer under the imprint of *LEF* publishing rather than Gosizdat, Tretyakov was 'LEF's tribune', the title of a hawkish article he wrote. Despite its lukewarm reception by the Communist Party, the journal was beginning to make a mark, and on 3 July a public debate, '*LEF* and Marxism', was held, chaired by the Minister for the Arts, Anatoly Lunacharsky, with Tretyakov, Brik and Kruchyonykh speaking for the journal, and a number of noted scholars speaking against it. Tretyakov spoke of how the revolution could not pass the arts by. A new art must be fought for, which was the purpose of *LEF*. This was an art which would not *represent* reality, but rather it would *make* reality. Art was no longer to be a free-floating item in a market-place. Contemporary art should focus instead on the particular audience or reader, the person to be influenced by art. The debate ended without agreement. And without Gosizdat's support, the journal languished for six months.

This was a setback, especially when its wings seemed to be spreading. Tretyakov talked of 'little *LEF*', referring to the Moscow group, the journal, a mere handful of people struggling to work out the problems of art in a revolutionary society, and 'big *LEF*', those across Russia and beyond who were also attempting to realize the 'new man' and who were mostly young, dynamic and promising, though there may have been an element of wishful thinking here. However, there certainly were *LEF* groups in Kazan, Ivanovo-Voznesensk and the Trans-Caucasus, as well as 'Yugolef', *LEF* in the south, Ukraine. Based in Odessa, where Nikolai Chuzhak joined them from Moscow for a while, and organised by the young Semyon Kirsanov, later a significant Soviet poet, this group produced four numbers of *Yugolef*, the last appearing in December of 1924.

But in Moscow, *LEF* was struggling. It was not appreciated by either the Communist Party or by the influential Party newspapers. In September, Gosizdat agreed to publish three more issues, but warned that after that *LEF* must become self-sufficient. And no journal appeared. In November, *LEF*, represented by Mayakovsky, Brik and Tretyakov, formally allied with MAPP (the Moscow Association of Proletarian Writers). The initial stimulus for this alliance was to complain of the inertia of the state publishers. MAPP's journal was *On Guard*, which was as militant as *LEF* but less theoretical, and published proletarian writers who tended to be more traditional in form as well as content than the radical *LEF* writers. Some respite was gained: the fourth number of *LEF* was published by Gosizdat. Dated September 1923, it did not actually appear until January 1924.

The autumn may have been disappointing for *LEF*, but Tretyakov was, as might be expected, also busy with other projects. With his 'comrade-in-arms', Vladimir Mayakovsky, he worked on two jointly-authored 'agit-poems' for Glavpolitprosvet, the department of the Commissariat of Education responsible for beyond-school education – libraries, adult classes, 'communist universities', and so on. The first, published in the newspaper *The Poor*, was 'The Tale of Klim from the Place of Black Earth, and of the All-Russian Exhibition and Rezinotrest', the latter being the rubber industry trust which liberally patronised *avant-garde* artists (especially Rodchenko); the second, which appeared as an independent pamphlet was 'The Tale of How Fadei Got to Know the Laws which Defend Working Class People'.

And he was still working indefatigably with Sergei Eisenstein at the First Workers Theatre of the Proletkult. Their next production was Tretyakov's *Are You Listening, Moscow?!* written and produced in the autumn months while *LEF* was languishing. The play's title was itself a challenge, and the action, set in an imaginary Germany, was perhaps comparable with *The World Upside Down*. Like the earlier play, it combined the pathetic-heroic with the grotesque-satirical, but Tretyakov described it as 'agit-guignol' and the guignol element was new. It was shorter and sharper than *The World Upside Down*. The plan was to stage it on 7 November 1923, the sixth anniversary of the Bolshevik revolution, which they did, but the premiere was partially upstaged by Hitler's 'Beer Hall Putsch' in Munich which took place at the same time.

In fact, the political situation in Germany was strictly relevant to the play. The idea of 'socialism in one country' had not yet been articulated, and as early as January 1918 Lenin had urged: 'It is the absolute truth that without a German revolution, we are doomed'.[67] In 1923 Germany again seemed to be on the cusp of revolution. Earlier in the year the French had occupied the Ruhr, and in October Ernst Thälmann led the Hamburg workers in an abortive Communist uprising. Trotsky even considered going to help, and the Russian Communist Party recommended, though not too enthusiastically, a further uprising on or around 7 November to coincide with the anniversary of their own October Revolution.

The play tells the story of a fictional uprising on this date in an imaginary province ruled over by the pseudo-Fascist Count von Stahl. In the face of a restless working-class, he has decided to order a public holiday when refreshments would be handed to the people, a pageant would be presented telling the story of his ancestor, the first Count, a benign figure (in Stahl's imagination) who particularly enjoyed his right to deflower any young woman about to be married, and a giant frieze depicting the first Count would be unveiled. But the workers, including those playing in the pageant and those making the frieze, have other ideas. At the climactic moment, the performers form the shape of the hammer and sickle, the emblem of communism. To cover the resulting confusion, Marga, the Count's mistress, waves her red handkerchief as a signal to uncover the frieze. The curtain is removed

---

67   Faulkner, Neil, *A People's History of the Russian Revolution*, London: Pluto Press, 2017, p. 226.

and the frieze is revealed. It is a giant portrait of Lenin. The revolution begins. The audience join the players in singing the 'Internationale', and an actor speaks directly to the spectators: 'Are you listening, Moscow?' 'Yes', the spectators in the auditorium shout in response, 'we're listening!'.

This finale is perhaps an ironic riposte to the contemporary joke: an *avant-garde* painter is commissioned to paint a picture of Lenin in Poland. When the painting is unveiled with suitable fanfares, it is seen to depict Trotsky in bed with Krupskaya, Lenin's wife. 'But where is Lenin?' splutters the Party *apparatchik*. 'In Poland', replies the painter. It also contains perhaps a reflection of Tretyakov's homeland. The seventeenth century Duke Jacob of Courland and Semigallia which included Kuldiga, Tretyakov's birthplace, was 'too big to be a duke, and too small to be a king'.[68] The Latvian nobility, descended from the Teutonic knights, enjoyed the *droit de seigneur* even into the nineteenth century. Curiously enough, a plaque to Duke Jacob was unveiled in the town in 2004.

However that may be, the play is incisive and fast-paced. Structurally it is built round the implicit comparison between the arrogant Fascist plotters and the determined Communist conspirators, and there is the strong central image onstage throughout the performance of the covered fresco on the cathedral wall around which is gradually built the festival platform. The 'attractions' Eisenstein incorporated into the production were fewer than in *A Wise Man*. They were less 'arbitrary' than Eisenstein had originally argued for, tighter and more disciplined. Perhaps the appearance of Judith Glizer as the Count's mistress on a camel, and the entrance of Grabbe, the court poet, on stilts could be said to be over-exuberant, but most were clearly relevant to the action.

Among these were the moment when Marga feels not enough attention is being paid to her. 'Tie my bootlaces', she suddenly cries.

> *They all throw themselves at her feet. The Count, wheezing, with difficulty, finally gets to his knees.*
> VOICES : What? – Marble! – A goddess!

---

68   Antoniśka, Daina, *et al.*, *Kuldiga*, Kuldiga: Tourism Information Centre, 2005, p. 24.

> POUND (*an American businessman*) : In a New York music hall she could make a load of money.
> MARGA (*squealing and giggling*) : Don't tickle! Whose are those whiskers? Count, stand up![69]

And so on. In fact, the attraction was pointed by Eisenstein directing the episode so that while the Count was doing up the lace on Marga's high boot, she placed her other boot on his neck in the pose of a big game hunter with a 'trophy'. The class war is pointed in an attraction later in the scene, when Marga encounters Kurt, a Communist. 'Look at this handsome fellow', she says. 'What pectorals – and his eyes!' He disdains her, but she persists, inviting him to kiss her leg. He refuses. 'But why? They say my legs are very beautiful. How can you possibly not want to?' She lifts her skirt higher. Kurt spits at her. She flies into a rage, attacking him and striking him with her whip until she is dragged away. This is both *grand guignol* and a moment of political penetration. Even more was this true of the final scene when the pompous poetic commentary on the pageant is interrupted:

> MARGA : Oh! Poetical enchantment!
> BISHOP : Yes, thoroughly edifying!
> (*In the pageant battle, the primitive people, as if by chance, cross a hammer and sickle.*)
> VOICES : – The hammer and sickle! Look, the hammer and sickle!
> – It's the seventh of November!
> – Remember Moscow!

The interruption forcibly reveals the kernel of the situation: in the oppression of the 'savages' there is the potential for revolution.

Characterisation here relies on what Eisenstein called 'typage' – the Count is a braggart and Marga the classic courtesan whose red handkerchief symbolises passion, not revolution. Other characters include the jittery Shtumm, the informer, and Grubbe and Grabbe, the Count's 'Michelangelo' and 'Shakespeare', self-satisfied 'artists' who are

---

[69] For a full translation of this play, see Tretyakov, Sergei, *I Want a Baby and Other Plays*, Glagoslav Publications, 2019, from which all quotations are taken.

Gas Masks in Kursk Station gasworks.

as silly as Tweedledum and Tweedledee. All this is set off against the down-to-earth workers, who wear their own everyday clothes.

The easily-recognized 'types', the dynamism, the merging of drama and reality at the end, and the montage's unexpected interruptions all helped to galvanise the play's audiences. They shouted, booed and clapped energetically throughout. One woman fled the auditorium when the man next to her started to scream imprecations at Marga. Groups of students attempted to swarm onto the stage at the end. One man with a gun tried to reach the stage to join the action, and was only restrained by another member of the audience. As Tretyakov desired, this was not a theatrical show, it was a theatrical blow. Margolin reported that 'the actors displayed brilliance in the emotional and rhythmical playing',[70] while Alexei Gvozdev wrote three years later that *Are You Listening, Moscow?!* 'was, and in the history of revolutionary theatre will always remain, a magnificent model'.[71] Nothing comparable had been staged before. It was perhaps one kind of fulfilment of Tretyakov's aim: 'Working on the agit-*chastushka*, the newspaper feuilleton, the agit-play, and the march song, the Futurists' calling was strengthened: art in life, towards its complete integration into life!'.[72] And the unexpected acceptance of *Are You Listening, Moscow?!* by the authorities was confirmed when it was chosen for a special performance at the Bolshoi Theatre before trade union organisers on 2 May 1924.

But meanwhile, on 21 January 1924, Lenin had died. It was a shock. Tretyakov was never a Party member, but he must have felt the reverberations as much as the rest of Russia. It was true that the previous summer had seen some unrest in Moscow and Petrograd – spontaneous strikes over pay and other vexations – but they had been contained. The question of the Soviet state's very stability became an unspoken fear now.

At this time Tretyakov, besides being heavily involved with the battles over the publication of new numbers of *LEF*, was deep in the

---

70   Margolin, S., *Pervyi Rabochii teatr Proletkul'ta*, Moscow: TeaKinoPechat', 1930, p. 40.
71   Christie, Ian, and Elliott, David, *Eisenstein at Ninety*, Oxford: Museum of Modern Art, 1988, p. 68.
72   Lawton, Anna (ed.), *Russian Futurism Through its Manifestoes, 1912-1928*, Ithaca, N.Y.: Cornell University Press, 1988, p. 209.

preparations for Eisenstein's production of his (Tretyakov's) new play, *Gas Masks*. This received its premiere on 29 February, not in a theatre but in the large hall of the water-powered Kursk Station gasworks for an invited audience of employees of the Moscow Gas Works. Indeed, the following two performances on 4 and 6 March also took place in the Kursk Station works for invited guests and newspaper critics. After this it was only performed four more times in the theatre proper before it disappeared from the repertoire. It appears that the director of the Kursk Station works was initially keen on the experiment and welcomed the acting troupe to his plant, but the disruption caused quickly led him to change his mind, and the experiment was discontinued.

The play, however, retains its interest. Publishing it in *LEF* in the summer of 1924, Tretyakov noted that he considered it an 'experiment', a transitional work in which the 'construction' of the play was less important than before, while the 'material' gained in significance, all in the search for greater sharpness of 'function'. The story was based on a report in *Pravda* of an accident in a factory in the Urals, for which the director's negligence was to blame. Tretyakov turned this into what he called a 'melodrama': a gas pipe in the factory has cracked but there are no gas masks for the workers to use while repairing it because the director has spent the money earmarked for masks on booze. Nevertheless, working three minutes each before they are overcome by toxic fumes and carried to the sick bay, the workers heroically save the plant. Their dilemma is clear: if they duck the hideous challenge and fail to save the works, their jobs (in the NEP period) will disappear. They are supposedly the new masters: have they the nerve and the strength of will to act on this? One worker, Foma, supported by his wife, wants to turn his back; the rest do what has to be done. The works is saved and the workers prove that they are equal to the new demands on their heroism. They are a 'mass hero'.

The melodrama is woven through this social-industrial action. It centres on the director's son, a good member of the Komsomol who only desires to help the workers. But he has a weak heart, and he wants to join the battle to save the works. His father desperately tries to persuade him that his heart cannot stand the strain of spending three minutes at the site of the gas leak. But the son takes his place among the workers. He faints and is carried away. The director demands special treatment for him from the medical staff and believes he is saved. He gulps down a drink which he takes from the box where the gas masks should have been stored. Then he learns that his son is dead, effectively murdered by his own father. He orders his own arrest.

The structure of the play interweaves the public and private worlds with exemplary skill, but the play retains Tretyakov's typical dynamism. As with his other plays directed by Eisenstein, *Gas Masks* employs a montage of attractions, the attractions now skilfully regulated and well integrated into the themes of the play. Thus, a scene of skulduggery between the director and Yegorych, a member of the factory committee, is interrupted by a specific attraction which also questions the residue of religion in everyday life. It takes the form of a comic chase and mock battle. Vaska, a worker, enters, carrying an ikon he is determined to destroy. The director nimbly climbs a step ladder to be out of the way. He is perhaps a dithering representation of God looking down on 'his' people below, as a gaggle of ikon-carrying women besiege Vaska, furious at his iconoclasm. They beat him with the wooden holy placards which, however, splinter and break, leaving Vaska holding his sore head and wondering 'Who did the lightning actually strike, me or God?'

Later, a different attraction has the young members of the Komsomol enter 'vaulting gymnastically over the benches'. They could enter more normally, but the use of biomechanics here allows the attraction to show them integrated into the factory world as well as demonstrating their revolutionary dynamism. The use of the attraction has thus gained considerably in sophistication: attractions are still startling interludes in themselves but they now do more than merely interrupt whatever is going on, thereby startling the spectator into new attention, they illuminate the themes and ideas as well.

The responses to the play were mostly positive. An audience member wrote: 'I see this as the first play of its kind. The play gives one a great shot of energy. It is not a rest, and it's good that it's not … When you left, you stood stronger on your feet'.[73] But there were those who questioned the use of the 'real' environment wherein the play was staged – the hissing gasometers, the pervading smell of gas, the attempt at 'purifying' the air with a spray before the performance

---

73   Tret'yakov, Sergei, *Slyshish', Moskva?!*, Moscow: Iskusstvo, 1966, p. 225.

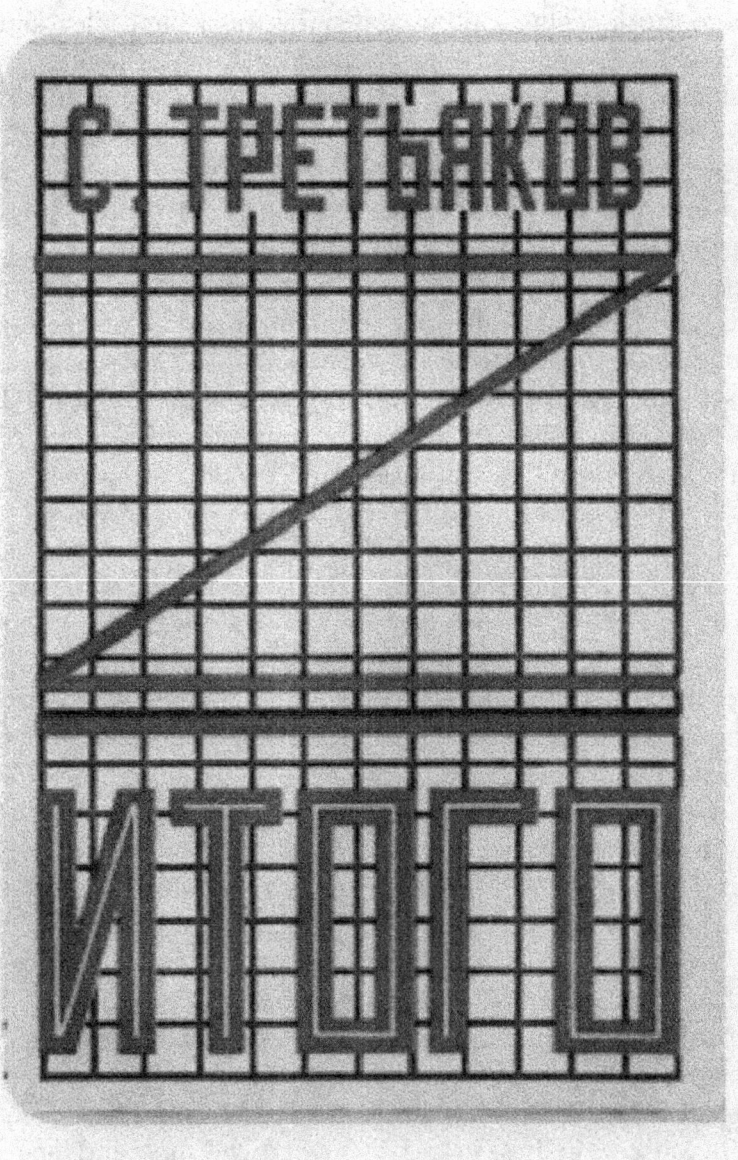

The cover of Tretyakov's poetry collection, *Itogo*.

began, and the appearance of the real workers arriving for their shift at its conclusion. One critic suggested this was a 'blind alley' and Boris Alpers called it 'prehistoric naïve naturalism' and maintained that 'the spectators were driven crazy'.[74] Eisenstein, on the other hand, asserted that 'when the men, facing certain agony and possibly death, went down the shaft to save the factory, "their" factory now, the minutes were tense with an actuality that no staged performance, with trained actors and modern lighting, could touch the fringe of'.[75]

The very contrast between the theatrical melodrama on the one hand and the harsh reality of the gasworks on the other set up the unique kind of *frisson* especially connected with what is now called 'site-specific' performance, and *Gas Masks* seems to have achieved something which Meyerhold's production of *The World Upside Down*, for instance, for all its real lorries and real field telephones, never reached. The problem of unifying life and art was perhaps not solved, but this production taught useful lessons. Its topicality was valuable in this context: the introduction of the 'worker-correspondent' in the cast list, for example, when the position had only been introduced in 1923, was daring but successful, while the depiction of the revolution which was continuing in the factories, and the workers gaining control of the process of production, hit hard in the wider social and political context. Over sixty years after Eisenstein's production of the play, Mark Rozovsky noted that 'the historical facts themselves, as set forth in this play, may cause us to wince today when we make the connection with Chernobyl',[76] and when it was produced at the Midlands Arts Centre in Birmingham in the summer of 1989, the local theatre critic wrote that the performance succeeded 'in bringing this long-neglected play to life … (and) breathed a remarkable immediacy' into it.[77]

Dudin, the worker-correspondent in *Gas Masks*, is significant as a positive character, not least because of Tretyakov's own work as a journalist. Tretyakov was extremely prolific throughout his career, and in Moscow in these years he wrote articles short and long for the

---

74 Alpers, B., *Teatr sotsial'noi maski*, Moscow: Gosudarstvennoye izdatel'stvo khudozhestvennoi literatury, 1931, p. 131.
75 Leyda, Jay, *Kino* (3rd edn.), London: George Allen and Unwin, 1983, p. 180.
76 *Sovremennaya Dramaturgiya*, Vol. 88, No. 2, p. 207.
77 *The Birmingham Post*, 10 August 1989.

newspapers and other journals. He also continued to write poems. In 1924 he published two collections of poetry, *Itogo* (*Altogether*) in Moscow, and in what now became Leningrad *Oktyabrevik* (referring to 'October' – the revolution – and amalgamating it with the last syllable of the word 'Bolshevik').

The poems were comparatively simple, agitational, often declamatory, and they aimed to be 'popular'. Osip Brik argued that in this the state was Tretyakov's true 'client'. Agitational poetry was easy to remember because it used repetition, catch-phrases and simple rhythms (like proverbs, nursery rhymes and so on), and thus the positive messages the agit-poetry contained would strike home most effectively.[78] Tretyakov concurred: 'The task of the poet', he claimed, 'is to make life, so it is necessary for the language to be concrete and of its time'.[79] One of his better-known poems from *Itogo*, which demonstrates how he attempted this task, is 'To the Living':

> Comrades!
> Let's move on.
> Are you listening?
> Promise!
> Maybe sometime after we're dead
> They'll decide to dedicate
> To us, the Futurists, who are fighting today,
> Something golden ...
> Fight the stone plinths, plinths
> Where we, cast in iron, are standing ...
> They just say to us: "Thanks
> For filling the gaps
> With your supreme genius
> And blah blah blah ...'
>
> Comrades!
> The eagle-cry of the workers is:

---

78   Barooshian, Vahan D., *Brik and Mayakovsky*, The Hague: Mouton, 1978, pp. 75-6.
79   Cheryomin, G.S., *V.V. Mayakovskii v literaturnoi kritike, 1917-1925*, Leningrad: Nauka, 1985, p. 229.

'Get on with it!
It's nearly nightfall'.
Swear
    On the Komsomol card
    In your Red grasp,
    On your cloth cap,
    The factory hooter
    And a comradely handshake,
And vow
In the night to place a stick of dynamite
Under the stone throne
Of the iron-cast Futurists.
And I'll dance
With whoever rewards you with kisses
Beside the smashed plinths of those geniuses.
        Fling them out – oh ho ho! Ha ha ha! at the explosion,
While the bits of the plinth fly by,
        Awesome in smithereens.

Comrades!
You who are young!
Promise!
Our lines
May be measured by a tailor's tape.
'Get learning! Learning, you so-and-sos!'
Where can you go further?
Don't be scared to contradict from the gloom!
Make up your own mind!

Comrades!
Vow
      With eyebrows singed in the 'shtooo',
      With fighting fists,
      With shots from the heart,
      With trade unions,
      With rifles,
      With five times five stars,
Vow!

Our very books
Which in our brains existed, existed, existed,
Exist now
Inside the brains
Of the obsolete.
    For the true flight
    To live and be known,
    Chuck
    Our books
    On the fire!
Promise?

The death of Lenin marked the end of the revolutionary period. It also marked the beginning of the end of the golden age of the Russian *avant-garde*. *LEF* was struggling and about to go under. Many of the radical theatre groups – those of Foregger and Ferdinandov, for example – were closing, while Eisenstein was moving into film. In 1924, AKhRR (Association of Artists of Revolutionary Russia), with the support of the Communist Party, issued a circular which deplored the 'so-called leftist trends in art', specifying their 'petty-bourgeois, pre-Revolutionary, decadent substance' and advocated 'a strong, precise, invigorating style … heroic realism'.[80] As for literature, the Party began to exercise its tendency towards control at the Conference held in May 1924, organised by the Central Committee's Press Section.

By the time of this conference, however, Tretyakov had already accepted an invitation to lecture on Russian literature at Beijing University, and indeed had departed for China.

---

80   Bowlt, John E., *Russian Art of the Avant-Garde*, London: Thames and Hudson, 1988, pp. 268, 269.

CHAPTER 6.
PROFESSOR TE TI-KO

It is not surprising that so restless an intellect as Sergei Tretyakov should want to go to China. He had become fascinated with the land, and had begun to explore it in 1920 and 1921. What is surprising, perhaps, is that he should withdraw from the battle for leftist art in Moscow, just as the struggle there seemed to be coming to its climax.

But he seems not to have hesitated when he was contacted at the end of 1923 by the Soviet authorities responsible for developing international cultural relations, and asked to go to Beijing. Perhaps his fascination with China remained, perhaps the fact of his father-in-law being in China was a reason for going. He also certainly believed in the ostensible motive – to foster cultural relations between Russia and China, and to help the Chinese to distinguish between the old tsarist foreign policy, aligned as it had been with imperialist exploitation, and the new Soviet policy of friendship. After all, it was less than thirty years since Russia had grabbed the Dalian peninsula, on which was the naval base known as Port Arthur. Now they were proposing a treaty of 'friendship between equals'. From the Communist point of view, there was also a pressing need to counter White Russian propaganda in China, to present 'true' information about contemporary Russian life and Russian political intentions. Much of this could be achieved if cultural links were developed between, for example, literary organisations and individual authors, and Tretyakov was well placed to build such links. There was, further, a need to correct the widespread perception in Russia of China as the 'mysterious' East, a land of 'fancifully curved roofs, little umbrellas, dragons, lanterns', as Tretyakov was later to characterise this misapprehension.[81]

Such was Tretyakov's agenda as he left Moscow for China in early spring 1924. He travelled by rail across the vastness of Siberia, entering China near Harbin and from there going through Changchun and Shenyang to Dalian. Here he took a boat to Tianjin, where he had lived four years earlier, and then the train again on to Beijing.

Tretyakov was housed in the Soviet Embassy where a few weeks later he was joined by Olga and the ten-year-old Tanya. The Embassy was situated in the Legation quarter, along with other foreign missions, most of whom maintained an obvious hostility to the new Communists of the Russian delegation. They were headed by the Ambassador, Lev Karakhan, a handsome, charming, cigar-smoking man, known as 'the Adonis of the Bolshevik Party', though this did not save him from Stalin's executioners in 1937. The building itself, with prominent white columns, surrounded by a high gated fence, contained the expected offices, a communal dining room, a club, and living quarters for the staff. The Tretyakovs stayed in a two-room flat in the building. Olga was employed in the Embassy as a typist, while Tanya attended the American school, learning, among other subjects, Chinese, which she soon knew far better than either of her parents. Tretyakov meanwhile quickly found opportunities to make up comic verses about the Russian diplomats and members of their families who were his neighbours, and he took part enthusiastically in sporting activities. He also gave mischievous names to places in the Embassy – the dining room was 'the Kremlin', their flat 'the Tretyakov Gallery'.

Tretyakov's primary reason for being in Beijing, of course, was to lecture on Russian literature at the National University. Founded only in 1898 to further Manchu ideals, after 1916 the University began a process of liberalisation which initially simply focused on the toleration of different opinions and outlooks. One typical result was the founding of the student journal, *New Tide*, the first edition of which appeared in January 1919, when it announced it was dedicated to the critical spirit, scientific thinking and 'reformed rhetoric'.

---

81 Tretyakov, Sergei, *I Want a Baby and Other Plays*, Glagoslav Publications, 2019, p. 197.

Tretyakov in China, 1924.

And in 1920 a Union of Socialist Youth was formed. In response, the 'old guard' of lecturers went on strike. The battle lines were drawn but the liberalisation continued, for instance with the introduction of a Russian Department.

Tretyakov was the third Professor of Russian in four years. Initially fifty students had enrolled on the course, but the first Professor was arrogant personally and a poor teacher. His knowledge of Russian literature seems barely to have extended beyond the anarchist writings of Pyotr Kropotkin and the stories of Leo Tolstoy. He was succeeded by a more approachable, more relaxed man, whose chief success seems to have been to add Chekhov to the pair of writers to be studied. However, by the time Tretyakov took over, only twelve of the original fifty students were left.

The Department was located in the three storey Languages Faculty. On one side was an old temple, on the other the Imperial Palace could be glimpsed through a window. Originally built as a dormitory for students, its lecture rooms were small, its corridors dark and narrow, and it had a poorly-stocked library. Those dozen students still attending in their third year were, however, 'new' Chinese, progressive, outgoing and keen to learn, and Tretyakov came as a breath of fresh air into their lives. At first they were apprehensive:

> What if we were unable to understand his Russian? If all the lectures were to turn out mere recitations in a strange language? ... The sound of sharp, quick steps came from the end of the corridor. An unusually tall, bald man appeared at the teacher's desk and said:
> 'Hello, comrades.'
> We answered slowly:
> 'Hello, how do you do.'
> He pronounced another sentence, which to our great horror we could not understand – he spoke too fast. Then he asked a question. A student rose and began to pull out slowly the necessary words, as one might take things out of a suitcase. The professor listened and then said slowly, separating each syllable, 'I will ex-plain very slowl-ly. If I be-gin to speak too fast' (from the expression on our faces, he saw that we did not

know the meaning of the last word) 'to hur-ry' (we nodded) 'you must stop me ...'[82]

Because he was so tall, they compared Tretyakov to a beanpole. But the nickname which stuck was 'Te Ti-ko' ('iron-sharp-conquer') which was as close as they could come to pronouncing his name. He soon became popular with them, however. He was patient, he smiled, and enjoyed a joke. The curriculum covered classical as well as modern literature, and he also used contemporary newspapers and journals, guiding them towards a 'truer' understanding of the Soviet state. He talked enthusiastically about the new Russia, and showed them magazines from Moscow, notably those with pictures of Lenin's funeral (*Krasnaya Niva*, *Ogonyok* and *Prozhektor*, for example). His lectures were full of warmth and passion, especially when he spoke of Mayakovsky's poetry. He often began his classes by asking, 'What's the news?' and discussed current concerns about which he easily became excited. He countered White Russian propaganda, and encouraged the students to write to the papers. He was interested in their lives, and even visited their rooms sometimes. It may be added that two of the twelve moved at the end of their course with him from Beijing University to the Sun Yat-sen University in Moscow. Tretyakov was obviously popular with his colleagues, too: the highly-regarded writer, Lu Xun, was a part-time member of staff teaching Chinese literature at the University, and he and Tretyakov worked together on a translation into Chinese of Alexander Blok's revolutionary poem, 'The Twelve'.

He was keen to explore the city, and his work is full of descriptions of it. The first typical element of the city was the dust: 'The west wind, called by the Europeans the typhoon, drove yellowish dust into our faces. It gritted our teeth, dried up our nostrils, formed small black crumbs in the corner of our eyes', he records at one point, and later:

> in summer the dust on the streets of Peking becomes unbearable. It comes from the grey tile roofs, from the wind-eaten, dove-grey bricks of houses, from the dung of camels and horses, left on the pavements by street cleaners. It swirls up from avenues and unpaved alleys which have been badly

---

82   Tretiakov, S., *Chinese Testament*, London: Victor Gollancz, 1934, pp. 343-4.

sprinkled by the jugs of the lazy municipal workers or splashed with the pails of slops by shop-keepers'.[83]

The streets were alive with pedlars, buskers, women in long robes with high chignons, coolie rickshaws, dogs and prostitutes. Tretyakov began to photograph scenes, making, in Christina Lodder's phrase, 'a visual chronicle of his experiences'.[84] He later published many of these photographs in *Prozhektor*, *Novy LEF* and other magazines, as well as in his later book of sketches of Chinese life, *Chzhungo*. They include an evocative picture of Beijing railway station, various street traders with their goods, and shots of the roofs of Beijing, almost abstract in their crazy geometry.

His students also introduced him to the classical Chinese 'opera' where, according to one commentator, he became a 'regular'.[85] He even got to know the star performer, Mei Lan-fang, who played female parts with extraordinary grace, subtlety and not a little irony. Mei's rivalry with the female performer, Lu Hsi-kuei, was legendary: for a woman to appear on the traditional Chinese stage – an innovation at the time – was regarded by many as decadent, if not disgraceful, Lu Hsi-kuei being one of the first women to appear in this tradition-bound theatre.

The classic Beijing opera was, in Tretyakov's view, stuck in the past, but with its ornate rituals, its flamboyant costumes, nimble and elegant actors and traditional music and singing, its presentations were always pointed towards a positive moral conclusion. And this, thought Tretyakov, led to the other form of Chinese theatre he was excited by, the street *agitki*, agitational propaganda pieces not unlike those he had conceived for Eisenstein at the Theatre of the Proletkult, which were also intended to lead to a specific ideological conclusion. He described one such performance he saw in detail: the actors made little attempt at 'realism'; posters were hung on the back curtain containing key information, either underlining the propagandist 'message' of the play or making some ironic comment on it; and the villains, the imperialists,

---

83   Ibid., pp. 283, 319.
84   Lodder, Christina, 'Sergei Tret'iakov – the Writer as Photographer', *Russian Literature*, Vol. 103-105, 2019, p. 100.
85   Parker, Stephen, *Bertolt Brecht: A Literary Life*, London: Bloomsbury, 2014, p. 342.

British, Japanese and so on, wore exaggerated costumes and masks or extravagant make-up. All this was not unlike Tretyakov's own dramas, especially the posters at the back of the stage, which were a direct counterpart to the projections in *The World Upside Down*. But the Chinese *agitki* employed a Narrator to ram home the meaning, which neither Tretyakov nor Eisenstein ever did. Ironically, the Chinese Narrator used a technique vaguely reminiscent of biomechanics or Expressive Acting:

> He (the Narrator) explains what the audience has just observed and hammers it into their brains by hurling furious, bitter, resentful words into the crowd, gesticulating not only with his arms but with all parts of his body, which shakes as if in spasm.[86]

His students took Tretyakov to see these street performances, and indeed he witnessed *agitki* which they created themselves and performed during actual demonstrations, reminding Tretyakov of the Blue Blouses and other agitprop troupes in Moscow. As he said, perhaps wishfully, perhaps eagerly, 'revolution was in the air. It blew about us like a wind'.[87]

These were indeed stormy times in China. For more than a century, it had been like some helpless, wounded beast, torn apart and devoured by the vultures of imperialism. British, French, American, Russian, Japanese and others demanded concessions, and forced China into increasingly humiliating 'unequal' treaties. The Manchu Empire was shredded in the process. In 1911 the last Emperor was thrown out and a Republic was founded under the charismatic Sun Yat-sen. But Sun was not power-mad, and early in 1916 he handed the reins of the republic to the cruel and over-ambitious Yuan Shihh-kai. The misery of China was not yet over.

Its worst manifestation was opium addiction. This was the result of the British exploitation of India, where cotton-growing fields had been cleared to make way for the cultivation of the poppy. When this

---

[86] Hofmann, Tatjana, 'Theatrical Observation in Sergei M. Tret'iakov's *Chzhungo*', *Russian Literature*, Vol. 103-105, 2019, p. 176.
[87] Tretiakov, S., *Chinese Testament*, p. 306.

was harvested it was shipped to China, and millions of Chinese were reduced to listlessness and beggary by it. Tretyakov's student, Den Shi-hua remembered a particularly bright, promising contemporary of his:

> His mother, a widow, used to smoke opium. Life to her was worth nothing without opium.
> Her house, her garden, and all her fortune, smoked away through her opium pipe. At that time her boy was receiving an inheritance from his bachelor uncle. His mother had no rights to the property. In order to get her hands on his inheritance, she taught her son, a schoolboy, to smoke.
> He stopped studying. His eyes lost their brilliance; he grew weak. During the day he would be dull and sleepy. He livened up only towards night. The smokers of opium are like bats; they live at night. He forgot even how to hold a brush. He was thrown out of school. His eyes would brighten only at the sight of the opium pipe through which his inheritance was disappearing in light smoke. When the money was all used up, he went out to a street corner of Hsien-Shih, and the first beggar-pennies clinked in his hand. But the pennies were for opium.[88]

Opium was a significant reason for the breakdown of the old, 'exotic' China, which depended on an interlocking system of feudalism, with its strict social hierarchies, Confucianism, which required quietism and acceptance of traditional rituals, and a family system which centred on the absolute authority of the husband in marriage and the father in the family.

All this was threatened by Sun Yat-sen and his Tung Meng Hui (Chinese United League) movement, who embodied the first genuine drive towards modernisation and some kind of democracy. Tung Meng Hui transformed into the Kuomintang political party and inspired not only the liberalisation of Beijing University but also the May Fourth movement, established in 1919 when a huge student demonstration in favour of democracy and against all foreign interventionism was launched. The movement developed and spread in many different ways but was always strongest among the students of Beijing.

---

88   Ibid., p. 46.

Meanwhile, warlordism, banditry, illegal taxation and naked power-seeking, usually backed by locally-recruited militias, was rife in the country, especially beyond the cities, while in the major ports and cities, imperialist forces continued to demand unrestricted domination. They stuck to their guns, literally. And with the development of the railways, and the introduction of steamboats, many coolies, river boatmen, porters and others lost their work. Against this, there developed a class of 'compradors', Chinese middlemen working for foreign companies, in effect ensuring the success of the invaders whose merchant vessels and gunboats plied the waters of the Yangtze and other trading highways. The situation was almost a prescription for violence, misunderstanding and crime.

One notorious, but not untypical, incident occurred on 19 June 1924, a few months after Tretyakov arrived in China. It involved an American, Edward C. Hawley, employed by the British firm of Arnhold and Co, who was supervising the loading of wood-oil onto his British steamship at the docks in Wanhsien (now Wanzhou). He was attacked by Chinese boatmen, who beat him and he fell into the Yangtse River. He was dragged out of the water, but died shortly afterwards. The boatmen apparently attacked him because he was breaching an agreement whereby wood-oil was to be carried by Chinese boats, not by British steamers. But in fact the legal position was – perhaps not surprisingly – confused. The British maintained that they were permitted to carry wood-oil during the summer months when the Yangtse was prone to flooding. It was also relevant that they were not subject to the wood-oil tax which Chinese boats had to pay.

Hawley had requested that a British gunboat, *H.M.S. Cockchafer*, would protect him during the loading, a request which he perhaps would not have required if his action had been entirely legal. In any case, the gunboat now arrived, under its commander, Lieutenant Whitehorn. When Whitehorn discovered that Hawley was dead, he demanded the death penalty for the perpetrator of his apparent murder. But the perpetrator could not be found. Whereupon Whitehorn demanded that two members of the boatmen's union be handed over to him for execution, and if they were not so handed over, he would bombard and make havoc with the city. Two boatmen were surrendered and executed. The Chinese protested to the British Legation, but Lieutenant Whitehorn was completely exonerated by the subsequent inquiry. It was not the last, or the worst, incident at Wanzhou in which *H.M.S. Cockchafer* was involved.

Incidents such as this helped to give progressive forces traction in the early 1920s. The May Fourth movement grew tenaciously, membership and support for Sun Yat-sen's Kuomintang Party increased, and the Chinese Communist Party was founded in 1921. By 1923 it was forming a United Front with the Kuomintang, giving further strength and apparent stability to the national, democratic forces. The May Fourth movement had been established with enormous student support, and now older members of the intelligentsia joined them, as did many industrial and other workers. The cry for change was spreading across China. In this sense, the 1924 Treaty of Friendship with Russia was a significant moment. 31 May 1925 was another significant moment, though for a different reason. On that day British police fired on demonstrators in Shanghai, killing up to ten people and wounding many others. More demonstrations flared, and fierce demands for a boycott of British goods were heard.

In Beijing, Tretyakov took his camera and ventured into the streets. He clung to the wall so as to be inconspicuous as those supporting the boycott confronted those who opposed it – mostly shopkeepers and the like who traded in British goods. On 10 June he was in the streets again, this time among the anti-boycott crowds.

> I was surrounded by policemen. They would not listen to me when I urged them to let me alone. I felt perfectly safe, and sure that nobody would touch me. They repeated a sentence learned by heart; 'Go back, we cannot guarantee your safety'. And when the crowd, attracted by our argument, surrounded us, asking what was the matter, policemen answered with one word, 'A foreigner!' and their eyes flared up with hate; their breath quickened; their hands reached towards me. The ring of policemen protected me from the wrath of the people. Who knows but that perhaps the next day the *Peking and Tientsin Times* might have published a dispatch telling how a

crowd of Chinese citizens had almost torn to pieces a hated Red agitator.[89]

It was this contemporary ferment in China which Tretyakov wanted to record. Over and over again he stresses his intention to debunk the traditional picture drawn so sensationally by popular romantic novelists of the mysterious orient, the exotic east, and China, the sleeping giant. To undermine these myths was of course part of the brief given him by the Soviet authorities, but there can be no doubt that he was entirely sincere in this. In the introduction to his play, *Roar, China!* he notes:

> The slow working Chinese, barefoot, in grey or blue clothing, at first glance apathetic, in the thick of whom are interspersed exalted officials, rustling in their formal black silk jackets, the staid and very corpulent merchants, the young intellectuals in glasses and with European style hats – this is the real China, which in our times we must contrast with false, exotic conceptions of the country, with all those vases, embroidered full length coats, the phoenixes, the princesses, the pagodas with their little bell towers, the refined courtesans, the cruel mandarins, the dancers ... – in a word all the pernicious nonsense with which till now our art has filled the head of the average person.[90]

And so, shortly after the Cockchafer incident, and with the noise and hustle of the revolutionary demonstrators in their ears, Sergei, Olga and Tanya left China.

One question remains tantalisingly poised before the biographer: during the nearly eighteen months the Tretyakovs were in China, what was their relationship with Olga's father, Viktor Gomolitsky? Gomolitsky was a White Russian refugee living in Harbin, about 1,200 kilometers from Beijing, but not difficult to reach by train. Years later, Gomolitsky stated that all contact with his daughter had ended in 1926.[91]

---

89   Ibid., p. 358.
90   Tretyakov, Sergei, *I Want a Baby and Other Plays*, pp. 196-7.
91   Information kindly supplied by Professor Mark Gamsa.

Given Sergei and Olga's strong support for the Soviet Government, was this rupture because of their political differences? Or did this severing of relations arise from some more personal problems? Perhaps, as so often with families, they broke off relations from a mixture of motives. It seems unlikely that we shall ever know.

CHAPTER 7.
ROARING CHINA

Tretyakov returned from China with an extraordinary range of projects in his head. He was perhaps over-ambitious, and by no means all his ideas bore fruit, but still his output concerning China was prodigious, varied and compelling. While still in Beijing, he sent home 'a series of brilliant reports',[92] over fifty of them published in *Pravda*, besides other articles, poems and photographs for different journals and papers. His anti-imperialist stance and solidarity with the victims of oppression gave a voice to the underprivileged, which still needs perhaps to be heard a century later. Many of these articles were reprinted in his 1927 book, *Chzhungo*.

Before that, however, he produced two other works, both called *Roar, China!*. The first was a sequence of poems, the second a hugely successful play. The poems, less than twenty pages in total, published as a pamphlet by *Ogonyok* in 1926, comprise a montage of vivid glimpses of the 'real' China which add up to a political statement: they work as a poetic equivalent to Tretyakov's dramatic 'montage of attractions'. The first poem in the sequence, 'The Wall', sets the tone:

> In China are many grim walls.
> They scratch the sky with the skin of their teeth.
> China is tired.
>   China sleeps.[93]

---

92 Kleberg, Lars, *Theatre as Action*, London: Macmillan, 1993, p. 90.
93 All quotations from the sequence, *Roar, China!* (*Rychi, Kitai!*) have been

The old myth of 'sleepy' China is resurrected. But it is a superficial view, and the poem goes on to undermine it. The fields may seem sleepy, but they are not a bed. The paddle wheels which water the rice paddy fields are turning, and 'the green rice shoots/Grow'. They will feed the people. And the poet exhorts the bullock-cart to 'keep moving/For China!'.

The next poem gives a different perspective on the reality Tretyakov is trying to convey – five hundred million souls clad in blue calico ('a blue/Anthill of peasants') on the red earth. They are the 'conquerors' of the land. 'The Well' more cynically tells how the 'ginger devils', the imperialists –

> French,
>   Japanese,
>   Yankee –
> Cut,
>   Suck,
>   Accumulate.

The poet is aware of his pen squeaking as he sings – or yells – his song for the Chinese – the rickshaw coolie, the grinder, the water carrier, the fruit seller. The sequence ends with a defiant student song, an anecdote about a French major angrily confronting a Chinese student in the buffet car of a railway train, and Tretyakov's own final assertion. The last poem is entitled 'I Know', and looks forward to a time when

> The courageous millions
> Bearing both bayonets and rage
> Step up from the textile factories
> And the steel furnaces,
> And stand for labour valued differently,
> Not with dosh,
>   But with the Red
>   International.

---

translated from Tret'yakov, Sergei, *Rechevik*, Moscow: Gosudarstvennoye izdatel'stvo, 1928, pp. 158-175.

The poems cohere as a montage leading inexorably to such a conclusion, and as such they are undoubtedly successful. They are poetically interesting for their jagged rhythms, for the unexpected swings from close focus to long distance view, and for the author's burning sincerity. But they were eclipsed by the author's next production, his play of the same name, *Roar, China!* (Vasily Fyodorov, the director, wanted to change the name to something like *R303*, explaining that this was the kind of name the British gave to torpedo boats. Tretyakov did not accept the suggestion.)

This was Tretyakov's fifth play, and it was based on the incident at Wanzhou when the American trading agent lost his life and the captain of the British gunboat, *H.M.S. Cockchafer*, threatened to bombard the town unless the perpetrator of what he described as murder was executed. An early version of the play was sent to Eisenstein in Moscow while Tretyakov was still in China, and he agreed to stage it with the First Workers Theatre of the Proletkult, who had presented three of Tretyakov's earlier works. But just at this moment, Eisenstein broke with the Proletkult on ideological as well as personal grounds, and *Roar, China!* remained unproduced. However, this pause allowed Tretyakov to revise and improve his play. It became a tendentious but searing critique of imperialism as it was then operating in China.

Tretyakov claimed that his time in China changed his dramatic practice, that now his drama was more fact-based. *Roar, China!* was indeed based on newspaper accounts of the incident, though the same could be said of his earlier play, *Gas Masks*. And as with *Gas Masks*, Tretyakov altered certain of the 'facts' for heightened dramatic effect, making it both sharper as polemic and funnier as satire. What was new, perhaps, in Tretyakov's dramaturgy was the subtler use of montage. Most obviously, this is seen in the way Tretyakov divides the action into nine 'links' rather than simply a compilation of 'attractions'. Each link consists of a few scenes, but each is self-contained, and could almost stand alone as a one-act play. Only when each link is joined with the other links does the full meaning emerge. A link is strong in itself, but only when joined with other links does it become a chain. It is this 'link montage', replacing the earlier 'collision montage', which constitutes Tretyakov's new dramaturgy.

Attractions – aggressive moments of theatre which grab the spectator's emotional attention – are also certainly in evidence here. They range from the foxtrot danced by Cordelia and Holey ('You foxtrot divinely, Mr Holey. You glide along like a swimmer') through the clownish comic scene when two grown men start kicking each other, to the appearance of the Captain 'transformed. He is in full dress uniform. His chevrons give him the appearance of a gilded idol'. In fact, the employment of attractions as such had further evolved and matured, as can be seen from the sequence after the Heshang tries to rouse the boatmen by brandishing 'a yellow, triangular piece of cloth with characters written on it' in a piece of emblematic theatre that could almost have come from the authentic oriental theatre. But the boatmen do not respond to this quasi-Buddhist prophet, especially when he refuses to face the executioner's axe. In the silence that follows, 'the sound of an orchestra playing a foxtrot carries across faintly from the river'. The scene changes to the British gunboat: searchlights probe the darkness ominously and the imperialists, the men in white dinner jackets, the women 'very décolleté and bejewelled', quaff their champagne. They mock a boy servant, make him drop the bowl of fruit he is offering round. He departs, but once his tormentors have gone, he reappears outside the Captain's cabin, 'humming a sorrowful tune'. He is carrying a rope. Slowly he ties the rope to the rail above the captain's door and makes a loop in the other end. Leaning on his elbows and staring into the darkness, he finishes his song, then with a groan, he grasps the swaying noose. The searchlights move away. There is 'the mournful sound of a distant factory siren'. When the searchlight moves back, the body of the boy hanging from the noose is lit up.

> Documentary? Or popular melodrama? Perhaps Tretyakov was being a little disingenuous when he wrote that the play is an attempt to demonstrate the facts, small, casual, forgettable facts, which are commonplace in China. Only this fact has been put under the microscope of comradely attention and stirred up on a theatre stage … It is a statement of fact. The strength of the production is not in the dramaturgy, but in the topical comments on current affairs. *Roar, China!* is a statement which falls into the consciousness of the audience not only from the pages of a newspaper but from the theatrical stage'.[94]

---

94 Fevral'skii, A., 'S.M.Tret'yakov v teatre Meierkhol'da', in S. Tret'yakov, *Slyshish', Moskva?!*, Moscow: Iskusstvo, 1966, p. 196.

Roar, China!: Chi and Holey fight on the boat.

The stage was now attempting to function in the same way as a newspaper – recording facts. This, of course, includes uncomfortable facts: the Chinese may be oppressed, but they are also, as the play shows, often venal, superstitious and lazy, while the imperialist intruders are haughty, racist and greedy. Small moments thus gain unexpected truth, as when the Heshang tries to convince the boatmen that his yellow cloth will protect them from being harmed by the enemy's bullets: this was believed by the Boxers who fought the imperialists at the turn of the nineteenth century. Similarly, the main thrust of the story is utterly plausible: the kind of bombardment the Captain threatens was exactly what the British (and other foreign powers) had been carrying out in China since at least 1834 when William John Napier, the supervisor of British trade in China, had used warships to bombard the forts at Humen in Canton.

A further interesting dimension is added to this authenticity by the use in the play of photography, most notably in the interventions by the American journalist with his camera, almost as Tretyakov himself had used it during his time in Beijing. When the boatmen clamour for his custom, the Journalist stops to photograph them, and later, at the scene of execution, he rushes towards the action, 'focusing his lens'. When questioned he exclaims eagerly: 'Gotta get a shot o' these bodies. It'll be one helluva sensation'. When the Boy hangs himself, Cordelia sees him and says 'in a choked whisper', 'Quickly – Mr Copper – quickly – get me –' but this is not shock at being confronted with this ghastly sight. Cordelia wants her 'kodak' to capture the scene.

Roar, China! was presented at the Meyerhold Theatre in Moscow on 23 January 1926. It was directed by the thirty-five year old 'student' of Meyerhold, Vasily Fyodorov, closely supervised by Meyerhold himself – so closely, indeed, that shortly after the premiere, Fyodorov resigned. The stage was divided into an upstage area, which represented the deck of the gunboat, orderly and gleaming white, and a forestage representing the messy, ramshackle wharf where the Chinese boatmen worked. The contrast was thus clearly marked visually and physically even before the action began. One British visitor wrote:

> At the back of the stage is a vast girder mast ... with a section of what purports to be the upper works of a British gunboat, 'The Cockchafer'. At certain moments in the action, this

> contrivance is made to advance upon the audience and to swing the muzzles of two large guns upon them with menacing effect.[95]

On this divided stage the characters were presented initially as groups rather than individuals, the Chinese presented with a sort of gritty realism while the effete Europeans are seen as grotesques, ridiculous but also merciless. Though it soon becomes clear that the various personages are distinct, they are actually presented as theatrical 'types'. Thus, the Captain in his dazzling dress uniform is a version of the traditional braggart soldier; Cordelia is the courtesan, or vamp; while the First Boatman is the stoical cynic. In the Fyodorov-Meyerhold staging, the Chinese characters actually wore masks with minimal but genuine traits outlined on them. And while the Europeans briskly foxtrotted and swigged champagne, the Chinese were presented in a slower tempo, their scenes sometimes accompanied by offstage voices chanting quietly and mournfully.

> The production, owing to its topical and daring subject, the unconventionality of its staging and the mixed character of its actors, aroused much curiosity. It became the leading show piece of Moscow to which every visitor who devoutly believed in the principles of the New Russia went to pay homage. Labour delegates from all parts of the world went to see it.[96]

Even Stalin attended a performance, and to increase its immediacy, up-to-the-minute despatches from China were sometimes read out from the stage. *Roar, China!* became Tretyakov's – indeed probably revolutionary Russia's – most performed play. The Meyerhold Theatre toured Europe in 1930 with *Roar, China!* in its repertoire, and though it was banned in Paris, in Germany and Poland it was enthusiastically acclaimed. In Cologne, 6,000 people were in the auditorium of the Rhinelandhalle for one performance.

---

95   Carter, Huntly, *The New Spirit in the Russian Theatre, 1917-1928*, London: Brentano's, 1929, p. 217.
96   *Ibid.*, p. 216.

Further productions proliferated. Across the Soviet Union there were performances in the Ukrainian, Georgian, Tartar, Uzbek and Armenian languages. Nikos Kazantzakis, the famous Greek novelist, saw it in Vladivostok. In Germany, in 1929 Leo Lania adapted it for performance in Frankfurt and elsewhere, and in Estonia in 1932 it was 'the greatest event in the theatrical world'. In Poland, the director Leon Schiller managed to produce it three times despite attempts by the police to intervene – in Lvov in 1932, in Lodz (also in 1932) and in Warsaw in 1933. More than three decades later, Janos Varminsky, the respected Polish theatre director, wrote to Tretyakov's widow that he recalled how it had 'provoked sharp opposition from the Polish *bourgeoisie* and the state authorities, and simultaneously the enthusiasm of the general public'.[97]

Herbert Biberman, who directed the play for the Guild Theatre of New York in 1930, when residents of Chinatown, most of whom had never acted before, were drafted in, similarly wrote to Olga Viktorovna Tretyakova, declaring, 'I do not exaggerate when I say that the experience of work on this play made me a politically conscious and progressive person'.[98] In Japan, Iosi Khidzikata produced it at the Tsukidze Theatre in 1933. Tretyakov himself recalled that 'the Tokyo police regularly dragged out spectators from every performance… when they had been fired by the revolutionary songs, cunningly inserted in the production by the producers, and they seized these spectators, often breaking their arms'.[99] Besides other productions in many countries, including Argentina, India, England, Canada and elsewhere, it was seen in several productions in China itself. It was first seen in Hangchow, in Canton, in 1930, and later in Shanghai, and when the Chinese Communist Party took power in 1949, their victory was celebrated in Shanghai with a new production of *Roar, China!*. Meanwhile, it had been seen in the Czestochowa Nazi concentration camp in 1944. It was staged by a former actor, now an inmate of the camp, Shie Tigel, who had somehow obtained permission to

---

97 Rostotskii, B., 'Dramaturg-agitator', in Tret'yakov, Sergei, *Slyshish', Moskva?!*, p. 236.
98 *Ibid.*, p. 235.
99 Pertsov, V., 'Sergei Tret'yakov', in Tret'yakov, Sergei, *Den Shi-hua*, Moscow: Sovetskii pisatel', 1962, p. 4.

run a Yiddish theatre there. With music by another inmate, named Katershinsky, and with new scenery and curtains, it must have seemed to those incarcerated there some sort of expression of their abominable oppression. It was only presented once, however, and soon after this the SS closed down the prisoners' theatre.

Tretyakov's third work about China, published in 1927, was *Chzhungo* (the old name for China, the 'Middle Kingdom'), which was largely a collection of his previously published articles sent to *Pravda* and other outlets. A revised version of the book appeared in 1930, considerably expanded and including photographs, most of them probably taken by Tretyakov himself. The work adds up to a series of snapshots of the evolving Chinese revolution, an examination of the historical process as it unfolds, with sharp insights into seemingly arbitrarily chosen details of its subject, failures and problems as well as successes and opportunities.

Each of the unnumbered chapters offers its own view of a particular facet of Chinese life. Some are intimate, some more public. The first is 'To Love China', which sets the agenda for the whole book: the exotic China may seem to be what is exciting about this country, but apparently dull reality is in fact more engaging as China emerges from feudalism into revolutionary possibility. The chapter on Beijing seems at first to be little more than a visitor's tour of the capital city, with its contrasting houses for the rich and the poor, its ponds, its alleys, its teahouses and brothels, and its streets filled with pedlars, buskers, market stalls and beggars. But the second edition of *Chzhungo* expands this chapter to include sections on dental practices, funerals and other matters, and a final section, tellingly entitled 'Roar, China'. This is more than mere sightseeing, and is complemented by and juxtaposed with later chapters, such as the description of Sun Yat-sen's triumphant appearance in Beijing, and his tragic death and funeral, as well as the graphic accounts of student demonstrations which Tretyakov had witnessed in the city.

The picture thus painted, though by no means comprehensive, is still surprisingly penetrating. The chapter 'Fathers and Children' is an incisive scrutiny of the clash of the generations – the fathers embody 'old' China, while their children are looking mostly to the west for inspiration for change. Yet, lacking as they do an understanding of Marxism or socialism, this hope is founded on a misapprehension:

Den Shi-hua.

it is towards Russia, Tretyakov maintains, that they need to look. The drift of the book is revealed as more than a mere compilation: the chapter on the theatre gives us both the traditional Beijing opera and the urgent agitprop of the streets and the protesters; the description of traditional funeral rites exposes religious superstition; and the essay on the status of women shows the reality of growing emancipation. Poor children are still cruelly exploited, but change is possible. Students such as those Tretyakov taught offer a necessary alternative, and he writes pen portraits of at least five of these, who, young and hopeful, perhaps hold the key to a brighter future.

Chzhungo jumps unpredictably from close-ups to endistanced effects – the individual is set against the crowd, the landscape against a small detail like the pond in Beijing. Its structure is based in these contrasts which are montaged, both between chapters and within chapters. Tretyakov himself is a liminal figure, more than merely an observer yet barely an involved participant. His work covers more than a year, so that clearly he is not just a tourist, but he is still a sort of outsider. This ambiguous standpoint gives the book much of its dynamism and power, as we see China moving towards the realization of its revolutionary potential. To see this process is, in Tretyakov's words, 'to know and love China, our relation and close friend'. For the benefit of his readers, Tretyakov quite frequently compares China to Russia, and Russia's good intentions are contrasted with the dirty deeds of the other foreigners in China, especially the British and Americans. Tretyakov does not attempt to conceal his anger at this, and also his impatience with Chinese superstition and what he considers backwardness, but nor does he shy away from expressing his admiration, especially of the politically active. Thus, not only are the contradictions of China in transition revealed, the author's own understanding of a country in flux is gradually deepened. These parallel developments, in the country and in the writer, interact almost dialectically. China no longer remains incomprehensible, and Tretyakov himself is learning as well as teaching in Beijing. He concludes the second edition of *Chzhungo* by predicting that 'a great social bonfire' will blaze across the country. Less than twenty years later, the Chinese Communist Party did indeed sweep to power.

Sergei Tretyakov's fourth major publication arising from his time in China, after the poetic sequence *Roar, China!*, the play of the same name, and the collection of essays and sketches in *Chzhungo*, was a long 'bio-interview', *Den Shi-hua*. First published in 1930, with a second expanded edition in 1932, *Den Shi-hua* was perhaps Tretyakov's most widely-read work, soon translated and published in Germany, Poland, Britain, America, Czechoslovakia, Hungary and elsewhere. It was the result of a long series of interviews with one of Tretyakov's former Beijing students, Den Shi-hua, most conducted in Moscow after Tretyakov left China and Den Shi-hua was attending the Sun Yat-sen University, a Soviet institution dedicated to training future Chinese Communist leaders, where Karl Radek, who was to feature again later in Tretyakov's life, was Rector. Tretyakov explained how the book was made by two people:

> Den Shi-hua provided the raw material. I put it into shape. To see one's own life in detail, and to tell its story, requires great skill. Den Shi-hua did not possess this skill. He accepted with enthusiasm my proposal to write an accurate biography of a Chinese student. For six months we conferred daily for four to six hours.[100]

He added that he had 'dug into' Den's recollections 'like a miner' and how he was, at different times, his 'examining judge, father confessor, interviewer, companion and psychoanalyst'.[101] Consequently the story is told in the first person, as if it were Den's autobiography.

As Tretyakov tells it, Den Shi-hua's life is a symbolic exploration of China's political awakening. Den is the son of an underground fighter in Sun Yat-sen's Kuomintang. The book covers his childhood, his relations with his parents and wider family, his schooling, and later, his marriage and divorce, as well as his time as a student. His childhood is bound by tradition. There is a screen in front of the gate to his family's house: 'I would never push or pull it down. It protected us, not only from the eyes of strangers, but also from evil spirits who swarmed in the wind, more numerous than flies over carrion'.[102] When he was small he ate with a spoon: it is a proud

---

100 Tretiakov, S., *Chinese Testament*, p. 7.
101 *Ibid.*
102 *Ibid.*, p. 28.

moment when he begins to use chopsticks. When his mother dies, she is given a traditional funeral, including the silk-covered mattress placed in the coffin, the white curtain hung to separate the house altar from the coffin, the porcelain bowl for burning prayer sticks, and the two whole days set aside for mourning, as people continually pass through the prayer-room, lighting incense sticks and placing gifts of gold or silver, paper gowns, horses, even a paper model house, on the table. A burial site has to be found which is dry and covered with flowers and from where the distant mountains and the mighty Yangtse River can be seen. There is a traditional funeral orchestra with trumpets, flutes, drums, gongs and little bells, and the monks chant their choruses.

Notably, the father was absent. He was still fighting for the modernisation of China. Earlier in the book, he arrives home and shocks his family because he is wearing European dress and has cut off his pigtail. And from out of his canvas suitcase (they have only seen leather or wooden cases before) he draws a gramophone, which is soon emitting 'the strong, hoarse measures of a military song'. It is a key moment in the book: modernity invades the traditional home.

Den Shi-hua's relationship with his father is perhaps the engine of the story. When the boy falls ill, the father never comes to see or comfort him. He is interested only in the political struggle. When the father is captured and sentenced to death, Den is horrified, and frightened: 'I was trying to imagine the execution. A sword... a shot... blood...' But the father is reprieved, and 'I was happy for the first time for months'. But the father is still cold towards his son. When Den enters the room where his father is sitting, he turns towards him 'without a smile'. When Den acquires a girlfriend of whom he is very fond, the father forbids them to marry. 'I felt as if he had split me in two with his straight, heavy sword'. But when his stepmother urges him to try to talk his father round, he has not the courage. He cannot go against his father. The old traditions are too powerful.

Instead, as tradition demands, a marriage is arranged for Den. He finds the chosen woman repugnant but the marriage is performed, with due and time-honoured ceremony, but without the father being present. However, tradition also states that if a husband ignores his wife for two years, he can 'turn aside' from her. And this he does. Tradition, seen usually as inhibiting, has now freed him. The question is problematized. China is changing – near the end of the book, Den looks again at his native village, 'remembering what it was like twenty years ago when my uncle brought me to school for the first time. I could not recognize it' – but the opium poppy is still flourishing. The government ostensibly deplores this, but whispers to the growers, 'Sow poppy. Sow poppy'.[103] Complexity gives *Den Shi-hua* its rewarding resonance.

And throughout, Den is moving towards social and political maturity. When there is a boycott of Japanese goods, he becomes the secretary of his school's boycott committee. He begins to read the newspapers and acquires a very partial understanding of the Russian revolution. When his father returns, he tries to teach him about Marxism, and is almost surprised by his father's response: 'I don't know about your Marx. But what you say sounds reasonable'. He takes his first tentative steps towards becoming a writer at a time when there is something of a literary renaissance in China. He becomes a student at the newly-liberalised Beijing University and he is active in the May Fourth movement. When he again meets his father, he is a promising writer and a political activist in his own right, and is planning to go to Moscow. '"Good-bye, son," father said… "If you seriously intend to go to Moscow, write to us, and we'll manage to get the money for you somewhere"'.[104] It is a reconciliation of sorts.

Critics and commentators have agonised over Tretyakov's description of this book as a 'bio-interview', and indeed Tretyakov backed off from the epithet once Stalin's 'socialist realism' had been promulgated as the only acceptable Soviet form of writing in the mid-1930s. But the difficulty remains. Clearly *Den Shi-hua* is not fiction, but nor is it history. A 'bio-interview' implies its authenticity, and today it might be called 'documentary' or 'oral history'. The fact that it is written from life but is not autobiography in the usual sense gives it a concrete materiality few books achieve. Perhaps the best way to understand it is as a witness statement by one who has been well coached by his lawyer.

This idea suggests how this book was made by two people. Another way of looking at its creation would be to see Tretyakov's role as akin to that of a film editor. Or – to revert to Tretyakov's formulation of his

---

103   Ibid., pp. 364-5.
104   Ibid., p. 368.

dramatic practice – Den Shi-hua supplied the material and Tretyakov the devices, while both agreed on the function. But questions remain. There are, for instance, echoes of Tretyakov's own experiences in the book – his childhood, for instance, and his observations of Beijing. How far did Tretyakov prompt Den Shi-hua? Was Den Shi-hua always completely truthful? And there were language problems: Den Shi-hua's Russian was not good, and Tretyakov's Chinese was possibly even worse: how effective was their communication? Furthermore, Tretyakov does not merely observe and listen to his subject, in a sense he is *producing* Den Shi-hua, helping him to be a writer and a revolutionary.

On another level, and a productive one, *Den Shi-hua* may be seen as a *bildungsroman*, though Tretyakov himself would probably have rejected such an approach as far too romantic. As he grows up, Den finds himself alienated from the society in which he lives, experiencing difficulties with love and unable to make meaningful relationships, for instance, with his wife. The central theme, the poignant relationship between the father and son, is interwoven with a 'public' story of China's development: the father's business of revolution is seen through the eyes of the son. Only when Den joins the May Fourth movement do the two achieve a kind of mature equality, and something like a resolution is reached. The difference, however, between this book and, say, *David Copperfield* or *The Catcher in the Rye*, is that this is not fiction, but is (as least supposedly) factual.

The style often emphasises the factuality, not least in its prevailing use of terse, direct sentences. But it frequently moves between the factual ('Some houses have salt wells. A long narrow pipe is driven through the ground, down to the rocky layer of salt. The pipe is filled with water. The water dissolves the salt', etc) and the lyrical ('At night, a crimson-breasted bird cries in Szechuan gardens… People say she cries until blood comes to her throat, and that in the morning she will be found under a tree, dead, with blood-stained beak'), between the objective and the subjective, and between the novelistic and the informative. Unity is attained in the way all these modes are inflected by Tretyakov's political stance. There is humour, as when the soldiers cut off the peasants' pigtails and Tretyakov reflects that 'they would have been less ashamed had the soldiers deprived them of their trousers', and sometimes surprising imagery: 'the fetters clinked their iron teeth', and 'people who had not seen one another now met and exchanged the rotting grains of gossip and news'. The vivid description of an execution and the complex emotions and reflections it evokes, spills into what Tretyakov no doubt thought of as montage, of which there are plenty of further examples, not least when the person of the narrator suddenly changes, and Tretyakov takes over from Den Shi-hua.

This book is therefore impressive by any standards, its fascination enhanced by the fact that it is impossible to slot it easily into any pigeon-hole, or categorize it simply by *genre*. And further evidence of its elusiveness is provided by its ending. The narrative finishes in 1927 when Den Shi-hua leaves Moscow to return to China, and Tretyakov has no idea what happened to him after that, though Den wrote a letter from Szechuan, reproduced in the book, suggesting that he was joining the revolutionaries. But nothing was known for certain. At the end of the Preface, Tretyakov acknowledges, somewhat ruefully, that the story should be continued, but 'I want the continuation to be written by Den Shi-hua himself'.

Besides these literary works, Tretyakov wanted to capture China on film. The place was inherently cinematic, he thought, and back in Moscow he laid out plans for a whole series of projects for Sergei Eisenstein. Fresh from his triumphant debut as a film director, Eisenstein responded enthusiastically, endorsing a proposed trilogy of major films, or what he called 'a gigantic Chinese film in three parts',[105] *The Yellow Peril*, *The Blue Express* and *China Roars*, the latter of which may have been a version of the drama, *Roar, China!* which Eisenstein called 'a superb play'.[106] It is possible that *The Blue Express* existed as a playscript, too. The whole undertaking would require considerable investment of time and money, as well as energy. As Tretyakov later explained:

> It is possible that to send such a film-expedition would have meant taking several risks, for there was the possibility that the Chinese revolutionary movement could take a sudden turn, even reversing itself. But I considered that such a risk should

---

105   Leyda, Jay, *Kino*, London: George Allen & Unwin, 1983, p. 221.
106   Rostotskii, B., *op. cit.*, p. 222.

be taken. I was so determined to have modern China (not its past) filmed, and absolutely as it is, that we came very close to a realization of this project.[107]

It was not to be, perhaps because the Soviet government seemed to find it difficult to form a clear policy towards China. Other proposals, too, including making a film about the making of the trilogy, a buffoonade using Chinese theatre techniques, up to ten documentary films about China, and a travel movie, *Moscow – Beijing*, though discussed extensively and ardently, all remained unmade.

A writer who engages with the social and political present runs the risk that the work will be overtaken by events. This was part of the reason why the Tretyakov-Eisenstein film projects floundered, and it also helps to explain why Tretyakov's books in later editions were changed or expanded. History was on the move. *Chzhungo* and *Den Shi-hua* recorded a moment in China's millennia-old history, they told with graphic immediacy of a country in transition to a new destiny. From that perspective, Tretyakov's work must be seen not so much as historical, as he might have wished, but as provisional.

What was happening in China fascinated and galvanised not just Tretyakov, but many Russians, particularly those who aligned themselves with communism. They saw hope, the possibility of a new, significant ally for the Soviet Union in the east, especially because of the United Front formed between the Chinese Communists and the nationalist Kuomintang Party. Then in April 1927, Chiang Kai-shek, the Kuomintang leader of the United Front, turned on the workers of Shanghai and their communist organisers, and killed thousands of them. There were similar massacres in Nanking, Canton and among the peasants in the countryside. For Russians – and presumably Tretyakov – it was utterly shocking. The more so as it became clear that, despite the United Front, Stalin, the General Secretary of the Soviet Communist Party, had long been conniving with Chiang Kai-shek over the suppression of the Chinese revolutionary movement.

Many Russian Communists were aghast. Trotsky and the left wing oppositionists were enraged, there were meetings, protests and arguments. But too many in the burgeoning Stalinist bureaucracy

---

107   Leyda, Jay, *op. cit.*, p. 220.

refused to budge. Victor Serge, a fiery oppositionist, records what happened at one meeting of Party workers:

> Despair was in us all when we met. The arguments within the Central Committee were repeated with equal violence in every Party cell where there were oppositionists. When I began to speak … I felt that a paroxysm of hatred was building up and that we would be lynched on the way out. I ended (my speech) by flinging out a sentence that brought an icy silence: 'The prestige of the General Secretary is infinitely more precious to him than the blood of the Chinese proletariat!' The hysterical section of the audience exploded: 'Enemies of the Party!'[108]

Tretyakov's own position at this time is not recorded – he was not a Party member – but it seems unlikely that he simply accepted Stalin's apparent betrayal. He was after all a leading member of the 'Left Front of the Arts'. Perhaps he was too canny to raise his head above the parapet, and, as noted, he did make changes to his books as new editions appeared, and perhaps further changes when Chiang Kai-shek failed to resist the Japanese as they marched into Manchuria in 1931. But he remained silent on the behaviour of Stalin's Government.

All this, however, was in the future. At his farewell dinner in Beijing in the summer of 1925, Tretyakov could still speak of the 'energetic heart of the Earth, whose distinct pulse we can hear in the young Beijing'.[109] On this gracious and optimistic note he departed the city, though his wife's secretarial work kept her and Tanya there for a further two months before they rejoined him in Moscow. He travelled north, where he even managed to interview a pro-Communist warlord, Feng Yu-xiang, who however was soon to defect to Chiang Kai-shek, and went on to Moscow via Mongolia.

---

108   Serge, Victor, *Memoirs of a Revolutionary*, New York: New York Review Books, 2012, pp. 253-4.
109   Hofmann, Tatjana, 'Theatrical Observation in Sergei M. Tret'iakov's *Chzhungo*', *Russian Literature*, Vol. 103-105, 2019, p. 174.

CHAPTER 8.
I WANT A BABY

Russia during Tretyakov's lifetime was a country in constant flux. Even eighteen months away from the Soviet Union must have made the country to which he returned in the summer of 1925 seem very different from the country he had left. It was not that hope or idealism had died but that the struggle to realize the true potential unleashed by the revolution was becoming vicious and more tangled. The title of Tretyakov's next play, *I Want a Baby*, symbolised the widely-held desire for a better tomorrow. But now there was a battle over what sort of baby it was that the revolution had borne.

Most obviously, on the political level, a titanic struggle for control of the future was being fought out with brutal intensity. It manifested itself in the manoeuvrings of Stalin against Trotsky, though it is arguable that neither man would have been strong in the creation of an open, pluralistic, tolerant society which would protect and enhance human rights. As the struggle proceeded, it became plain that Trotsky's naïve self-belief was no match for Stalin's greater political cunning and ruthlessness. On 25 January 1925 Trotsky had been ousted from the War Commissariat. In 1926 he was removed from the Politburo, and in 1927 from the Communist Party altogether. When he tried to speak on the tenth anniversary of the revolution which he more than anyone had orchestrated, he was heckled, booed and driven from the platform. In January 1928 he was exiled to Alma-Ata and the following year banished altogether from the Soviet Union. And once Trotsky was out of the way, Stalinisation accelerated. This was particularly evident in the fates of other leading Bolsheviks whose victimization now began: the revolutionary leader Lev Kamenev was expelled from the Communist Party in December 1927, Anatoly Lunacharsky, the cultured Minister for Education and the Arts, was replaced by Andrei Bubnov, and soon Nikolai Bukharin, for long Stalin's closest ally, was removed from the editorship of *Pravda*.

Victor Serge called the years between 1926 and 1928 the 'deadlock of the revolution'. Indeed progress was deadlocked. The old Bolshevik Party was no longer what it had been: the idealists who had fought for the revolution were being elbowed aside, outnumbered, sidelined and outvoted by new members, careerists, ambitious, efficient, but hardly motivated by altruism. As early as 1925 Bolshevist internationalism, which Tretyakov, of course, expressed in plays such as *Are You Listening, Moscow?!* and *Roar, China!*, as well as in *Den Shi-hua* and other works, had been replaced by the slogan 'Socialism in One Country'. A counter-revolution, giving power to the bureaucracy, was under way.

This inexorable counter-revolution with its accompanying political strife is what historians tend to focus on, not least because of what came after it in the 1930s. But its undeniable historical significance conceals another side to this turbulent period. For those who believed that the route of revolution must lead towards the sunny uplands of a different society, these political struggles were almost irrelevant. Even Trotsky, to the end of his days, believed that the Soviet Union, if only because of its socialised economy and its Marxist foundations, was bound to enter its true inheritance eventually. This was the road, and if it proved to be bumpy, or even dangerous, all the more must eyes remain fixed on the destination. The left especially, and left artists notably, refused to be distracted by the shenanigans of the intra-party contentions. They continued what they considered the prime struggle. Things were still in flux, and those who cared for the values of the revolution never doubted that they must continue to drive towards them. Tretyakov was firmly of this persuasion.

When he reappeared in Moscow in the summer of 1925, the two most immediate factors which affected the work he wanted to do were, first, the discontinuation of *LEF*, the literary journal to which he had devoted so much of his energy, and, second, the Communist Party's Resolution on Literature, which had been adopted in June 1925. This Resolution was a forewarning that the Party claimed the right to control literary production, though, as it also made clear, it refused for the time being to exercise that right by endorsing any particular literary school. However, it did favour proletarian writers, who tended to be more interested in content than in form, over the *LEF* group, whose claims to Communist legitimacy were denied. It was therefore threatening in its intentions but for the moment quiescent. There were still openings for Tretyakov and his comrades.

The only place Tretyakov had been able to find to live when he returned from China was, according to his daughter, a 'ghastly', L-shaped, one-bedroom flat, which was freezing even in summer, and it was here that he began work on his major play, *I Want a Baby*. He showed a draft of this to Vsevolod Meyerhold in September 1926, and Meyerhold quickly agreed to stage it. This drama is perhaps its author's most significant work, and has claims to be one of the most remarkable plays of the twentieth century, perhaps still waiting for the major productions across the world which it deserves. It centres on Milda, a Latvian Party cadre, who wishes to further the aims of the new society by bearing a child with an impeccable proletarian heredity. She does not wish to burden herself with a husband, however. She lives in an overcrowded Moscow apartment block surrounded by an extraordinarily diverse cross-section of contemporary citizens, from a drug-addicted poet to eager Party workers, and from violent hooligans to a grumbling 'aunty' run off her feet by the children she looks after. Milda invites the down-to-earth proletarian building worker, Yakov, to father her baby, despite the fact that he is already virtually engaged to a postal worker, Lipa. He is astonished by her proposal, but finally agrees, and soon Milda is pregnant. Yakov becomes sentimental at the thought of fatherhood, but Milda sends him back to Lipa. Her behaviour has aroused the ire of her neighbours, but she shrugs this off, and in a dream foresees the Soviet future when her baby will win the prize for the brightest and healthiest Soviet child. But her triumph turns sour when she has to share the prize with the child of Yakov and Lipa, and the next prize is won by the child of the drug addict, whose partner Milda had counselled to have an abortion. Yakov is left to salute the children in an uncanny pre-echo of Stalin himself: they are 'the heroes of the age!' The play's ending is thus highly ambiguous.

I Want a Baby is about creating a new kind of person for the new age. 'The play isolates and examines dispassionately the expenditure of sexual energy which has as its aim the birth of a baby', Tretyakov asserted somewhat primly, though he added that it thereby 'aims to discredit the so-called love intrigue, that commonplace of our theatrical art and literature'.[110] One of the methods he uses to achieve this is to present a bewildering array of love or sex partnerships – Saxoulsky seduces the naïve Kitty; Barbara is infatuated with the poet, Filirinov; the Block Superintendent makes clumsy advances to both Angelica and Milda; Andryusha's attitude to Ksenichka is hopelessly romantic; she is gang-raped by a group of hooligans; and so on. Milda's own approach to sex and love is utterly anti-septic and ingenuous. 'Up to now on stage', Tretyakov maintained, 'love has been a spicy stimulant. The tension of it gripped the spectator, turning him into an "illusory lover". In the play, *I Want a Baby*, love is put on the operating table and traced to its socially significant result'. Sex and love were subjects of considerable anxiety in early Soviet Russia[111], and it is no surprise to find Tretyakov taking an active part in debates such as that on 5 March 1927 in the Communist Academy, when Professor V.P.Polonsky spoke on 'Mass Decadence in Life and Literature in Connection with Questions of Sex'. On this occasion, Tretyakov roundly attacked the editors of popular papers and magazines for pandering to the lowest tastes with titillating smut: 'you maintain the things you print are necessary for Soviet youth. Such lies and nonsense', he snorted.[112]

Tretyakov's concerns were always sociological rather than psychological. In the play, Milda is a typical female Communist bureaucrat with briefcase and leather jacket. She is interested in child-bearing, not sex. Yet she is just one among the teeming crowd of undertakers, supervisors, prostitutes, flower sellers, working women, nappy-changing fathers, drama students, drunkards and poets who form a vivid kaleidoscope of contemporary society. They are shown with an absolute lack of sentimentality, but also with a good deal of humour, and they are connected to the play's theme rather than its overt 'plot'. How can this jostling, unruly multitude, which includes Milda, conjure a happy future for the Soviet Union?

---

110 Fevral'skii, A., 'S.M. Tretyakov v teatre Meierkhol'da', in Tret'yakov, Sergei, *Slyshish', Moskva?!*, Moscow: Iskusstvo, 1966, p. 198.
111 See Naiman, Eric, *Sex in Public: The Incarnation of Early Soviet Ideology*, Princeton: Princeton University Press, 1997.
112 Volkova, N.V. (ed), *Vstrechi c proshlym*, Moscow: Sovetskaya Rossiya, 1983, p. 168.

Milda: the Freedom Monument in Riga.

The question is asked, but not answered, and Tretyakov explained:

> I will not bow any more to plays which end with some kind of approved maxim, which emasculates any struggle towards understanding. The intrigue has been worked out, the conclusion has been presented, and the spectators can go and put on their galoshes in peace. I think plays which stimulate in the spectator something that lasts beyond the theatre are more valuable.[113]

I Want a Baby is thus a highly unconventional play, which rejects the expected notions of theatrical naturalism. This is exemplified as early as the second scene when Saxoulsky performs an incident of extreme pathos from the Civil War to the Club Secretary. An old general lies dying in Paris, and his Bolshevik son comes to visit him. But he rejects him even on his deathbed. 'No Bolshevik's a son of mine', he declares. 'There are no commissars in the Polyudov family. In my veins flows the blood of Catherine's court'. But at the scene's conclusion, the Club Secretary is shocked: 'Ideological claptrap!' he asserts. So Saxoulsky performs the scene again. An old general lies dying, but this time in Moscow, and his White Guard officer son comes to visit him. The old man rejects him: 'No White Guard's a son of mine. There are no tsarist cavalry captains in the Polyudov family. In my veins flows the blood of Pugachev's warriors'. The tears now are for a valiant Bolshevik, and the Secretary exclaims: 'Now that's artistically valuable and ideologically consistent'.[114] By presenting the two scenes in exactly the same way, and achieving totally opposite responses, Tretyakov undermines the very basis of psychological drama.

Besides specific vignettes like this, Tretyakov creates a virtually unique cacophony of voices – snatches of overheard conversations, a jigsaw of apparently ill-fitting pieces which appear to have no connection with the 'plot' of the play. But this montage is in fact its

---

113   Fevral'sii, A., *op. cit.*, pp. 203-4.
114   Tretyakov, Sergei, *I Want a Baby and Other Plays*, Glagoslav Publications, 2019, pp. 283-4. All quotations from *I Want a Baby* (both versions) are taken from this book.

life-blood. And because they are carefully orchestrated, they make up an endlessly echoing context for Milda's search.

Beyond this, Tretyakov also trawls his own past as a Latvian-born Russian for one thread which runs through the play. Milda is from Latvia, and occasionally she finds herself stumbling over Russian words or phrases, because Latvian is her first language. Yakov, when he learns where Milda is from, mutters that Latvians are 'good snipers' and indeed there had been a moment during the revolution, in the summer of 1918, when a small detachment of Latvian riflemen and snipers had in effect saved the revolution.[115] But Milda herself has perhaps a deeper significance. In giving his protagonist this name, Tretyakov almost certainly was referring to Milda as the Latvian goddess of love. This legendary figure was perhaps originally Lithuanian, or Polish, but the Latvian people claimed her as their own, and though her mythical status was much disputed, by the end of the nineteenth century, when Tretyakov was a boy in Latvia, her eminence was widely and popularly accepted. Her rise in the public consciousness owed much to the 'Young Latvian' movement. 'Milda' became a common name for girls, and in the mythology she came to symbolise hope and patriotism. Today, in the centre of Riga, stands the Freedom Monument, erected in 1935 and around which ceremonial guards parade. At the top of the monument is Milda with her arms aloft, holding up the three stars of freedom.

But Tretyakov's Milda is also very much an exemplar of the 'new' society which Tretyakov saw evolving. In his programmatic essay, 'From Where to Where?' published in *LEF* in 1923, he wrote of the 'new type of worker' who

> finds it difficult to love nature the way the landscape painter, the tourist or the pantheist once did. He is repelled by thick pine forests, untilled steppes, unutilized waterfalls which tumble not according to our order, rain and snow, avalanches, caves and mountains. He finds beauty in those things upon which one can see the mark of the organising human hand.[116]

---

115   See Deutscher, Isaac, *The Prophet Armed*, Oxford: O.U.P., 1987, p. 404.
116   Lawton, Anna (ed), *Russian Futurism Through its Manifestoes, 1912-1928*, Ithaca: Cornell University Press, 1988, p. 214.

Early in the play, Milda shows she is well in tune with this leftist extremist position during a conversation with Dr Softer after she has refused to buy flowers from a street seller, saying she doesn't like flowers because they are 'the plant's sex organs':

> SOFTER : You don't like nature then? Mountains, waterfalls, wild places?
> MILDA : I love it when there's a turbine on the waterfall, mines in the mountains and sawmills in the wild woods, and regular plantations.

Here is the nub of the dialectical contradiction Tretyakov wishes to explore between the mythic love goddess and the contemporary Soviet woman. In the process, *I Want a Baby* meets head on a range of crucial sociological questions in ways which demonstrate the author's intellectual and artistic engagement with his time.

Most noticeable is the challenge the play poses to conventional bourgeois attitudes to sex and gender which the Communist Party, as part of its counter-revolution, was in the process of re-incorporating into the 'normal life' of Russian society. Female sexuality is at the centre of the dramatic action. From the beginning, Milda is not seen as the conventional woman: she wears masculine clothes and carries a briefcase, and Grinko, seeing her from behind, mistakes her for one of his pals. She is busy and active in social life, an organiser and a campaigner. She suggests to the Block Superintendent that he doesn't 'need' a woman, he can solve the problem which his wife's absence causes him by masturbating. After all, female 'sexiness' is merely a matter of waving your hair, putting on make-up and wearing a low-necked dress. In her relations with Yakov, it is always she who takes the lead, even if Tretyakov's skill as a dramatist makes a scene like his seduction by her one of high comedy bordering on farce. By subverting gender roles, *I Want a Baby* is also able to query the possessiveness which conventional love relationships always seem to demand, though in a brief moment very near the end of the play Milda's own doubts are revealed, when, momentarily wistful, she asks Yakov: 'Do you think it was easy for me back then to give you the brush-off?' Tretyakov's sense of irony, and his human sympathies, constantly complicate this brilliant play.

Questions of gender and sexuality are further problematized by the play's exploration of eugenics and social and racial stereotyping. Eugenics, that is, selective breeding, implies both parental selection and perhaps forced sterilisation of those deemed unfit to bear children, and was widely discussed at the time *I Want a Baby* was being written. It grew out of the nineteenth century's fears of over-population, the dangers of which had been graphically prognosticated by Thomas Malthus. But it was suggested that the danger Malthus foresaw could be countered by what was actually a misreading of Darwin's theory of evolution, the 'struggle for existence' and the 'survival of the fittest'. The waters were further muddied by another misreading, this time of Nietzsche's concept of the *übermensch*. In 1895 Alfred Ploetz published his theory of 'racial hygiene', in 1908 the British Eugenics Society was founded, and the similar Russian Society was established in 1920. At the same time, the Austrian eugenicist, Paul Kammerer, was invited to set up a laboratory of 'experimental biology' in the Soviet Union. Alexandra Smith notes:

> Kammerer was a proponent of the Lamarckian model of eugenics which views all genetic material as modifiable by social conditions and transferable to future generations in an enhanced form. Tretyakov himself was apparently aware of Kammerer's works, and the name by which Milda's friend is known – Stoneturner – evokes Kammerer's statements comparing genetics to sculpting.[117]

It should be added here, parenthetically, that Tretyakov's name for the character called 'Stoneturner', one who leaves no stone unturned, in the English version, is actually 'Distsiplinyor', which would be more accurately translated as 'discipliner', one who disciplines others, or whose approach to life is disciplined.

For Marxists, the human personality was unimportant, indeed it might be constructed, as in Brecht's play, *Man Equals Man*, written in 1926 and therefore an exact contemporary of Tretyakov's *I Want*

---

[117] Smith, A., 'Reconfiguring the Utopian Vision: Tretyakov's Play *I Want a Baby* (1926) as a Response to the Revolutionary Restructuring of Everyday Life', *Australian Slavonic & East European Studies*, Vol. 25, No. 1-2, p. 111.

a Baby. The implication was that humans could control their own future, as Milda imagines is possible in Tretyakov's play. There was a belief that with eugenics 'the ordinary person in socialist society would be the equal of five Pushkins'.[118] And Marxists were not the only people toying with this idea: Daylanne English has pointed out that 'from eugenics' inception in late nineteenth-century England to its peak in the United States during the post-war years of the late 1910s and 1920s, few challenged the view that modern nations, especially those beset by immigration, must improve their stock, in order to remain competitive, indeed viable, in the modern world'.[119] And theory became practice: we know about the Nazi drive to produce an ever-purer Aryan race, and it seems that there are still sperm banks in the USA storing the genetic inheritance of 'men of genius' for use with suitable mothers (such sperms can also be bought). Genetic engineering remains a thorny moral problem for our society: in Sweden in the years after the Second World War over 60,000 young men were forcibly sterilised in the interests of 'racial hygiene'; in 2002 the US state of Virginia formally apologised for its programme of eugenics which had led to more than 7,000 people undergoing forced sterilisation; and in 2005 a Dutch reality television show featured women choosing the most suitable competitor to father their child.

The continuing relevance of Tretyakov's play could hardly be plainer, but it must be added that it has often been misinterpreted and even denigrated by critics who have failed to recognize Tretyakov's pervasive and subtle irony, not to mention his sense of humour. The comment that *I Want a Baby* 'concludes by advocating selective breeding'[120] is typical of remarks made by commentators from Stalin's censors onwards, and reveals a sad misapprehension about how this play operates. Of course, it does not advocate anything, nor does its author endorse the behaviour of any of its characters. As he himself said:

---

118   Rozovskii, Mark, 'Etyud o Tret'yakove', *Sovremennaya Dramaturgiya*, No. 2, 1988, p. 208.
119   English, D.K., *Unnatural Selection: Eugenics in American Modernism and the Harlem Renaissance*, Chapel Hill: University of North Carolina Press, 2004, p. 1.
120   Braun, Edward, *The Theatre of Meyerhold*, London: Eyre Methuen, 1979, p. 224.

> The play is constructed deliberately problematically. The task of the author is not so much to give a kind of single final prescription as to demonstrate possible variants, which could challenge the healthy discussion society needs on the serious and important questions which are touched on in the play.[121]

It is worth adding that – as we would expect with Tretyakov's work – the play is not complete fiction. Many of the incidents are based in fact such as the Healthy Baby Competition which is held at the climax of the play. The Soviet Union's first Healthy Baby Competition was sponsored by the magazine, snappily titled *Hygiene and Health of the Worker and Peasant Family*, and announced in September 1926. Tretyakov, using this to tie up the ends of his play, and treating it both sardonically and comically, asks: is this the future of the Soviet Union?

The same question is posed with considerably more trepidation in the scene of the gang rape, which probably derives from a notorious – even sensational – case which took place as he was writing *I Want a Baby*. In Chubarov Alley in Leningrad on 21 August 1926, about twenty-five young men, several of whom were members of the Komsomol, the Communist Party youth organisation, raped a young peasant woman, Lyubov B., a student at the local Rabfak school for young working people, who wanted to enter higher education. The perpetrators of this outrage were employees of the nearby Kooperator works. They dragged the woman onto some waste ground, the San-Galli Gardens in the rundown district near the Oktober railway station, and beat and raped her over a period of hours. She was left near death, and barely able to communicate. It was the worst, but by no means the only, such incident: shortly before it there had been two cases of rape committed after noisy parties at the Medved Hotel, an impoverished doss-house in Zhelyabova Street. But the Chubarov Alley occurrence was not only appalling it itself, it attracted huge publicity, including an angry poem by Vladimir Mayakovsky, and it led to a widely-reported trial. This resulted in five of the offenders being sentenced to death and most of the others receiving long prison terms. The affair was not imported into *I Want a Baby* merely for sensational or melodramatic

---

121   Fevral'skii, A., *op. cit.*, p. 198.

Tretyakov by B. Antonov.

purposes. It was central to Tretyakov's concerns, and spoke urgently to the anxieties about sex and gender which the play addresses.

The fierce and often sanctimonious tone of the furore surrounding the Chubarov Alley case also hinted at the danger of Tretyakov's whole artistic project, a danger which became unexpectedly apparent as the tortuous and fraught possibility of its presentation on stage began. When he presented the draft script to Meyerhold in September 1926, the latter was excited by it, and immediately commissioned the *avant-garde* artist, El Lissitzky, to draw up designs for it. Tretyakov had been stirred by Meyerhold's production of Ostrovsky's classic, *The Forest*, which he had seen soon after returning from China, and when the Meyerhold Theatre had celebrated its fifth anniversary, scenes from *Roar, China!* as well as excerpts from Mayakovsky's *Mystery Bouffe* and other plays had been presented. Now the chance to work with 'the Master' again on what Mayakovsky was 'firmly convinced could become a second *Battleship Potemkin*' was certainly tempting.

A contract was signed, and at the end of November Meyerhold took the now-finished script to Glavrepertkom, the official censor, for permission to stage the play. Publicity was generated in the newspapers and posters were printed. The first read-through took place and casting was announced. Before the first rehearsal began, on 16 February 1927, Meyerhold spoke to the company, pointing out the prevalence of 'banality' in so many contemporary plays. 'Tretyakov', he said,

> has banished the banal. He transformed *Night* into *The World Upside Down*. Eisenstein beat down banality in the Theatre of the Proletkult aided by the exertions of Tretyakov. In *I Want a Baby* Tretyakov is doing the same again. And whereas in *Roar, China!* he did not present questions, in *I Want a Baby* he does pose questions (to which he does not provide simple answers). When this play is produced, people will never stop talking about its subject matter.
>
> This thing is not complete, in the sense that *Roar, China!* was. It is not a single complete play.
>
> But the play will become complete when we begin work on it. The schematic characters will begin to live, if they are played properly. When we read *I Want a Baby*, I saw in your faces that it fascinated you. It caught you in its trap. The play will create an

incredible outcry and plenty of noise. I award Tretyakov a gold medal. It's not certain he'll take it. To put on *I Want a Baby* is more difficult than to act it. I will not cut it. Tretyakov himself can change whatever may be necessary to change during our work on the production. Many are saying that that's weak, but actually it's because the play is strong.'[122]

Then Glavrepertkom banned the play, and rehearsals were stopped. The censor's agent, N.A.Rozer-Nirova, contacted Tretyakov, and suggested that if he made certain major changes, he could return with a revised script to see whether a new version could be agreed to.

Tretyakov might have recalled Trotsky's words, written less than five years previously:

> If your comedy will say: 'We are building a new life now, and yet how much piggishness, vulgarity and knavery of the old and of the new are about us; let us make a clean sweep of them', then of course the censorship will not interfere, and if it will interfere somewhere it will do so foolishly, and all of us will fight such a censorship.[123]

But he set to work again to create what was virtually a new version of *I Want a Baby*. The story of Milda's search for a properly proletarian father for her baby is the same, but is now given a rural agricultural setting. Milda is an agronomist, and the story is framed by discussions of crop-growing, insecticides and animal husbandry.

Gone, therefore, are the fast-changing glimpses of the stresses of everyday life in the Moscow apartment block, and the play is peopled by peasants rather than urban misfits and city slickers. Eugenics as a theme becomes even more important, so that Milda's professional attention is taken with the problems of breeding pure white rabbits, the harvesting of gherkins in a greenhouse, and the growing of cabbages on peat. The prevailing conditions at the time of gestation must be factored in, as with the native tribe where

---

122 *Ibid.*, pp. 199-200.
123 Trotsky, Leon, *Literature and Revolution*, Ann Arbor: University of Michigan Press, 1971, p. 239.

prospective parents are not allowed to drink alcohol if they wish to conceive. Milda worries about the seeding machine, while she knows that plenty of blossom in the spring may still mean very small fruits on the trees in autumn. Finally, the baby competition at the end is infused with considerably more bite by the implicit comparison between humans and farm livestock – both are exhibited with medals awarded to the finest children as to the finest piglets.

Though not so stark as the first version, and perhaps lacking some of its originality and daring, this second version of *I Want a Baby* is by no means merely a paler version of the first. It is able to link more effectively genetic heritage with female sexuality and a woman's control over her own body. And the play's ending, apparently different, is just as ambiguous. Stoneturner has invented an electric rattle, and in the final scene he leads the whole cast, Pied Piper-like, round the stage and away. 'Those who would like to give their best babies to the Soviet Union', he cries, 'not deformed or abnormal little monkeys, but healthy, bouncing, beautiful Soviet babies, follow me'. Brandishing his device, he goes into the heart of the kindergarten, and the crowd follows him. Again we are faced with the question about the nature of any future society.

In spite of the fact that the new version was clearly a challenging and original work, Tretyakov was feeling melancholy. 'The confrontation of "art" and "life" is over', he wrote. 'What is left are confrontations between different styles within "art". Theatre has returned to its channels, constructions have become decent wooden sets, and biomechanics a peculiar kind of plastic movement'.[124] It was no doubt with a sinking heart that he attended the recalled meeting of Glavrepertkom, which was not held until 4 December 1928.

In the meantime, after Meyerhold had appeared to hesitate about *I Want a Baby*, perhaps because of the ban, perhaps because of the complexity of Lissitzky's design, which might not be appropriate for the second version, another possible director had appeared on the scene. This was Igor Terentiev, a friend of the poet Alexei Kruchyonykh, an extreme Futurist with four slim volumes of poetry to his name. Over the previous few years he had created several wildly *avant-garde* productions, including an extraordinary *Government Inspector*

---

124 Kleberg, Lars, *Theatre as Action*, London: Macmillan, 1993, p. 115.

in which real mice were let out on the stage, and the Mayor and his councillors carried on their debate while in small cubicles, their voices deformed by the strains of defecating. It was, among other things, a satirical sideswipe at Meyerhold's own controversial and brilliant production of Gogol's comedy, which had opened four months before Terentiev's. Now Terentiev had the opportunity of producing Tretyakov's new play at the Theatre of the Revolution in Moscow. He was clearly fascinated by *I Want a Baby*: he saw Milda as 'a female Hamlet, in a major key' who tested the limits of rationalism. Tretyakov found his ideas provocative and attractive. Maybe the play should be given to him?

The Glavrepertkom meeting was chaired by the perhaps-appropriately named Fyodor Fyodorovich Raskolnikov, an old Bolshevik who had joined the Party in 1910. He was the husband of Larissa Reissner, a considerably more charismatic figure whom some said served as a model for Milda. He was the editor of a literary journal, *The Young Guard*, and a playwright in his own right, best known for the dull and utterly predictable drama, *Robespierre*. He had only recently become chair of the censorship committee. After Tretyakov had read the new version of *I Want a Baby* to the committee, Raskolnikov, perhaps unnecessarily, indicated that it would be considered from two points of view: whether it was ideologically sound and whether permission to stage it should be granted.

Then came the comments of the various members of the committee. Comrade Rafes thought the overemphasis on the 'physical elements' was a 'peasant approach' and incorrect. Comrade Ravich found the play 'schematic' and coarse, and thought it might arouse 'unhealthy' interest, though with some cuts and careful treatment a single performance might be permissible. Comrade Petrov from the Hammer and Sickle factory, disagreed. He thought it propagandised masturbation, and a sixteen year old girl should not hear such words. Families go to the theatre for a rest, he asserted, though he admitted that the play could perhaps be reworked. One can almost hear Tretyakov groaning, even from this distance in time. However, Valery Pletnev, with whom Tretyakov and Eisenstein had crossed swords at the Proletkult, agreed that it should be reworked, and could be tested by being presented before a small number of spectators before it was shown to the public.

The discussion remained rather unfocussed. Comrade Khenkin thought the play oversimplified and primitive, but that was not a reason to ban it, and Meyerhold would be able to 'transform the face of this play'. The theatre critic Vladimir Blyum, on the other hand, thought *I Want a Baby* one of the best Soviet plays, and the film director Abram Room welcomed its honesty – 'we need to stop lisping to our audiences', he said. Arguments for banning the play came from Comrade Novitsky, who found it vulgar and the fact that psychology was banished from it 'wrong', and Comrade Gens, representing 'the Guardians of Motherhood and Babyhood', who pleaded that 'we are not so bad' as the sexual anarchy depicted in the play implied. Comrade Rozer-Nirova, who had carried the bad news of the original ban to Tretyakov, admitted that its subject matter was topical, but stated that 'without radical change, the play must not be performed'.

Vsevolod Meyerhold cut through the discussion. He was obviously upset that Tretyakov had talked with Terentiev about a possible production, and especially that Tretyakov was excited by Terentiev's ideas, which he called 'absurd'. Meyerhold needed this play for his own repertoire, which was under constant fire for its lack of contemporary Soviet plays, and he even threatened to put on a different play, but to change its title to *I Want a Baby*. He flattered Comrade Raskolnikov for his conduct of the meeting which he said, for him, had been 'a creative process'. He suggested now what he thought Terentiev would find 'extremely unpleasant', that is, a further meeting at which each director would put forward his plan for how the play could be amended and the production could work, but without the author being present. Tretyakov, obviously trying to assuage Meyerhold's anger, welcomed the scheme, but insisted on his presence at any further meeting, and his *imprimatur* for any changes to the text. Comrade Raskolnikov, noting that both the Guardians of Motherhood and Babyhood and the Women's Section of the Central Committee were resolutely opposed to the play, nevertheless accepted Meyerhold's suggestion of a further meeting, though he also agreed with Tretyakov that the author should be present. Terentiev, on a personal note, said that he wanted the production, not for himself, but for the Soviet theatre, and added that he was aware that 'the path of Meyerhold was carved out long before mine'.

Olga Viktorovna Tretyakova.

Before the meeting was reconvened, the chairman received a telling letter from Boris Isaakovich Goldberg, the managing director of the Meyerhold Theatre, presumably at Meyerhold's request. He urged that 'the play is interesting, strong, though many of its positions arouse completely fair objections. But', Goldberg continued, 'to ban it (especially now when the repertoire is in such crisis) in no way follows'. This letter probably had some effect.

When Glavrepertkom's deliberations resumed on 15 December 1928, Meyerhold laid out his plans. He suggested a 'discussion play'. He said that there were 'mistakes' in the play, and he had done a lot of work on it, including with El Lissitzky on his stage model. In their plan, the auditorium and the stage would not be divided off from each other. Some spectators would sit on the stage, while some of the action would take place in the auditorium, and the play would be interrupted at pre-ordained moments for discussion, in which the actors would participate as well as the audience. 'The discussion will be in the form of a dialectical argument, and will give pointers to the future discussions at the end of the show'. He accepted that Glavrepertkom could from time to time send representatives to participate in the discussions, but his plan had the advantage that 'every full stop and comma of the author' would be respected. Meyerhold even proposed that Tretyakov himself could come from the stalls and speak. 'And sometimes you could come out, too, Vsevolod Emilievich', Comrade Raskolnikov hinted brightly to Meyerhold. Tretyakov, perhaps scenting that this was the only way the play would be produced, even though he preferred what Terentiev was to propose, said he welcomed Meyerhold's scheme. For the actors to be challenged over their characters' roles was refreshing. 'The play is not in any way apologetic', he added. 'It is not correct to say that I want to make the public identify with Milda. I myself include a series of moments when she is discredited'. And Meyerhold had one final proposal: 'On the poster will be written, not "First Performance", "Second Performance", "Third Performance", etc, but "First Discussion", "Second Discussion" and so on'.

Raskolnikov summed up: 'The play *I Want a Baby* is banned. By way of exception, Comrade Meyerhold is permitted to produce it according to this interpretation'.

'But', Tretyakov interposed, 'you've got to listen to Comrade Terentiev too'. So Terentiev laid out his plan, which was for a discussion to be held at the end of each performance. But the committee was wary of Terentiev. Meyerhold, eager to capitalize on the advantage he thought he had obtained, now suggested that Terentiev was copying him, for his ideas about a discussion play had long been known. In any case, under Terentiev's plan the spectator could slip away without staying for the discussion. Terentiev roundly disputed this, saying that the idea of discussion is built into the play, and anyway he (Terentiev) had only begun to think about the play a year or more ago after Meyerhold had indicated that he didn't want to do it. 'I didn't refuse it!' rejoined Meyerhold. Comrade Pikel calmed the flaring tempers in a long speech, which however got round to the point that 'if we allow *I Want a Baby*, it's for one theatre only'. For him, that theatre must be Meyerhold's. Terentiev backed down: 'Obviously this is the kind of play which must be given to Comrade Meyerhold'. But he still hankered after *I Want a Baby*. Perhaps he could be permitted to direct it in 'another city', probably Leningrad where he had done most of his work. Meyerhold cattily pointed out that his theatre toured Leningrad, but at this point Raskolnikov intervened for the last time to state: 'The play remains banned. Comrade Meyerhold is permitted to produce this play on a trial basis. But the possibility is not closed to Comrade Terentiev to mount a production in another city. If Comrade Terentiev rehearses with another theatre, we will consider the question again'.[125]

Was it all a storm in a teacup? Meyerhold never did stage *I Want a Baby*. The setting he had requested from Lissitzky was so complex and overpowering that he decided he needed a completely new theatre in order to do the design justice. As fortune would have it, the authorities had just agreed that a new theatre should be built for him. The work on this went on for years. Meyerhold lost favour with the Communist Party. His theatre company was liquidated, the new theatre became a concert hall and he himself was arrested and in 1940 judicially murdered. Terentiev's fate was perhaps even bleaker. He was arrested the following year, 1929, but released quite quickly. He was re-arrested in 1931, released again, and arrested a third time in 1936. He died in the gulag camp in 1937. *I Want a Baby* was not staged in Moscow – or indeed anywhere in Russia – until 1990.

---

125   For both meetings of Glavrepertkom and Boris Goldberg's letter, see *Sovremennaya Dramaturgiya*, No. 2, 1988, pp. 238-243.

CHAPTER 9.
FACTOGRAPHY

Because of Olga Viktorovna's work at the Soviet Embassy, she and Tanya did not leave Beijing for several weeks after Sergei had departed. When they did reach Moscow they soon found that the 'ghastly' flat which Tretyakov had found when he returned was not suitable for three people. Olga indeed could not stand it, and in 1927 she went to the State Insurance Co-operative for help to find better accommodation. They moved to a smart, two-bedroom first floor flat at 21/13 Malaya Bronnaya Street, a 'severely functional' apartment block built in a thoroughly modern style. The flat was comfortable and contained a gas water heater, a rare luxury in Moscow at that time. On the other hand, the refuse chute outside their door was often sealed off and unusable because there seemed to be no-one to service it. In the kitchen there was a wall cupboard, an extractor flue, a gas cooker and a kitchen table where the family ate their meals. Tanya shared a bedroom with her mother, Olga sleeping on a divan bed while Tanya slept on an ugly armchair-cum-bedstead with a green imitation leather bed cover. There was also a table with Olga's typewriter, a shared wardrobe and a so-called Swedish glass-fronted bookcase. Tretyakov's bedroom also did duty as his study. He had a divan bed with a sprung mattress, a writing-desk, a small armchair, a small plain wardrobe and book shelves which stretched from the floor to the high ceiling. One further room with a large round table was a kind of reception room, but was also used sometimes as a guest room, though male guests more usually slept on a mattress on the floor of Tretyakov's bedroom.

Sergei and Olga, being naturally convivial people, did much entertaining in this room. All three directors of his films made in

Georgia, for instance, Nikolai Shengelaya, Mikhail Kalatozov and Mikhail Chiaureli, stayed with the Tretyakovs when they were in Moscow. Ivan Kirillovich Martovitsky of the Communist Lighthouse kolkhoz, who stayed there several times in the 1930s, recorded that his reception was always cordial and friendly: Olga Viktorovna and Tanya made every guest feel at home and would have been offended if anyone had suggested staying somewhere else. Tretyakov took Martovitsky to the theatre and concerts, and to the offices of newspapers, and showed him the sights of Moscow. One evening he took him to Herzen House to hear Vsevolod Vishnevsky read his play, *The First Horse Army*, to invited guests. Martovitsky accompanied Tretyakov, and remembered how Vishnevsky read for three hours without interruption: when he asked whether his listeners would like a break, they all implored him simply to continue.

Tanya commented, perhaps wryly, that Tretyakov was 'gay and witty, true to his friends and active in their defence', and during these years the family was happy: 'the three of us, he, my mother and I, were very close friends', she remembered. If Olga did most of the housework, she was also 'always ready for fun', which Sergei gladly joined in. He made up comic rhymes for Tanya on her birthdays, and sometimes even versified little stories for her. Occasionally, if she made a witty remark, he would give her ten kopeks as a reward. He played ball, ping-pong and other games with her and with Olga, they went skiing together as well as on other excursions, to the theatre and to poetry readings by Mayakovsky and others. When either his wife or his daughter was ill, 'he nursed us very skilfully and was always ready with a joke to cheer us up'. His father, Mikhail Konstantinovich, was a very frequent visitor, coming for his evening meal three or four times per week. He was Tanya's adoptive grandfather, and she loved him dearly. He helped her with her school work, especially a few years later when she was preparing for the maths examination which could gain her a place at the Technical Institute, which she had set her heart on entering. His coaching was instrumental in her success at this exam.

As with most writers, home was also of course Tretyakov's main workplace. Olga was often happy to act as a kind of unpaid secretary for him, typing to his dictation and keeping his papers in order. An American visitor, Alfred Hamilton Barr, wrote at this time: 'His study is filled with books and periodicals on China, modern architecture, and the cinema. In this laboratory atmosphere, behind the mask of what seems ostentatious efficiency, there is a profound seriousness and very real sensibility'.[126] And this showed itself not only in the works on China and the plays that he wrote, but in an extraordinary range of other work which he now embarked on.

Film began to excite him. He had already suggested to his friend, Sergei Eisenstein, that he should film an early version of *Roar, China!* In September 1925, shortly after he returned from China, and perhaps thanks to Eisenstein's influence, he became Vice-Chair of the Artistic Council of the First State Cinema in Moscow (Goskino). That autumn he spent time in Odessa with Eisenstein as part of the team working on what would become *Battleship Potemkin*, probably Eisenstein's – and Russia's – most admired film. Tretyakov honed the script and supplied subtitles, all of which, according to Grigory Alexandrov, was 'integral' to its success when it premiered in December 1925.

Early the next year, not only was much time devoted to the China film projects, but Tretyakov, Eisenstein and Alexandrov were also working on a projected film of Karl Marx's *Capital*. Nothing came of these projects, but in November 1926, Tretyakov went via Sukhumi on the Georgian Black Sea to Baki (formerly Baku) on the Caspian Sea, Azerbaijan, where Eisenstein was filming *The General Line*, and the two discussed another project, a film to be called *Five Minutes* about a strike on a foreign ship at the time of Lenin's death. Further aborted scenarios by Tretyakov without Eisenstein's involvement included *Neurosis Today* which he worked on in 1927, and *I Want a Baby*, after its second banning from the stage in 1929, with its slightly creepy opening shot:

> In the shot a million fibres are moving, and this movement looks like a ripened field, swayed by the wind in one direction. On this swaying there appears a huge, semitransparent sphere, glimmering with radiating filaments from the luminous nucleus at its centre. The sphere rolls on the swaying field. The delicate flagella with their fat little heads, wriggling swiftly, move towards the sphere. They surround the sphere with

---

126   Hofmann, Tatjana, and Ditschek, Eduard Jan (eds), *Sergei Tret'jakow: Ich Will Ein Kind!*, Vol. 2, Berlin: Kulturverlag Kadmos, 2019, p. 276.

twitching rays on all sides. One of them pierces the membrane of the sphere. This membrane becomes glassy as soon as it is pierced, grows turbid, and through the murk one can see how the head of the flagellum moves towards the nucleus and joins with it. With a sharp movement this entire picture is jerked out of the shot. This is Milda the agronomist-cattle-breeder working with the microscope.[127]

The film of *I Want a Baby* was never made.

Tretyakov also wrote more than fifty texts about film between the mid-1920s and the 1930s. Lenin and Stalin both emphasized the importance of film for the U.S.S.R., both as a propaganda vehicle and as a means of exhibiting the country in a favourable light both within and beyond its borders. Tretyakov probably shared this view. Perhaps the clearest exposition of his ideas can be found in 'Our Cinema' in *The Film: The International Language of Understanding Between Peoples* which was published in several languages in Moscow in 1928. His observations in this essay are shot through with incisive insights. In Esther Shub's *The Fall of the Romanovs*, for example, he notices how

> the beads of perspiration on the faces of the Princesses dancing with naval cadets is being shown together with the sweat of the hard-toiling peasant. This combination gives a cinematic phrase, fully spiced with perfect irony.

And in Vsevolod Pudovkin's *The End of St Petersburg*, he notes that

> the glass of hot tea on the table in a workman's room is not being touched, nobody drinks it.
> In regard to its original purpose, it does not work. But this same glass serves as a measurement of time, by showing how the steam from it is getting thinner and thinner. The same glass, alone on the empty table, characterises lack of land and poverty.

---

127   Kiaer, Christina, and Naiman, Eric (eds), *Everyday Life in Early Soviet Russia*, Bloomington: Indiana University Press, 2006, p. 184.

But Tretyakov went further than merely commenting on existing films: he developed his own hard-edged theory of film which began by contrasting films from the 'old' society with films from the 'new' Soviet Union. From the capitalist world came films whose intention (like the twenty-first century's social media) was to give the *illusion* of intense living, or, as he put it rather more colourfully, which wanted to 'manicure the dirty finger-nails of society'. Instead he proposed that cinema should be a 'fact factory', with an emphasis on documentary material, such as Shub had achieved with *The Fall of the Romanovs*, which was made entirely out of old newsreel, or as Dziga Vertov was creating in his *Kino-Eye* series:

> The director ordinarily *invents* the plot for the scenario – Dziga Vertov *detects* it. He does not, with the aid of authors, actors and scenery-carpenters, build an illusion of life; he thrusts the lens of his camera straight into the crowded centres of real life.

'We do not need fairy tales, nor do we need fables', he wrote, 'we need real life, shown on the screen just as it is'.[128] The last phrase was perhaps disingenuous, because of course Tretyakov required the facts to be ordered and controlled. The process of film-making, like theatre, relied on the dialectical interaction of the three basic elements – the material (what), the construction (how) and the function (why). Montage, how these elements were woven together, was key: 'Montage is a means of linking (confrontation, opposition) of facts, such that they begin to emit a social energy and the truth hidden inside them'.[129] Depending on the function, the facts could be used either for informational purposes or for agitation, or both. This was 'factography'. Finally, it should be added that Tretyakov saw film production as an industrial and collective enterprise, and as such intrinsically socialistic.

In March 1927 Tretyakov was invited to become Drama Consultant at the Georgia State Film Institute in Tiflis (Tbilisi), the capital of the Georgian state. The political situation in Georgia, however, was

---

128 Quotations from 'Our Cinema', in *The Film: The International Language of Understanding Between Peoples*, Moscow: VOKS, 1928.
129 See Reischl, Katherine M.H., 'Where Have I Been with My Camera': Sergei Tret'iakov and Developing Operativity, *Russian Literature*, Vol. 103-105, 2019, p. 126.

precarious. The region is bound by the Caucasus mountains and the Black Sea, and skirted by Russia, Azerbaijan, Armenia and Turkey. It had been incorporated into the Russian Empire by Catherine the Great in the eighteenth century, but the Georgians are a rugged, no-nonsense people in a rugged, even wild, landscape, and the relationship between Moscow and Tiflis was never smooth, even when Stalin, a Georgian, acquired supreme power. In 1918 Georgia had declared its independence, but by 1921 Russia had swallowed it again. Unrest among the peasant population, however, rumbled on. In the summer of 1921 in Svanetia they rebelled forcefully, and another peasant uprising in 1924 was suppressed with notable brutality. Sporadic terrorist acts were still occurring at the time Tretyakov arrived in Tbilisi.

The State Film Institute was founded in 1923 with ambitious plans to expand the Georgian film industry, and was soon attracting *avant-garde* film makers and other artists from Moscow. The radical film director and *LEF* supporter, Lev Kuleshov, and his wife, the film actress, Alexandra Khokhlova, were opening a film workshop there, and Viktor Shklovsky and Esther Shub also arrived. Tretyakov received a much warmer welcome here than he had at Goskino, and he was soon organising workshops and lectures for young aspiring Georgian film makers, as well as other artists – writers, theatre workers, visual artists and so on. He also brought with him many ideas for films, the first of which was *Locomotive B-1000* which Kuleshov agreed to direct. It seems that the film centred on a train crash, but after some months, filming was halted and the work was never completed.

His first scenario to be realized was *The Blind Woman*, which was also the first film of its director, Mikhail Kalatozov, one of those eager young Georgians who had worked as a cameraman on *Locomotive B-1000*. Unfortunately there seems to be very little record of this film, and it is presumed lost. It was, however, followed by what Jay Leyda called 'a triumph',[130] *Eliso*, also known as *Caucasian Love*. Directed by Nikolai Shengelaya, a Futurist poet and former assistant to the well-known theatre and film director, Konstantin Mardzhanishvili, Tretyakov's scenario was based on an 1864 novel, *Eliso*, by Alexander Kazbegi. Perhaps surprisingly in view of Tretyakov's rejection of 'fairy tales and fables', Kazbegi's book was itself a re-imagining of a folk tale.

---

130 Leyda, Jay, *Kino*, London: George Allen and Unwin, 1983, p. 273.

Nevertheless, the film powerfully evokes the age-old struggle between Russia and the Caucasian peoples, the Chechens and Cossacks, and evokes not only Tolstoy's masterpiece, *The Cossacks*, but also pre-echoes Stalin's later ethnic cleansing of the 1940s. And its relevance stretches further, reminding us of Russia's present-day struggles in Chechnya, the never-ending contention between Muslims and Christians, and more.

The story begins when the tsar's government decides to use the Cossacks to evict rebellious Chechens from the Empire and to steal their land. In the village of Verdi in Terek province the people implore the Russian governor not to drive them out, but the Cossack *ataman*, Seidulla, tricks them into signing by finger-print (they cannot read or write) a letter which actually calls for them to be re-settled in Turkey. The eighteen-year old daughter of one of the village elders, Eliso, is in love with a Christian from the next village, Vazho, who, seeing what is happening, is fired up to fight for Verdi. He saves their cattle and takes on a group of Russian guards in a guard post single-handedly. But his heroics are too late: the villagers are already leaving. In the mayhem a young mother is killed, leaving her child an orphan, and Eliso herself sets fire to the village. The climax comes when the villagers turn their despair into the *lezginka*, a folk dance of the people of the Caucasus, in an episode which Eisenstein particularly admired. Then Vazho, who has done so much for them, appears. But he is a Christian and of a higher class than they: he cannot go with them. Reluctantly, Eliso tells him: 'You will be a stranger among us'. He turns to her. 'Remember your vow, Eliso. You must go with me'. She embraces him. Then she steps back. Her face changes. 'No. I cannot abandon my father'. As the villagers are departing, silhouetted against the sky, a woman appears with the orphan child of the murdered mother. She gives Vazho the child which he hoists onto his shoulder and steps out with a firm step. As with Tretyakov's *I Want a Baby*, the child is the future.

The film is notable for its hectic editing which urges its concerns into the viewer's consciousness. Shot in the Caucasus region, the magnificent landscapes, vibrant traditional costumes and the determined, weather-beaten faces of the characters give the film an appropriately epic sweep. Horses are depicted stark against the sky, a villager treks determinedly across the boulder-strewn hillside, and at night the shadows conjure fear, hope, the pain of the endless struggle.

Yet the epic can also contain moments of humour, as when the Russian officer is seen ceremoniously eating a cucumber, and occasional filmic parodies, as when Vazho, having invaded the Russian guard post, strides over the officer's desk and leaps, Errol Flynn-like, out of the window.

Eliso was released in October 1928, almost two years before the next film with a scenario by Tretyakov appeared. This was *Salt for Svanetia*, the province in which *The Blind Woman* had also been set. Tretyakov was obviously fascinated by this distant, almost inaccessible region to which he paid at least two fairly extensive visits. The first of these was in May 1927, and after his second visit, the following year, he published *Svanetia*, a compilation of sketches, essays and photographs. The film was directed by Mikhail Kalatozov, who had directed the lost *Blind Woman* and was to go on to find world fame with his film *The Cranes Are Flying* in 1957. More clearly according with Tretyakov's trenchant views on fact as the necessary basis for film, *Salt for Svanetia* demonstrates just how powerful this 'factography' can be.

Salt for Svanetia concentrates on the primitive, patriarchal society of Svanetia in the far north west of Georgia, cut off by mountains and glaciers. The people are subjected to merciless tax gatherers who carry guns. They can only defend themselves with rocks hurled from ancient stone towers. They have no salt. The cows give no milk. They are verging on starvation. From sheep's wool they make their own coarse clothes, as well as the ropes which hold together bridges across the river gorges, bridges so fragile that even the donkeys fear to venture onto them. A man urinates against a wall, and the domestic animals gather like hungry wolves round a wounded deer, waiting to lick the salt from the urine. Some of the young men work on the tangerine farms below, and they can bring salt back to their villages, but an unseasonable snowstorm may cut them off, or an avalanche destroy them. A rich man's death is cause for an imposing funeral involving the whole community, but the event actually serves to enrich the money-grubbing priest. And it is a disaster for a young pregnant woman: giving birth at the time of a funeral is a curse. She is flung out of her home, and while the procession of mourners perform their rites, she is alone, bearing her child in the cold open air. A dog licks up the placenta. The baby – Tretyakov's symbol of the future – dies, and the mother's milk is dripped onto its unmarked burial place. Religion and

1928: Gorky returns. Welcoming him are Lunacharsky, nearest Gorky, Mayakovsky, standing behind Lunacharsky, Tretyakov behind Mayakovsky with camera round his neck.

superstition consume Svanetia. But help is coming. Muscular young men with picks are digging a new road. The earth is moved, trees are felled and as they blast their way into this inaccessible place, they bring more than salt to what is now Soviet Svanetia.

The film is in black and white with no sound, but perhaps all the more powerful for that. The striking photography – awesome scenery, craggy human faces, tired, anxious, sometimes hopeful, and the tense, urgent editing – makes not only the hardship and relentless struggle for life all the clearer, it also permits a fierce lyricism. For the American film critic, Jay Leyda, *Salt for Svanetia* was 'the most powerful documentary I've ever seen'.[131] And it is a classic of factography – informational for most of its length, its climax moves to the agitational.

A third Georgian film for which Tretyakov supplied at least the idea for the scenario was *Khabarda!*, also known as *Out of the Way!* which was not released until December 1931, more than four years after he had left his six-month posting to the State Film Institute in Tiflis. It was the third film directed by Mikhail Chiaureli, a former painter, cartoonist, sculptor and theatre director. He was in the early stages of what would become a glittering career which would include no fewer than six Stalin Prizes and a seat in the Supreme Soviet of the U.S.S.R. The film is set in Tiflis at the end of the 1920s. In an insalubrious district of the city, the Town Council decides to demolish the jerry-built houses which regularly collapse, causing deaths, and a nearby little church which is in a parlous and much-dilapidated state. But it is suggested that this church is a historic building, and so should not be knocked down. The energetic Komsomols, however, find a plaque in the foundations of the building which shows that the church was in fact erected in 1890. It is no historic monument. They take matters into their own hands and pull the church down, allowing the rebuilding to begin. Thus, communism sweeps away the remnants of the now-useless *bourgeois* life. Despite the apparent crudity of the story, which may or may not have followed Tretyakov's original idea, the film is made with pace and radical filmic expressivity.

Khabarda! was not quite the last film in which Tretyakov had a hand. That was *A Song About Heroes*, directed by the young Dutch director, Joris Ivens, with music by Hanns Eisler. The lyrics for the two

---

131   *Ibid.*, p. 310.

songs the film contains were written by Tretyakov. The film concerns the building of the city of Magnitogorsk in the Ural Mountains, the steelworks and blast furnace, the coking works and tractor production. One of its most interesting features is that it shows work available for women and the nomads of the steppe, and indeed workers of all ethnicities are welcome and productive. Tretyakov's songs were 'The Ballad of the Komsomols' and 'The Magnitogorsk Song' with its march-like refrain, 'Ural, Ural, magnitaya gora' ('Ural, Ural, the magnetic mountain') referring to the uniquely rich iron ore found in the soil here. In the hotel where the film-makers were staying, a piano was brought to Eisler's room and he and Tretyakov banged out the music and sang the words together. Guests of the hotel all down the corridor opened their doors and poked out their heads to listen to this 'modern' music, which was originally rejected by the film company, though it was later accepted. Due to open in 1932, it did not actually premiere until January 1933, when it did not receive unanimous praise.

Tretyakov's work in film ran alongside and complemented his work in photography, of which he became a master. The post-revolution Russian *avant-garde*, especially the Constructivists, were early to recognize the potential of photography: thus, Alexei Gan, in *Kino-Fot* in 1922, stressed the importance of photography, not just as an adjunct to film, which he called 'living photography', but in its own right. Alexander Rodchenko was beginning his experiments at this time, photographing social scenes and portraits, soon expanding into photo-montage which he used for book covers and poster designs. 'The photograph presents a precise moment documentarily', he asserted, and urged: 'Photograph and be photographed'.[132]

Tretyakov discovered the use of the camera in China in 1924, after Osip Brik had suggested he should 'kodak' what he saw. He followed this advice enthusiastically to document not only the place, but the people, including their angry political demonstrations, and then published them so that they became integral with his written reports. He was therefore among the very first photo-journalists. As Christina Lodder notes, this also distinguishes him 'as one of the first members of the Russian *avant-garde* to actually take and publish photographs.

---

132   Bowlt, John E., *Russian Art of the Avant Garde: Theory and Criticism*, London: Thames and Hudson, 1988, pp. 251, 253.

Even the artist and Constructivist Alexander Rodchenko, who later became renowned as an innovative photographer, did not start taking photographs until 1924 and only began publishing them in 1926'.[133]

Tretyakov practiced this new art on his family. His sister Nina remembered:

> He was always ready to help anybody, despite being madly busy himself. Seryozha never flung aside anything that was half done, and most of what he did was brought to perfection. When my daughter was born, Seryozha on occasion came to photograph her and unless everything was satisfactory he would come again and again until the photograph was perfect.

He photographed all the members of his family, especially his wife and daughter and his father, as well as making photo-portraits of his friends and acquaintances. He developed and printed his own photographs, using the bathroom in the flat on Malaya Bronnaya Street as his dark room, and carefully catalogued every photograph taken, which was then stored in his archive. This contained several thousand photographs by the time of his death.

As with Tretyakov's other explorations of art forms, he insisted from early in his career as a photographer (or 'photographist' as he preferred, in order to distinguish his kind of work from run-of-the-mill 'photographers') that every photograph must have a function. Thus, he moved quickly from a position where he was taking 'documentary snapshots' to one where he organised his subject in advance, in order to clarify its purpose. But he also insisted that any alteration or touching-up to a published photograph must be admitted and explained in an accompanying caption. If one looks, for instance, at his photographs from Svanetia, included in his book of the same name, it soon becomes apparent that each has its specific function, or purpose. To take a single example, he reproduces a photograph taken in the countryside of the ancient, dilapidated stone towers which feature in *Salt for Svanetia*, and are set in the open fields. Perhaps it seems merely like any tourist's snapshot. In

---

133   Lodder, Christina, 'Sergei Tret'iakov – the Writer as Photographer', *Russian Literature*, Vol. 103-105, 2019, p. 97.

fact, his purpose is to demonstrate the contrast between the old and the new, the time-weathered, empty towers and the growing crops in the neatly organised fields, sterility and fertility: factography again.

Factography can then often be extended from the single snapshot to the photo-series, that is a sequence of photographs juxtaposed as a montage which can reveal the – usually political – meaning. Thus, the ancient stone towers of Svanetia are implicitly in contradistinction to the adjoining photographs of modern agricultural buildings, medical clinics, busy workers in the fields, and so on. He noted:

> If a more or less random snapshot is like an infinitely fine scale that has been scratched from the surface of reality with the tip of a finger, then in comparison the photo-series lets us experience the extended massiveness of reality, its authentic meaning. We build systematically. We must also photograph systematically. Sequence and long-term photographic observation – that is the method.[134]

The series can then be accompanied by text, as in the *Svanetia* example, and text and photographs interact, contradict or complement one another, and this is often further enhanced by the positioning on the pages of the photographs and the text, and perhaps of the white spaces around them. This is seen perfectly in his photo-series published in 1933 in the journal, *Pioneer*, entitled 'Where Have I Been With My Camera?'. The written title in capital letters on the right hand side of the first page is matched on the left by a photograph of Tretyakov himself taking a photograph, apparently of the title caption, with his camera. The following pages document in words and photographs his travels from Beijing in 1924 to his actions as a reporter in 1929, so that he himself becomes a kind of protagonist moving between these places and witnessing revolutionary developments. In 1934 he was able to state confidently: 'One thing remains undeniable:

---

134 Cited from Kim, Soo Hwan, 'Sergei Tretyakov Revisited: The Cases of Walter Benjamin and Hito Steyerl', *e-flux* journal, No. 104, November 2019 <https://www.e-flux.com/journal/104/298121/sergei-tretyakov-revisited-the-cases-of-walter-benjamin-and-hito-steyerl/> [accessed December 2019].

photography has begun to occupy an increasingly prominent place on the visual arts front'.[135]

The photograph seemed to many, not just to Tretyakov, to be replacing the easel-painting, and in a technological, mass-culture age this was certainly consequential. Moreover, photography was accessible to anyone with a camera, and it denied a special place in the artistic creation to the 'author', whose 'authority' was undermined. As Tretyakov put it, 'Each boy with his camera is a soldier in the war against easel painters'.[136] Photography was not elitist, but it was useful and powerful in ways which were to be embraced – it informed, it taught, it organised. As such, it could be the key to a new kind of art centred on ordinary people.

Among his contemporaries, Tretyakov was widely acclaimed as a photographer and a photo-journalist, more so probably than Rodchenko. In 1929 he worked to establish an Association of Workers in Revolutionary Photography, though this failed. However, what was long remembered was his wry observation that he didn't know whether his Leica camera or his notebook and pen were more important for his work.

Tretyakov also wanted to resurrect the now-defunct *LEF* journal in some form. He probably chivvied Mayakovsky, whose name at least was useful, to join him in an approach to the State Publishing House in August 1926 with a proposal for its resurrection, and on 1 September, surprisingly rapidly, the proposal was accepted for a journal to be called *New LEF*. On 1 January 1927 the first issue of *New LEF* appeared, with a poem by Mayakovsky and a strident call to arms from Tretyakov. *New LEF* appeared at regular intervals over the next two years, each issue of 1,500 copies containing 48 pages. Unlike *LEF*, the layout was not particularly striking, but *New LEF* used more photographs than its predecessor and pursued a considerably more consistent line ideologically. Initially Mayakovsky's flat in Hendrikov Alley was the new journal's headquarters, and there were regular '*LEF* Tuesdays' held there when members of *LEF*'s informal collective gathered – Tretyakov, Aseyev, Pasternak, the young Kirsanov from *Yugolef*, Osip Brik, Viktor Shklovsky, Vsevolod Meyerhold, Lev Kuleshov and others. They were often assailed by other literary groupings as a good deal

---

135   Reischl, Katherine M.H., *op. cit.*, p. 121.
136   Willett, John, *The New Sobriety*, London: Thames and Hudson, 1978, p. 107.

of jockeying for position within the Soviet state took place. Given the state's apparent favouring of 'proletarian' writers groups, it is not surprising to find in January 1927 Tretyakov and Mayakovsky writing an angry letter to the Press Bureau of the Central Committee of the Communist Party and the Federation of United Soviet Writers, from which they had been excluded:

> The Writers of Left Front demand that they be included in the Federation of United Soviet Writers ... Left Front is a union of the most qualified sections of the new Soviet literature.
> Without the representatives of Left Front it will be impossible to carry out the tasks set by the new Federation ... We consider it a sad misunderstanding that the Left Front has not been invited from the very beginning into the organisation of the Federation, as the work of the Left Front since the very first days of the Revolution is well known to all workers of literature.[137]

They appended a list of 38 supporters, ending 'and many others'. The 'proletarian' writers, however, were not amenable to this approach. *New LEF* remained on the outside.

Meanwhile it soon became apparent that Mayakovsky was not much interested in the day-to-day business of producing the journal. Tretyakov, disciplined, strict with time and demanding both of himself and of his colleagues, took over more and more of the work, and the editorial tasks were increasingly performed at the flat on Malaya Bronnaya Street. Here, Olga Viktorovna became the effective secretary of the operation, typing, keeping the papers in order and creating a *LEF* archive.

New LEF was less concerned with 'literariness' than with shaping a response to social experience. Futurism gave way to factography, even for Mayakovsky, who wrote in 'Very Good':

>   Stanzas now
>   like telegrams
>   fly!

---

137   Marshall, Herbert (trans and ed), *Mayakovsky*, London: Dennis Dobson, 1965, p. 21.

> Bend
> 　　and drink
> 　　　　through lips parched and cracked
> 　from the river
> 　　　known as – 'Fact'.[138]

The emphasis now was on non-fiction and prose – sketches, essays, travel notes and the like. There were critical essays, such as those by Shklovsky on Pushkin and Tolstoy, and by Brik on proletarian writing, and the journal also included photographs, both stills from contemporary films and single photographs, though surprisingly few of Tretyakov's own photographs. For the radical young, the journal was inspiring: 'We read with pleasure the thin volumes of *New LEF*, with their brilliant photomontages on the covers, because we liked their militant, provocative tone', wrote one later.[139]

Tretyakov's many contributions consisted of both factual pieces – sketches, excerpts from ongoing work, such as *Den Shi-hua*, and so on – and programmatic statements of *New LEF's* theoretical stance. In the first issue he asserted that art had become a swamp, its participation in class struggle nullified, and *New LEF* was to be a stone thrown into the swamp. '*LEF* caresses neither the ears nor the eyes', he proclaimed, 'and art as reflection of life is replaced by the work of building life'.[140] A year later, in the first issue of 1928, he noted '*LEF's* uncompromising focus on the literature of fact and on the photograph'. Marking out *LEF's* position in contradistinction to the emphasis on content of the proletarian writers – and that of most of the Bolshevik leaders as well, of course – he argued that it was the *form* of the work which counted. Whereas for the '*passséist*', as he called those writers who opposed *LEF*, 'the one compromise – changes in theme – is sufficient', for *LEF*, 'only *expediently formed* material can become a thing with direct social function. Changing a theme is trivial' (my italics).[141] He noted 'the growth in demand for memoirs and sketches' and complained that

---

138　Ibid., p. 364.
139　Gladkov, Aleksandr, *Meyerhold Speaks, Meyerhold Rehearses*, Amsterdam: Harwood Academic, 1997, p. 64.
140　Lawton, Anna (ed), *Russian Futurism Through Its Manifestoes, 1912-1928*, Ithaca: Cornell University Press, 1988, p. 250.
141　Ibid., p. 265.

'at publishing houses, a good article, requiring a trip, research and selection of material, brings less than half the pay for an ordinary belletristic novella, for whose realization one needs only a finger to suck on'. He commended the Komsomol member who had written: 'One technician is much more necessary than ten bad poets', adding that 'we would be agreeable even to omitting the word "bad"'.[142]

But partly as a result of Tretyakov's unwavering focus on factography, a serious split developed among the *LEF* collective. Several members repudiated what they saw as the over-emphasis on 'the naked fact', even though they still held to what Mayakovsky called 'the primacy of the goal over content as much as form'. In early 1928 Mayakovsky led these writers and artists, who included Brik, Aseyev, Rodchenko and others, out of *New LEF*. 'All literary coteries have outlived themselves', Mayakovsky declared,[143] though in the summer he and Brik attempted to establish *REF* (Revolutionary Front of Art), which would have been another 'coterie' had it got off the ground. Tretyakov took over the sole editorship of the journal for its last five issues. Who was to blame for this rupture? There was intransigence on both sides, but as Pertsov noted many years later, 'in disputes on literary themes, Tretyakov was sometimes too inflexible … like an iconoclast repudiating the worship of images'.[144] He certainly held his ground, proclaiming now in *New LEF* the continuing 'fight for fact against fiction' and 'the memoir, travel notes, the sketch, articles, feuilletons, reportage, investigations, documentary montage – as opposed to belletristic forms of novels, novellas, and short stories'.[145]

Such statements indicate how far Tretyakov's ideas had evolved since his days – barely over ten years before – when he was a practising Futurist poet. Now the slogan was: 'From composition to construction'. 'Tretyakov is against aesthetics', Shklovsky wrote at this time. 'He speaks not of the end of verses but of the end of aesthetic influence in

---

142   *Ibid.*, p. 267.
143   Jangfeldt, Bengt, *Mayakovsky: A Biography*, Chicago: University of Chicago Press, 2014, p. 452.
144   Pertsov, V., Introduction to Tretyakov, Sergei, *Den Shi-hua, Lyudi odnogo kostra, Strana-perekrestok*, Moscow: Sovetskii pisatel', 1962, p. 21.
145   Lawton, Anne (ed), *op. cit.*, p. 270.

general'.[146] In his 1927 essay, 'The New Tolstoy', Tretyakov called not for a new writer, but for a new kind of writing – factography.

The basic premise for factography was set out by Boris Arvatov in a small book published in 1928, *Art and Production*. Arvatov notes that in pre-capitalist societies the artist was a workman like any other, but the one who organised the patterns of social living. He (or occasionally she) was the one who decided the cut of a smock, the carpenter who shaped the handle of the axe, the sculptor of the stone for the church windows. He was, in other words, one craftsman among many, but with the particular task of shaping social life. With capitalism, and its concomitant, *bourgeois* society, this position changed. With capitalism came specialisation, the alienation of work, and the introduction of the machine.

> In addition to this, the old commissioner of art – the city – was gradually receding. The heads of the city now were state officials; the collective way of life of the previous community had disintegrated; there was nothing left to organise; and the artist, who once was the organizer of everyday life, had no direct connection with it any more. He was confronted by the new ruler of society: the spontaneous, indifferent and faceless market, with its almighty powers of conformity.[147]

The artist was no longer another worker among many: his contribution became purely decorative, and his products were sold as rarities and displayed in private houses or exhibited in galleries. But, Arvatov argued, art must be re-integrated into life – hence the 'modernist' chairs and costumes created by the Constructivists. Use value must replace exchange value, and in a socialist society, when alienation has vanished, the artist must again be the prime organizer of social living.

For Tretyakov, a similar history of the work of the writer could be told, and if it were, the necessity for factography would be clear. Factography is more than mere reportage or documentary, because as Tretyakov stressed, it must include the organizing purpose or function

---

146   Papazian, Elizabeth Astrid, *Manufacturing Truth: The Documentary Moment in Early Soviet Culture*, DeKalb: Northern University Press, 2009, p. 26.
147   Arvatov, Boris, *Art and Production*, London: Pluto Press, 2017, p. 30.

which Arvatov indicates in his analysis. The function might be simply to impart information, but it was usually more agitational than this. Thus, it might be compared, perhaps superficially, with a newspaper. Few newspapers are impartial. Almost all try to persuade the reader of something. But the other similarity is that the newspaper is written by different journalists, whose work is laid side by side to form a kind of montage. Factographic writing therefore may be collectivized, a practice which immediately democratizes its practice. And as with newspaper journalists (of which Tretyakov was a prolific example), the factographer must expect to use pen and notebook (and camera) and to research his subjects.

The classic example of factography which Tretyakov posited was the biography of the thing, which would replace the biography of an individual person, thus replacing psychology with sociology. He acknowledged that 'books like *Forests, Bread, Coal, Iron, Flax, Cotton, Paper, Locomotive, Factory* have yet to be written,' but added, 'we need them, and the only satisfactory way to write them is on "biography of things" lines'.[148] He pointed out that the novel 'subjectivizes' all reality, but in the biography of the thing, the inanimate subject has no psychology, it moves between people and experiences without any inner turmoil, thus exposing the means of production, the forms of consumerism, and so on. Soo Hwan Kim has pointed to the filmmaker, Hito Steyerl's 2010 *In Free Fall* as an example. Its subject is a Boeing 707 aeroplane.

> It opens with an image of the Mojave Air and Space Port in the California desert, a junkyard-cum-cemetery where planes are brought to die. The story of the deceased thing thus begins with its grave. The story of the Boeing is truly dramatic. After serving in the fleet of TWA, the passenger airline founded by the American business tycoon, pilot, engineer and film mogul, Howard Hughes ... the plane was sold to the Israeli air force. They then used it in the famous 1976 raid on Entebbe, the mission mounted to rescue hostages on another passenger airliner, which had been hijacked by Palestinian and German militants from the PLO and commandeered to Uganda.

---

148   Willett, John, *op. cit.*, p. 107.

After the raid on Entebbe, the plane was used as a prop and blown up for the 1994 Hollywood blockbuster *Speed*. This was not the vessel's end, however. After being blown up on the set of *Speed*, the left over aluminium parts were sold to a Chinese DVD manufacturer, and so the airliner eventually became a laser disc. The plane thus lost its former materiality, becoming another thing, a disc for storing, among other things, footage of the explosion that destroyed it.[149]

As Soo Hwan Kim comments, 'the film is a literal realization of Tretyakov's ideas'. Providing more than information, it opens up to agitation international air travel, the American business tycoon, the Israeli-Palestinian conflict and the Hollywood film scene.

One must therefore ask: was factography a break with the *avant-gardism* of the 1920s? Or was it a step further on the *avant-garde's* exploratory path, moving it towards new uncharted places? Was it a bridge for the *avant-garde* to reach the safety of Soviet 'socialist realism', or was it a radical new move towards merging art into life? Georg Lukács, the pre-eminent Marxist literary critic of the Stalin era, wrote dismissively that 'the "cult of facts" is a miserable surrogate for intimacy with the people's historical life'.[150]

As suggested already, the primary model for factography was perhaps the newspaper. A useful precedent was the fact that many of the pre-revolution Bolsheviks had been journalists, and the underground newspaper had been their lifeline. Now, for Tretyakov, the newspaper was the 'epic of our time', comparable with *The Iliad*, *The Odyssey* or *The Bible*: each day each page of the newspaper revealed more of the epic which was contemporary Soviet life, whose heroes were ordinary workers. He depicted something of this in the character of Dudin, the worker-correspondent in his play, *Gas Masks*, and it was in the hands – or pens – of these worker-correspondents that he believed much of the future lay. He noted in 1933 that there were 6,775 newspapers in the Soviet Union reporting on matters such as the repairing of tractors for the spring sowing, shock brigades of

---

149 Kim, Soo Hwan, 'Sergei Tretyakov Revisited: The Cases of Walter Benjamin and Hito Steyerl', *e-flux* journal, No. 104, November 2019.
150 Lukács, Georg, *The Historical Novel*, London: Penguin, 1981, p. 303.

tractor women receiving awards, problems with creches on collective farms, and so on. The Soviet newspaper, he asserted, 'is truth, active truth, stubbornly reconstructing the world'.[151] He wrote tirelessly for the newspapers himself, including his photo-journalism published in illustrated magazines like *Prozhektor*, which was edited by Nikolai Bukharin.

Perhaps Tretyakov's most famous piece of reporting was of the motorised sleigh ride he took in February 1929 as a reporter for *Moscow Worker* and *Moscow Evening News*. New forms of this vehicle, introduced in the First World War, were being developed, somewhat like crude hovercraft with wings and skis for travel over snow and ice. A group of these aeroplane-sledges were now being trialled, with newspaper reporters, including Boris Gromov of *Izvestia* and of course Tretyakov himself, aboard. He described, almost breathlessly, how they raced past horses, churches and on to the house of the nineteenth century poet, Nikolai Nekrasov. Exciting and perilous, the journey took them onwards, down roads and over rivers. At one point, over a river where the ice had melted, catastrophe struck – two of the vehicles plunged into the water, and Tretyakov helped to rescue his wrecked comrades. They dashed on. The reader can almost feel the future speeding to meet him. The trial made a perfect subject for Tretyakov's photo-essay, which he then published as a slim book with Gromov, *The Complete Slide*: it was the essence of factography.

Equally powerful, and equally dependent on technology, though in a different form, was Tretyakov's work in radio. In his view his contemporaries preferred a concert on the radio to listening to a live balalaika, and in March 1926 Trotsky, still clinging to the shreds of power, had given a speech, 'Radio, Science, Technology and Society' at a congress held to promote the radio. Many more people than just Tretyakov saw the radio as able to end the isolation of the artist, replacing the individual with the collective and subverting the concept of art which could be possessed and consumed in private. He organised a 'writers brigade' to report live on radio about the events on public holidays. They would prepare the outline of what was to be included

---

151   Tretyakov, S., 'Words Become Deeds', *International Literature*, No. 3, Moscow, July 1933, p. 55.

in the broadcast, but this was not a script, merely a skeleton to keep the report on track. The spoken words were spontaneous.

From the late 1920s Tretyakov became the voice of May Day and Revolution Day, as he commentated on the celebrations live from Red Square, and soon his commentary itself was an integral part of public holidays. 'Outside' broadcasts were rare at the time, and these made a very strong impression on listeners. The buildings in central Moscow were decorated with flags and slogans, thousands thronged the streets, all marching towards Red Square where the *Internationale* was sung, banners hoisted and speeches made. The first broadcast Tretyakov and his team made from Red Square was both farcical and hair-raising. Outside the GUM multi-storey department store, a rickety, hastily-improvised scaffolding was erected, and Tretyakov clambered through a window onto this precarious perch while his assistant, the writer Lev Kassil, clung onto his trouser legs and he spoke to the whole nation. As the years went by, he became less excited by the adventure of it all, and more nervous for the actual performance. Fearing to lose his voice, he would eat a raw egg before he started, apparently believing this would ensure his voice would hold out during the broadcast. His sister Nina, by now a successful actress, recalled listening to his reporting of the October and May festivals from Red Square, and she concluded: 'completely professionally, as an actress, I judged his unusually sonorous voice, beautiful diction and obvious talent as an improviser!' His last broadcast was on May Day 1937.

The evolution of factography meant the end of poetry for many of the Futurists, and certainly for Tretyakov. His last collection of poems, *Speechnik*, is dated 1928, though there is some reason to think it did not actually appear until 1929. It contained 35 poems, most of them several pages long, and at the end of each the date of their composition was carefully recorded. It may be telling that the majority were written in 1923 (nine poems) and 1924 (thirteen poems). Seven had been written earlier than these, and only six between 1925 and 1927, though one written in 1923 had been revised in 1927. Now his mantra was:

> Fewer poems – more journalism
> Fewer reading rooms – more radio

> Less theatre – more cinema
> Fewer lyrics – more usefulness[152]

The suicide of Tretyakov's close comrade-in-arms and friend, Vladimir Mayakovsky, in the spring of 1930 seemed a tragic confirmation of this conclusion for poetry. Before his death, Mayakovsky put together an exhibition, 'Twenty Years of Work' which he said was 'an account rendered of my work'. He had withdrawn from the *LEF* group in 1928 because he could not follow Tretyakov into 'factography', and he had tried to establish a new group, *REF*, which failed. Now he announced he would join *RAPP*, the association of proletarian writers, whose concerns seemed far from his own, but which found favour with the Party elite. It seemed like poetic suicide for him.

The exhibition opened on 1 February 1930 in the Moscow Writers' Club, and most of those who came were young and radical. Osip and Lilya Brik and Viktor Shklovsky attended, as did Olga Viktorovna Tretyakova and her sixteen-year-old daughter Tanya, but Sergei Mikhailovich was away. Mayakovsky was gloomy and uncommunicative. He complained that the 'grey beards' had failed to show up, though one young man shouted: 'to hell with the grey beards, Vladimir Vladimirovich – you're our poet, the poet of the young, and we love you!'.[153] Mayakovsky read one of his poems, but the whole affair was dismal, anti-climactic. Less than three months later, on 14 April, he shot himself.

---

[152] Kruchyonykh, A., *15 let russkogo futurizma, 1912-1927*, Moscow: Vserossiiskii soyuz poetov, 1928, p. 56.
[153] Tret'yakov, Sergei, *Strana-perekrestok*, Moscow: Sovetskii pisatel', 1991, p. 561.

CHAPTER 10.
TO THE *KOLKHOZ*

1928 was a momentous year for the Soviet Union, and for Sergei Mikhailovich Tretyakov. While Tretyakov was busy with his books on China, with fighting for and rewriting *I Want a Baby*, with editing *New LEF* and with his various film projects, the Soviet Union brought Lenin's New Economic Policy to an end, and inaugurated the first Five Year Plan. It was this which would drive Tretyakov, whose energy was astonishing, into new, genuinely original paths.

It was ironic that the Five Year Plan put into practice many of the ideas which the 'Left', Trotsky and his followers, had for years argued for: taxation of rich peasants, the end of NEP, industrialization, and so on. But it went further, giving industry, especially heavy industry, targets, or quotas, to fulfil, and forcing rapid agricultural collectivization in the vast Russian hinterland. It seemed like a great leap forward, and one which won the approval not only of many of the Trotskyites, but also of more sceptical, 'left' intellectuals, like Sergei Tretyakov. This was, it seemed, the true road to socialism. After all, it promised to bring not just tractors but other machinery to the countryside—and it succeeded. New forms of political representation were established, new management and bureaucratic procedures were introduced, libraries were opened, the reach of radio was extended, new modes of production were developed, infrastructure was built. As the capitalist west seemed to collapse in the wake of the Wall Street crash, the Soviet economy looked to grow at a furious pace. But to achieve this, the Soviet Union was turned inwards, effectively cutting itself off from the outside world, and then limiting free movement within the country by introducing internal passports.

Tretyakov, a *kolkhoznik*.

The collectivization of agriculture, which was the focus of Tretyakov's attention, was an extraordinary and enormous undertaking. The Bolsheviks' policy towards the peasantry had been muddled from the start, resulting, in the ten years to 1927, in only three years of good harvests, with five poor harvests and two famine years. Any agricultural policy would require the active co-operation of the more than twenty-five million peasant smallholders across the land. But collectivization was mostly carried through with a brutal ferocity, and met with furious resistance. Agents sent to enforce the policy were attacked, beaten up and even murdered. Peasants slaughtered their own livestock, ate or sold the meat themselves and made shoes out of the hides. Bread rationing was introduced in the cities, a black market inevitably sprang up, and, after Stalin announced in 1929 the need to 'liquidate' the *kulaks* (rich peasants), executions and mass deportations began. By 1930 there was famine in some areas: people literally starved, bands of orphaned children could be found on roadsides begging for food, and there were revolts: Armenian rebels seized control of several districts, while in Azerbaijan the dissenters took the opposite course of action and fled into neighbouring Iran.

Did men like Tretyakov know the full horror of what was happening? Probably not. And if there were outrages, revolution was a nasty business, and, as the old saying had it, 'you can't make an omelette without breaking eggs'. The fact was that many believed that the Soviet Union was on the right track, and dangers and difficulties had to be faced and outfaced. The compromises of N.E.P. were over, construction was beginning. Probably Tretyakov and others only knew a fraction of the truth. And it was not long before the fruits of the struggle began to be seen: the extraordinary White Sea Canal, for instance, was completed in 1933 (the use of slave labour in its building was never acknowledged) and then the Party's hard line seemed to be softening when it readmitted leading 'old' Bolsheviks, previously expelled, like Zinoviev and Kamenev. Construction was difficult and tiring, mistakes were inevitable, but it seemed that the country was moving in the right direction, despite the 'problems'. With hindsight it is easy to see how, with the temporary readmission of Zinoviev and Kamenev, for instance, Stalin was relying – as tyrants usually do – on creating uncertainty in the minds of others, being deliberately unpredictable; for Russians at the time, however, especially for those willing the revolution to succeed, yearning for the future Communist Utopia, such clarity was elusive at best. 'I want to build', Ivan Smirnov told Victor Serge, 'and in its own barbaric and stupid way, the Central Committee is building for the future'.[154] Many shared this position.

It was approximately Tretyakov's attitude when he heard the call, 'To the *kolkhoz*!' The Five Year Plan aimed to take writers and artists to the factories and the collective farms, where they would find new subject matter and write about the construction of the new country. The idea was a distant echo of the early socialists of the 1870s, the Narodniks, who had gone out into the country in an idealistic effort to bring enlightenment to the peasants. This was like a repeat of that fresh morning. The *LEF* group strongly endorsed the cry. Mayakovsky wrote 'To the Workers in Poetry and Prose on their Summer Visit to the *Kolkhozes*' which included the lines:

> To you, Tretyakov,
>   a subtler task,
> you are
>   an inveterate controversialist.
> To the interior of the earth!
>   Press yourself to the brownness!
> and thus
>   you will controversialize splendidly,
> for not any
>   old fool
> can go
>   into the bosom of the country.[155]

Nikolai Chuzhak and Viktor Pertsov were others of the group who answered the call. They had no orders concerning what they should write, though controversy was not necessarily what was wanted. But they were certainly expected to be more than simply writers: Stalin himself said: 'Writers must not sit still, they must be familiar with the

---

154   Serge, Victor, *Memoirs of a Revolutionary*, New York: New York Review Books, 2012, p. 294.
155   Tret'yakov, Sergei, *Slyshish', Moskva?!*, Moscow: Izdatel'stvo 'Iskusstvo', 1966, pp. 211-12.

ways of life in their own country. Man is reshaped by life itself, and you must assist in reshaping his soul. That is what is important', adding that writers were 'the engineers of the soul'.[156]

Tretyakov went to the 'Communist Lighthouse' *kolkhoz* situated in the Stavropol region in the far south of Russia on the plains north of the Caucasus mountains. The Communist Lighthouse had actually been established in 1920. Its President, Ivan Kirillovich Martovitsky, had driven the first tractor seen there in 1923: he was to become a staunch friend of Tretyakov. He was a skilled organizer: 'he is given a problem in very difficult circumstances and he solves it easily and gracefully where other people would tear their hair out. He manages (the *kolkhoz*) like Caruso sings', Tretyakov told Brecht later. If Martovitsky learned something of contemporary culture from Tretyakov, Tretyakov learned a good deal about rural economics from Martovitsky. And after Tretyakov's death, Martovitsky insisted that documents and pictures of him at the commune should be preserved in the local museum.

There was no thought of that when Tretyakov paid his first visit in July 1928. He described this later with characteristic humour. On his arrival by train at Stavropol, he went to the District Kolkhoz Association office there. He was immediately informed that there was no value in 'desultory work', and the official tried to talk him out of his planned excursion. In any case, he said, 'Right now everyone there is busy threshing'. 'Which is precisely why I'm interested', Tretyakov replied. The official, a not untypical bureaucrat, it seems, was exasperated:

> 'What are people thinking when they send the visitors on outings that end up burdening the *kolkhozes*?'
> 'I'm not on an outing. I'm a writer'.
> 'A writer was just there a little while ago'.

Tretyakov, it seemed, was not wanted. However, he proceeded on his way, but when he reached the *kolkhoz*, the people there seemed almost equally dubious. 'They thought that I was some strange guy snooping

---

156   Westerman, Frank, *Engineers of the Soul*, London: Vintage Books, 2011, p. 34.

around. And in general I was wandering around like a fool,'[157] he added, echoing Mayakovsky's poem.

After a few weeks at the Communist Lighthouse, he began to realize his own ignorance of the collective farm, its management and its operation. He remained an outsider, finding it hard to come to terms with what was for him, a city-based intellectual, a strange and even alien world. He expected all peasant farmers to have Tolstoyan beards, and was surprised when he came across a pair of clean-shaven young men squaring up to each other in a field. He was an outsider, a guest, who fitted nowhere in the *kolkhoz* scheme of things. Was he to write descriptions of the leaves of the poplar trees rustling in the breeze, or of the wrinkles in the old peasants' necks? He could uncover facts from documents and records, but the real question was how was he to understand and explore these people's lives and attitudes, and the workings of their society? They seemed utterly uninterested in both him and his enquiries.

He felt a failure, but the visit had whetted his appetite. He was determined to return, to find out more about collectivization so that he could focus on more than the summer winds whispering in the trees. Consequently, in the spring of 1929 he went with a young Communist, V. Machavariani, to investigate collectivization in the Tuva People's Republic on the northern edge of Mongolia, south-west of Irkutsk. In January 1929 Moscow-backed Communists had overthrown this semi-independent state. Buddhist temples had been destroyed and the lamas in the government thrown out. What interested Tretyakov was the fact that the nomadic cattle herders were now being collectivized. But it seemed that this was ongoing, and it was too early to provide much illumination, at least for deepening his understanding of life in the Communist Lighthouse *kolkhoz*. Though he and Machavariani wrote a thin book about their visit, *To Tannu-Tuva*, published in Moscow in 1930, it was to the Caucasus that Tretyakov returned that summer. 'I would understand nothing unless I made a long stay there' he reflected.[158]

---

157   Tret'iakov, Sergei, 'The Writer and the Socialist Village', *October*, Vol. 118, Fall 2006, p. 63.
158   *Literature of the Peoples of the USSR*, VOKS Illustrated Almanac, Nos 7-8, 1934, p. 116.

His second visit lasted for considerably longer than his first, and he stayed with one of the *kolkhozniki*. He wanted to share directly in the life and work of the Communist Lighthouse, which had, while he was away, been amalgamated into a larger combination of collectivized farms called 'Challenge'. Now he found a place as a cultural worker, still somewhat outside the daily work of the *kolkhoz*, but contributing to its development: he strengthened ties with Moscow, organised leisure activities, worked for the improvement of the schools and libraries, and established a stencilled wall newspaper (perhaps remembering Trotsky's contention that 'the factory news-bulletins, pasted on their walls, represent a very necessary, though very remote, promise for the new literature of the future.'[159]) He was making progress.

He returned for a third time in January 1930 and this time stayed in the single men's dormitory until the autumn. In March he took a brief break and returned to Moscow, and it was while he was there that his friend, Vladimir Mayakovsky, the mighty voice of the revolution, its foremost poet and lionized advocate, committed suicide. Moscow, and especially revolutionary Moscow, was stupefied, appalled. Tretyakov attended his laying out, formed one of the guard of honour as his body was carried to the cemetery, and was the first speaker at his funeral.

Nothing changed with the death of Mayakovsky. And yet everything changed. The Meyerhold Theatre, which had staged two of Mayakovsky's plays in the previous two years, continued. Shostakovich, who had composed the music for *The Bedbug*, went on writing music. And Tretyakov returned to the *kolkhoz*. Yet in a few years, the Meyerhold Theatre was to be liquidated. Shostakovich would be accused of 'muddle not music'. And Tretyakov, whose star was now apparently in the ascendant, found that his focus shifted towards internationalism as the clouds of Stalinism darkened the revolutionary skies. The *avant-garde* project in the Soviet Union, of which Mayakovsky had been a central pillar, came under growing pressure. Without Mayakovsky, its future took on an ever gloomier appearance.

Immediately after Mayakovsky's funeral, however, Tretyakov returned to the Communist Lighthouse still full of hope for the

---

159   Trotsky, Leon, *Literature and Revolution*, Ann Arbor: University of Michigan Press, 1971, p. 227.

revolution. Now he managed to establish a proper newspaper, 'The Challenge', and he was able to acquire two 'culture caravans', sort of mobile libraries which also carried portable projectors to show films, and which travelled from place to place throughout the larger commune. And he went further, calling mass meetings where he explained the Communist Party's policies and collected money for new tractors and for the 'state fund'.

His approach was fundamentally democratic. He became 'Uncle' to the *kolkhozniki*, and they became his new family. Several of them stayed with him in Moscow in the next few years. He knew he was learning all the time. When he took a photograph, he would develop and print it and then ask the subject and his or her friends and neighbours to comment and judge it, before sticking it on the wall of the club, or into an album. He took charge of the village reading rooms and clubs where he organised art exhibitions, formed drama groups to perform for other members of the commune, and ran courses. He administered the creche, occasionally finding himself making peace between arguing mothers, and he investigated and set right various complaints of members of the *kolkhoz*. He also worked to change the minds of those who opposed the collectivization, those who took their animals out of the communal fields, or their children out of the communal nursery. He held meetings to reconcile 'old' and 'new' members of the *kolkhoz* in their bitter disputes about private property as against what was shared, always arguing that 'old' and 'new' were meaningless categories now because everybody was new in this new commune, 'Challenge'. And he consistently reported on developments for the Moscow papers.

The more he entered the life of the *kolkhoz*, the more he found to do. At meetings he joined discussions about topics as varied as the purchase of spark plugs for tractors, the patching of tarpaulins and the erection of threshing machines. He was asked about the timing and procedure of the spring sowing, a matter he struggled with since he had no idea whether a horse collar was suitable or whether a plough needed new parts. To those who thought this was not the business of the writer, he pointed out that only thus could he gauge the mood of the workers, their attitudes, what made them willing or unwilling to play their part. It was actually the basic means by which he could produce the work which as a writer he believed was necessary. And if he learned from people in these meetings, he also taught them skills, such as were needed in publishing the *kolkhoz* newspaper, educating would-be contributors to it, training typesetters and so on. He also spent many hours negotiating with Moscow suppliers for paper, type and the other necessaries for the newspaper. He took over two thousand photographs himself, but he also showed others how to use the camera to best effect. In all this, he realized that 'specialization' of the conventional sort was inappropriate here: every member of the collective could contribute to various areas of the work, and he himself learned to be not just a writer. He was going a long way towards realizing the reconfiguration of the artist's relationship with society propounded in Boris Arvatov's *Art and Production*.

For his own work as a cultural organiser, he constructed a diagrammatic plan of the various areas he covered and how they inter-related.[160] The various activities which grew from the central cultural base included political education, the library, the newspapers produced by the *kolkhoz*, protection of mothers and babies, adult education, the clubs and their activities, art work, exhibitions, and the radio and film centre. From the gauche newcomer of 1928, Tretyakov had become by 1930 an integral part of the working of the twenty *kolkhozy* of the Challenge combination, and his work was to influence the development of Russian collectivized agriculture for years to come. And not least he learned practically and for himself about living and working with ordinary people, something which not enough Marxist philosophers or cultural *animateurs* have managed.

This emerges from the works he wrote about the *kolkhoz*. Here factography gives place to 'operativism', and the *avant-garde* project which had begun with the Futurism of the Silver Age now reached its furthest point. Fact alone had become fetishized in factography. The Five Year Plan forced a writer like Tretyakov beyond the simple narration of facts towards the process of social construction itself. The result of this for Tretyakov was operativism, by which he meant written works with 'direct practical efficacy'.

The first of these works was *The Challenge: Collective Farm Sketches* which was published in 1930. The book is in three parts, each part

---

160   Reproduced in Papazian, Elizabeth Astrid, *Manufacturing Truth*, DeKalb, Ill: Northern Illinois University Press, 2009, p. 57.

corresponding to a year in which he visited the Communist Lighthouse. In the first part of *The Challenge* he records his own awkwardness when he first arrived there, and gives something of a history of the *kolkhoz*. In Part 2 the Communist Lighthouse has become part of the larger 'Challenge' combination, and the main focus is on the methods he began to adopt. In conjunction with the *kolkhoz* leaders, he helps the people to transform from traditional peasants into *kolkhozniki* through supporting and developing work in schools, the expansion of the library, the streamlining of the newspaper production and so on. And in the third part of the book, Tretyakov discusses the work he does as a fully integrated member of the collective and the further development of all sorts of ambitious cultural schemes.

In the final sketches, Tretyakov has become fully active within the collective, and indeed he assumes various leadership functions. Thus, in 'The Purge' he makes two impassioned speeches in public meetings about the expulsion of uncooperative rich peasants (*kulaks*) and the need for unity among the remaining *kolkhozniki*: 'someone has to take the floor', he realizes, and so he speaks himself. In 'The Women's Rebellion' he describes how some women on a particular *kolkhoz* in the Challenge collective wanted to reject communality, and how he took a leading role in persuading them to end their rebellion. The last essay in the book, 'We Are Sowing', shows how the new-found unity among the remaining *kolkhozniki* enables them to overfill their quotas. Perhaps the most interesting feature of the book is the way the growth and blossoming of the *kolkhoz* itself gradually unfolds, and how this proceeds in step with the writer's own growth and development from awkward incomer to fully operative participant. The book almost seems to show a concrete realization of the Experimental Laboratory of Kinetic Construction dreamed up by Tretyakov, Eisenstein and Arvatov in the heady early days of post-revolutionary Moscow. And it was received with delight by the members of the *kolkhoz*, who between them bought 181 copies of it. He admitted that, unlike them, he was not ploughing up the soil, but he was, he hoped, ploughing up their brains, and planting new seeds there. In return, they made up a poem which parodied his own verses in 'Roar, China':

> Roar, *kolkhoz*,
>   pressure

>   doesn't slacken.
>   Treble
>   the blows
>   in the autumn ploughing!

In 1931 a second book, its title parodying Turgenev's nineteenth century play of *bourgeois* hypocrisy and passion, *A Month in the Country: Operative Essays*, was published. It takes a more uncompromising, less reflective tone: 'Every minute, every word, and every step of a citizen has to be full of the fight for the reconstruction of our life', he writes, and the essays 'don't simply enumerate recurring facts; rather they see these facts in their development and demand immediate intervention in occurring events'.[161] He 'operates' on the facts to make a better outcome. He holds himself responsible for failures as well as successes. He points a way forward and depicts the struggle to reach the new end.

A selection from *The Challenge* and *A Month in the Country* was immediately made, translated and published in Germany, under the title *Field Marshals*, where it aroused considerable attention and controversy. A third volume, *A Thousand and One Work Days*, this time parodying the *Arabian Nights* in its title, was published in 1934, containing further essays, stories and sketches. The stories are simple but effective. 'Guards of the Harvest', for instance, is a tale of a poor twelve-year-old boy, Yasha, an orphan and member of the Appolia Pioneers, who guards the growing fruit in the *kolkhoz* garden and tries to defend it against those who would steal from it, though he takes a few nuts for himself, too. But he admits his transgression and is elected to go to the regional Pioneer meeting, where he is given a prize, and later goes on to the circus in Rostov. Tretyakov enters the world of the young *kolkhozniki* convincingly, and tells his story with gusto and amused irony. He is still capable of fine writing – the workers' 'backs ache so that the skin cries with large tears of sweat' and later 'the wind is in a rush to count the leaves on the poplars' – and, most interestingly, he introduces the figure of a 'tall writer' who follows the children and even writes a song for them:

---

161   Papazian, Elizabeth Astrid, *op. cit.*, p. 59.

> Let the rain come down in showers,
> Or the sun burn hot and strong,
> No Appolia Pioneer
> Leaves his post a minute long.[162]

The story of 'Nine Girls' concerns the brigade of the famous heroine of the Second Five Year Plan, Pasha Angelina. Five of the girls in her brigade are of Greek origin, and Tretyakov opens his story with an implicit comparison with Greek sculptures and the ancient Greeks' epic achievements in making civilization. It is a significant reference point. The story starts in 1930 when almost insurmountable difficulties arose – 'The *kulaks* fought back savagely, radicals took policies too far, lamps kept going out at meetings and Party organizer Angelin (Pasha's father) and his children were pelted with corncobs'. But Pasha is soon enabled to form her own women's tractor drivers' brigade and they are quickly seen to be outstripping the men's brigades. When her husband treats her badly, she simply jumps onto her tractor, and the women plough 1,225 hectares each. The nine girls are called to Moscow, where they are feted and rewarded. She is nervous, but 'when she mounted the tribune of the Kremlin Palace, Stalin stood up applauding', and three thousand audience members followed his example. Pasha vows to do yet more – 1,600 hectares each!

> And then she fell silent. She wiped her brow with her hand and, leaning to the side, said quietly, like a little girl:
> 'Working is easier than talking ...'[163]

It is hard today to assess these operativist stories objectively. They were certainly admired in their time, but they are perhaps too similar to the ballooning number of Soviet stories by hack writers of the 1930s hailing the heroes of the Five Year Plan and their Stakhanovite achievements in overfilling their 'quotas'. Tretyakov's stories are not so banal as most of these, but they seem to lack some of the energy found

---

162   Tretyakov, S., 'Guards of the Harvest', *International Literature*, No. 2, 1934, p. 51.
163   Tretyakov, Sergei, 'Nine Girls', in von Geldern, James, and Stites, Richard, *Mass Culture in Soviet Russia*, Bloomington, IN: Indiana University Press, 1995, p. 227.

in his best work – *A Wise Man, I Want a Baby, Den Shi-hua*. Perhaps the difference lies in the function: Tretyakov's operativism goes well beyond the typical propaganda purposes of most Soviet writers of the time. Operativism depends on prolonged absorption in the subject of the writing, and on avoiding writing merely for consumption. The operativist writer is fully involved alongside his subject, which is why he is responsible not just for the writing, but for the processes he describes as well, a responsibility which the propagandist of course never considers. It is why the presence of the 'tall writer' in 'Guards of the Harvest' is crucial to the story.

All this work saw Tretyakov's star rising in the U.S.S.R. A mark of status was the sign on the wall of the Actors' Club in Moscow which Rybakov remembered:

> Remember one truth only,
> When coming to the club, bring a wife.
> And don't be like the *bourgeois*,
> Bring your own, not someone else's.

'The first two lines were by the writer, Tretyakov, and the last two by Mayakovsky, just before his death'.[164] His reputation was further enhanced by the enormous range of writing projects which he undertook in the first years of the 1930s. These included *The A-Y Country*, a book of sketches and essays written after a visit to the Angara region in Siberia which was rapidly industrialising under the Five Year Plan; *Chelyuskin: A Country Saves its Sons*, in which he collaborated with Leonid Muchanov, Mikhail Goldberg and Sergei Dikovsky to tell the story of a Soviet steamship which tried to navigate the northern Murmansk to Vladivostok route through the polar ice floes in the autumn of 1933 and became stuck the following February near Kolyuchin Island, the crew escaping onto the ice where they built a makeshift runway so that a plane (fitted with skis) could land to rescue them; a new kind of Guide Book to Moscow in collaboration with the cartoonists, Ilya Ilf and Evgeny Petrov, the writers Yury Olesha and Isaac Babel, as well as Boris Agapov and Tatyana Tess; and a book, never published, about Soviet scientific research laboratories and their

---

164   Rybakov, Anatoli, *Children of the Arbat*, London: Arrow Books, 1988, p. 521.

leading members, provisionally entitled *The Brains of the Country*. He proposed a further project to Rodchenko in February 1934, this one centred on photographs. The latter recorded in his diary:

> On the phone today, Seryozha (Tretyakov) proposed going to Tiflis and shooting the entire trip for a book, winter and summer. And moreover to travel with the Kultprosvet train to the Far East, where writing would be possible.[165]

Rodchenko seems not to have been keen on the idea, and it too came to nothing. Tretyakov was also working on two more plays, one about Svanetia, the other about the Communist Lighthouse, to be called *We Fill the Earth*. This was intended for the Theatre of the Revolution but it seems neither of these plays was completed.

A feature of much of this work, which could be characterized as 'operativist', was his willingness – perhaps his eagerness – to collaborate with other writers, several of whom were young and at the start of their careers, such as Sergei Dikovsky, who was to go on to become a prominent Soviet writer. His home was sometimes more like a studio, or collective, of young writers. They formed a brigade, and he was the leader. He was interested in their lives, checked on their work, and gave them literary tasks which he oversaw. He was indefatigable in his supervision and his encouragement, a stern taskmaster but a sympathetic and humorous fellow-worker, and they regarded him as their 'master'. The individual worker, even the writer, was thus dissolved in the process of revolutionary production and collectivization. Tretyakov was creating a kind of laboratory for new ways of organising artistic production and seeking a new place for the writer or artist in a collectivized society to replace the lonely author of *bourgeois* imagination, stuck in a garret and wrestling with his soul. The old ways served *bourgeois* society: now new ways must be found.

Conscious that contemporary reality was changing quickly, operativist writers found new forms – the essay, the sketch, the photo-series – which were brief, sharp, and able to keep up with the rapid and vast movements of the time. Operativism documented, energised

---

165   Lavrentiev, Alexander N. (ed), *Aleksandr Rodchenko: Experiments for the Future*, New York: The Museum of Modern Art, 2005, p. 309.

and pushed forward. Critics have often preferred to use the Russian word, '*ocherk*', rather than essay or sketch, for what Tretyakov came to practice. The *ocherk* may perhaps be thought of as an expansion of the newspaper article. It relates the facts, draws conclusions and urges its readers towards the next steps. Elizabeth Papazian explains its importance in the period of the Five Year Plan:

> It was seen as fulfilling the perceived need to document industrialization and collectivization; as engaging the public in the process of documentation; and as helping teach new writers to write and new readers to read by virtue of its accessibility and clarity (as opposed to fiction). Thus its documentary character, its dual promise of objectivity and instrumentality, was the source of its specific appeal.[166]

The operative writer is involved rationally and emotionally, and is well enough informed to give the reader a vivid and true insight into people, events and a way of life, and, consequently, an indication of how to judge these. And this leads the reader to act, even if the acting is only a refocusing of ideas, a comprehending of possibilities, or an engendering of solidarity. Thus Tretyakov's project was essentially democratic not only in its effect on the reader, but also because he wished every worker to become an artist and every artist to become a worker. All this gained him prestige, and he was high in the Party's favour.

But the underlying question which was becoming ever more urgent was: how far was this inherent democratization in step with the Communist Party and its creation, the Soviet Union? The Soviet Union's project seemed to be moving ever more clearly towards centralisation, and was thus ever more anti-democratic. The signs were increasingly ominous. 1928, for instance, had started with a new kind of 'show trial' when over fifty engineers and administrators in Shakhty in what is now the Rostov region were charged with sabotage and spying. Of the fifty, five were executed and most of the rest imprisoned without any convincing evidence. It was a menacing first glimpse of Stalin's ruthlessness, the beginning of the 'second'

---

166   Papazian, Elizabeth Astrid, *op. cit.*, p. 15.

Tretyakov, about 1931.

revolution, the 'cultural revolution', which might also be called the counter-revolution, the Bolsheviks' Thermidor.

This counter-revolution could be detected in the world of the arts by seemingly unconnected straws in the wind: the resignation of Anatoly Lunacharsky as Minister for Education and Culture; the aggressive attacks on 'Rightism' in the arts by spokespeople like Platon Kerzhentsev; the condemnation of the *avant-garde* by an international Congress of Revolutionary Writers in Kharkov in Ukraine; the emigration of Mikhail Chekhov, probably the country's finest actor and nephew of the great playwright; the suicide of Vladimir Mayakovsky; and the arrests during these years of *avant-garde* or satirical writers like Daniil Kharms, Alexander Vvedensky, Nikolai Erdman and Vladimir Mass.

On the other hand, in 1932 all the fractious literary groupings were abolished and a single USSR Writers' Union established, which was to provide housing (*dachas* as well as flats in the cities), care homes, sanatoria and medical care, not to mention special access to travel, domestic goods and even publication. Meanwhile, the Moscow Art Theatre, so long denigrated by Bolshevik hangers-on as 'mystical' and 'idealistic', now became 'the greatest theatre in the world' and the Stanislavsky acting system the exemplar for all Soviet actors.

In the summer of 1934, Tretyakov organized an All-Union Conference on the Artistic *Ocherk*. It was a sign of the form's growing importance, and it was practiced by writers such as Boris Agapov, Marietta Shaginyan, Mikhail Prishvin, and Boris Galin, whose *ocherki* in *Komsomolskaya Pravda* were arousing special interest. Moreover, the movement was supported by Maxim Gorky, the Party's most favoured writer, who had returned to the Soviet Union in 1928 and was now President of the new Writers' Union. His journal *Our Achievements* devoted space to *ocherki*. The search for an art which could be theorized as specifically socialist or Soviet had led from factography to operativism. Was it Tretyakov's hope that operativism would be adopted at the All-Soviet Writers' Congress, which was to meet in August and September of that same summer, immediately after the Conference on the Artistic *Ocherk*?

He was chosen as one of the lead organizers for the All-Union Writers' Congress, which was chaired by Union President Maxim Gorky, whose membership card was number one. Viktor Pertsov described the opening in the Hall of Columns in the House of the Union:

> In the morning of a hot August day there prevails here a cool shadiness, which is cut through with bright spotlights. There is a row of small windows, almost under the ceiling, above the circle which is the place for guests, giving enough light for people to see one another. A single lamp burns on the rostrum. The speaker is Maxim Gorky. In the intense silence of the crowded hall, his voice is listened to, hard to catch, and cut short from time to time by a slight coughing.[167]

There were six hundred delegates to the Congress from over forty different Soviet nationalities, as well as representatives of industry and agriculture and not a few foreign delegates. The excitement was intense: 'Everyone was enthusiastic and striving to put literature "in touch with the times"'.[168]

The Congress is usually thought of as a significant turning-point in Soviet literary and artistic history, but this seems only partially accurate. It was certainly another sign of increasing dangers to come, but as such it was one more step down an increasingly steep slope rather than a turning-point. It was certainly important for the fact that it cemented 'socialist realism' as the only permissible form for the Soviet artist, though precisely how to define 'socialist realism' was never very clear. For Gorky, it meant a continuation of the Russian realist tradition which had reached its apogee in the novels of Leo Tolstoy. For others, crucial features included typicality in the choice of character and action, the accessibility of the material, and optimism in the tone, as well as what Andrei Zhdanov called 'revolutionary romanticism'. This, it was understood, meant that the writer had to show how reality accorded with the Party's policies, though romanticism also, of course, negated modernism. Socialist realism thus demanded political orthodoxy, and its adoption by the Congress inevitably handed to the Party the right to jurisdiction in matters of art. This was the danger.

However, it was certainly not spelled out. Indeed, Alexei Stetsky, one of the emissaries of the Party, asserted that the Congress 'is not passing any resolutions on literary questions that are binding on all

---

167 Pertsov, V., Introduction to Tret'yakov, Sergei, *Den Shi-hua*, Moscow: Sovetskii pisatel', 1962, p. 3.
168 *Ibid.*

writers', and that 'we do not have a guiding line in literature', though he added, confusingly, that 'our guiding line is that of socialist realism', and Karl Radek reminded writers that 'literature is a weapon of the (class) struggle'.[169]

Nevertheless, Tretyakov's work could be seen as not far from all this, and in any case he was now enjoying great esteem in influential literary and Party circles. If it seemed that small *genres* like the *ocherk* were downgraded in value compared with the thick novel, the full-scale opera or the feature film, there were other signs that were definitely positive. Thus, Andrei Zhdanov may not have endorsed operativism as such, but he did advocate drawing 'subject matter, images, artistic language and speech' from such things as 'the life and experience of the men and women of ... Magnitogorsk', which was the subject of *A Song about Heroes*; from 'the heroic epic of the Chelyuskin expedition', about which Tretyakov had already published; and from 'the experience of the collective farms', which was his primary subject at the time.[170] Stetsky recommended that the book about the Chelyuskin expedition should be distributed among the delegates, because it would 'teach the artist that he cannot confine himself to mere photography ... to a mere chronicling of events'.[171] And Radek seemed to endorse Tretyakov's approach: 'the great creations of socialist realism cannot be the result of chance observations of certain sections of society; they demand that the artist comprehend the tremendous whole'.[172]

The conference's implications did not seem – at least at the time – to be the threat to Tretyakov and others which has sometimes been imagined by those wise after the event. Actually it was a measure of Tretyakov's high standing at this time that he was chosen to edit the published transcript of the proceedings of the Congress.

---

169   Gorky, Maxim, Radek, Karl, Bukharin, Nikolai, Zhdanov, Andrei, *et al.*, *Soviet Writers' Congress 1934*, London: Lawrence and Wishart, 1977, pp. 263, 264.
170   *Ibid.*, p. 20.
171   *Ibid.*, p. 270.
172   *Ibid.*, p. 157.

Friedrich Wolf, photographed by Tretyakov.

CHAPTER 11.
SHARING A BONFIRE

The speech by Sergei Tretyakov at the 1934 All-Union Congress of Soviet Writers concerned not operativism or socialist realism but the international dimension for Soviet writing which he urged writers to remember. He had sought an international perspective for progressive artists since the earliest days of *LEF*. In Europe his strongest focus had always been on Germany (the notional setting for *Are You Listening, Moscow?!*): he had spoken German from his childhood and his work on the *kolkhoz* had very quickly been published in Germany. His speech was punctuated by enthusiastic applause.

He began by stating that the books of Soviet writers must be seen as ambassadors for their 'astonishing' country. He referred to some good examples, such as Lidia Seyfullina's *Virineya*, about a young woman from a community of Old Believers who falls in love with a Communist, *Kostya Ryabtsev's Diary: Scenes of School Life* by Nikolai Ognyov, Alexander Fadeyev's *The Rout*, which told the story of the defeat of Japan in the Far East after the revolution, when Tretyakov himself was there, and *The Story of the Five Year Plan* by M. Ilin.

These books, he said, 'go into battle, they enter the Fascist fire, and by the light of the flames they face the frightful mugs of the gorillas with their swastikas'. He gave further examples, including his own drama, *Roar, China!*, at performances of which in Japan spectators sang revolutionary songs, even while being dragged out of the auditorium by the police. A major task for Soviet writers, he said, was to 'destroy in the consciousness of foreign readers false and exotic representations' of the Soviet Union. 'Our invasion into the literature of foreign countries is a process, which presses forward alongside the creative work of our friends abroad, our friends in the real struggle'. And he went on to mention John Dos Passos, Theodore Dreiser and Bertolt Brecht, suggesting their works should be read by Soviet readers. 'That's why I want to make a concrete proposal here: every writer should have a second language', a proposal greeted with applause from the hall. Writers 'who possess real eyes and pens', he said, would then be able to 'communicate about us' to foreign readers, and they would also be able to make reports about foreign countries.

He echoed calls for international solidarity among revolutionary writers, but questioned the term, 'revolutionary writers' as it seemed to him too narrow, too exclusive, and to deter many determined anti-Fascist writers who were not yet Communists. He concluded by saying that writers from the capitalist west were aware their society was 'sinking in the rotten mud': Soviet writers could show 'the fresh air of tomorrow's youth'. Then capitalism's 'final moments will reveal our writers' pens as weapons to shoot and cut down'. Applause.[173]

Tretyakov's internationalism had always sat alongside his support for the Soviet experiment. It was perhaps a somewhat dangerous, even contradictory, position at this time. Nevertheless, he had spent much of the Congress translating both from and into German for the delegates from that country. His German, though, was Baltic German – the word order and the pronunciation of some words was different, and sometimes the German guests had difficulty in following him. Still, he was the obvious person to lead a group of them who had attended the Congress on a long tour of Russia, mostly in the south of the country. Most of these were exiles from Hitler's Nazi regime, and several of them were in the process of settling in the U.S.S.R. They included Oskar Maria Graf, novelist and playwright; the anarchist writer Theodore Plievier; John Heartfield, political artist and stage designer; the playwright Ernst Toller, now based in England; Johannes Becher, writer and active Communist; and Ernst Ottwald, also a writer who was fated to die in the gulag camp in 1943. Meanwhile, Olga Tretyakova took charge of further visitors to the Congress, who also went on the tour, notably the Spanish writers Maria Teresa León and her husband, the poet Rafael Alberti Merello, the British journalist

---

173 *Pravda*, 28 August 1934.

Ada Chesterton, and the Danish author Karin Michaëlis. The tour lasted for two months.

Perhaps the most poignant – or terrifying – moment came when Maria Teresa León offered to tell Olga's fortune. She could, she said, read a person's hand. Olga offered her hand and Maria Teresa studied it before pronouncing that after she reached forty years of age, a terrible tragedy would occur in her life. Olga was thirty-seven at the time. She would be forty in 1937.

Many of the German writers were already known to Tretyakov from his visit to Germany four years earlier. He had arrived there in December 1930, after a short stay in Vienna, and remained in Germany till the following May. For most of his time in Berlin he stayed with the graphic artist and film-maker, Hans Richter, who helped him to purchase a Leica Camera, the most up-to-date available at the time. It became one of his prize possessions, and he put it to immediate use in Germany, taking a series of sharp photographs, including of Bertolt Brecht and members of his family. It was this that he said a few years later was as important to him as his pen and notebook.

His work had already been seen in Germany when the Meyerhold Theatre had toured to Berlin and other cities earlier in 1930. Included in the repertoire of that theatre was *Roar, China!* which the progressive intelligentsia had hugely admired. Herbert Ihering, the theatre critic, for instance, had written that the scenes depicting the Chinese in the play were 'among the most extraordinary I have ever seen',[174] though it may be added that the foremost left-wing theatre director, Erwin Piscator, did not agree: for him, these scenes provided 'detail, not elucidation'.[175] Most of the theatre-going public had certainly enjoyed it, though it had also aroused controversy, having been abominated by the rising right wing in pre-Hitler Germany. Nevertheless, Tretyakov was widely welcomed across the country, which he traversed, giving lectures and meeting many of the leading artists and intellectuals who opposed Hitler. Besides those already mentioned, Tretyakov met Friedrich Wolf, the writer and medical doctor, Hanns Eisler,

---

174 Bullivant, Keith (ed), *Culture and Society in the Weimar Republic*, Manchester: Manchester University Press, 1977, p. 151.
175 Willett, John, *The Theatre of Erwin Piscator*, London: Eyre Methuen, 1978, p. 125.

the composer for the film *A Song About Heroes*, Gregor Gog, the founder of the Brotherhood of Vagabonds, and, most significantly, Bertolt Brecht, who had defended *Roar, China!* vigorously. In a side trip to Denmark he also became acquainted with the writer and socialist, Martin Anderson Nexø. He wrote lively portraits of many of these, using the *ocherk* form, and publishing the collection in Moscow in 1936. Its title referred to the notorious burning of books by the Nazis – *People Who Shared a Bonfire* (*Lyudi odnogo kostra*).

He met Friedrich Wolf in his square white house in Stuttgart. Wolf, whose writing as well as his medical work sprang from his commitment to communism, was keen to show Tretyakov how he lived. He demonstrated the calisthenics he performed each morning, showing how fit his body was, and explained his diet and its importance for a healthy life. This was what he preached to his proletarian patients, and Tretyakov even attended a meeting in a Berlin sports hall where Wolf explained to his audience his ideological commitment.

He struck up an even more meaningful relationship with Bertolt Brecht, which was to last for the rest of his life. Brecht took him to Augsburg, where he had been born and had grown up. Founded by the Roman Emperor, Augustus, the city had seen witches burned and fortunes made; it had a medieval castle and modern factory chimneys, and the tallest chimney of all was that belonging to Brecht's father's paper mill. They visited the local cemetery, noting how the class system operated even after death, as the rich had huge gravestones and stone crosses to mark their burial places, whereas the poor and destitute were huddled away in the corners, often with no marker at all. In Berlin, Tretyakov was intrigued to have to take an extremely rickety lift to reach Brecht's flat, from the window of which could be seen street fighting between Communists and Nazis. Brecht smoked cigars endlessly, sang ballads with his banjo across his knee, and they talked. Sometimes it was fun, as when Brecht described his career as a medical orderly:

> I bound up wounds and painted them with iodine. I administered enemas and gave blood transfusions. If a doctor had said to me: 'Brecht, amputate this leg!' I would have replied: 'As you order, Herr Staff Doctor!' and cut off the leg. If

somebody had given the order: 'Brecht, trepan!' I would have cut open the skull and poked about in the brain.[176]

(It seems a shame that some critics, not understanding either Brecht's or Tretyakov's sense of humour, should have taken this comic flight of fancy seriously.) But much of their talk, now and in after years, concerned ideas, politics, theatre and commitment. As Brecht had admired *Roar, China!* so now Tretyakov admired *Man Equals Man* which he saw on 2 February 1931 in Brecht's own production with Peter Lorre and Helene Weigel in the leading roles. Only Meyerhold's *The Magnanimous Cuckold* had made a deeper impression on him, he said. But what struck Tretyakov perhaps most forcibly was the audience reaction to the play:

> Women stamped their heels, lawyers foaming with anger hurried from the theatre, hurling their crumpled programmes at the actors as they left. In the cloakroom a sobbing woman tore her coat from her husband's grip and went to a far corner to put it on alone. Her husband was unbearable, for he had watched the play without being nauseated.[177]

It was the kind of reaction Tretyakov and Eisenstein had been seeking nearly a decade earlier at the Proletkult theatre, but one which was not in accord with Brecht's developing theory. Brecht also took Tretyakov to a party at the home of the Marxist sociologist and politician Fritz Sternberg, where the talk turned to the Soviet collectivization of agriculture. Some of the other guests began to attack the policy and the way it was being carried out, making Tretyakov, probably the only person present who had actual experience of working in a *kolkhoz*, distinctly uneasy. Exactly what was said, and how much was known, is unclear, but it may be that this altercation planted a seed of doubt in Tretyakov's mind, even if no doubts existed previously. It was certainly not mentioned in *People Who Shared a Bonfire*, nor in the many reports

---

176   Witt, Hubert (ed), *Brecht as They Knew Him*, London: Lawrence and Wishart, 1974, p. 71.
177   Ibid., p. 73.

Tretyakov sent back from Germany to several newspapers and journals in Moscow.

Tretyakov's main purpose in visiting Germany was the lecture on 'The Writer and the Socialist Village', which he gave at the Society for the Friends of the New Russia in Berlin on 21 January 1931. In this he followed in the footsteps of Anatoly Lunacharsky, Sergei Eisenstein and others, who had spoken to the Society in previous years. He went on to give further lectures in Königsberg, Dresden, Stuttgart, Frankfurt am Main, Hamburg, Aachen and Heidelberg. Back in Berlin, he spoke again at the Theatre am Nollendorfplatz, where he also met and chatted to young German writers.

'The Writer and the Socialist Village', which was accompanied by slides made from the photographs Tretyakov had taken at the Communist Lighthouse *kolkhoz*, made a significant impact on the German intelligentsia at this fragile time in the dying years of the Weimar Republic and just before the coming of Hitler. Beginning with a riposte to Ezra Pound, who had suggested in an 'Open Letter to Tretyakov' published the year before, that to understand the Russian revolution, a reading of the classic nineteenth century novelists would be more helpful than a study of 'Marxian theories', Tretyakov pointed out that Turgenev or Dostoyevsky would not even understand contemporary Russian vocabulary, words such a 'kolkhoz', 'rabfak' or 'komsomol'. The new reality demanded a new kind of literature, focusing on man's social and intellectual aspects rather than the biological and emotional life of a protagonist. The author who visited a *kolkhoz* seeking material for a traditional novel or the artist who wanted to paint a conventional portrait of an agricultural activist would produce only superficial work.

'The quest for the correct method of grasping and holding reality is one of the most burning questions in Soviet art', Tretyakov maintained. And he suggested three steps which needed to be taken to give any meaningful answer:

> First: the choice of object, investigating the facts in their specificity, and in their concrete manifestations.
>
> Second: the journalistic processing of found factual material. Enhancing its characteristic moments. Extracting the

> dialectical chain from the process in which the fact is the essential, determining link. Drawing the fact in an effective agitational form. Testing the fact's public, social interest and significance. The fact thereby becomes an argument, a signal, a concrete proposal.
>
> Third: the practical conclusions. Operationalizing the literary contribution within the organization of reality in accordance with socialism.[178]

The writer thus has a social responsibility, which requires an organic, personal connection to his material beyond simply the business of observing, a responsibility which includes the future fate of the material. 'I call participation in the material itself an operative relation ... Inventing something important is bellesletristic novelism; discovering something important is reportage; constructing something important is operativism'.[179] Literature thus becomes a tool or weapon engaged in socialist construction, and the writer a person who is first engaged with this struggle but who is also – secondarily – equipped with literary skills. And by incorporating himself into the work of construction, the writer is no longer the romantic isolated figure of yore, nor is his work something merely to be consumed. He has learned 'not only the art of drawing life's likeness, but also how to change life'.[180]

> Thus the *kolkhoz*, my literary subject, has become the site of my civic activity. I integrated myself not just to get to know the heroes of my book, not just to record their transformations. Side by side with my heroes, I struggle for the reorganization of their life.[181]

The lecture contained many startling new ideas for Tretyakov's hearers, and it certainly set the cat among the pigeons of German left wing

---

178   Tret'iakov, Sergei, 'The Writer and the Socialist Village', *October*, Vol. 118, Fall 2006, p. 68.
179   *Ibid.* p. 69.
180   *Ibid.*
181   *Ibid.*, p. 70.

Bertolt Brecht, from
People Who Shared a Bonfire by Tretyakov.

artists and writers. Many on the left were excited by what he had to say; others worried about what seemed to be a discrediting of basic humanist values as they saw them. Siegfried Kracauer, for instance, while pointing out that social conditions in Germany and the Soviet Union were not the same, accepted the need to jettison idealism and concentrate on social reality. But Alfred Döblin, who also rejected utopian idealism, was much more pessimistic about the social function of the writer. To Gottfried Benn such an idea was anathema. He thought the writer's task was 'to exclude life, to constrict it, and actually to fight it, in order to give it form', and he spoke of the 'inner emptiness of this Tretyakov presentation'.[182] He even suggested Tretyakov might be an agent for the Cheka (secret police). It may be worth adding that in 1933 Gottfried Benn joined the Nazis.

Other, less maverick left wingers took issue with what they believed was Tretyakov's desire to finish with literature as they knew it. His ideas displayed the formalist-aesthetic attitude of the discontented petty *bourgeois*, they contended, and they welcomed the advent of 'socialist realism' in the Soviet Union, unaware perhaps that Tretyakov's new formulations might be regarded as one pathway amid many within the socialist realist project. This was probably how Tretyakov himself regarded it. Nevertheless, Walter Benjamin, perhaps Tretyakov's most sympathetic and most perceptive critic, set Tretyakov's ideas against socialist realism, which he (Benjamin) rejected because of what he saw as its tendency towards emotionalism, especially the emotionalism of identifying with a hero. Tretyakov's operativism, on the other hand, he saw as a literary practice from which one might learn. Benjamin's essay 'The Author as Producer', unpublished at the time, but greatly respected in decades to come, articulated amazed admiration for Tretyakov's work at the *kolkhoz*. Benjamin understood that Tretyakov was proposing nothing less than the transformation of the means of literary production – a genuine cultural revolution. 'In the case of the writer, this ... consists in conduct that transforms him from a supplier of the productive apparatus into an engineer who sees it as his task to adapt this apparatus to the purposes of the proletarian revolution'.[183] It is ironic

---

182   Völker, Klaus, *Brecht: A Biography*, London: Marion Boyars, 1979, p. 161.
183   Benjamin, Walter, *Selected Writings*, Vol. 2, Part 2, 1931-1934, Cambridge,

that so much critical and intellectual attention has been paid to Benjamin's essay, and so little to Tretyakov's work which inspired it.

Tretyakov's most formidable opponent in these disputes and controversies was the Hungarian Marxist, Georg Lukács, who became the leading ideologue for the specifically Soviet form of socialist realism. Lukács arrived in Germany from Moscow in 1931. He soon began to publish critical essays in the left wing journal, *Die Linkskurve*, in which he attacked the 'open' epic forms in contemporary literature, and advocated a return to the 'bourgeois cultural heritage', the tradition of Balzac and Tolstoy. It was a position he would develop and refine over a period of decades. In 'Reportage or Portrayal', published in 1932, he attacked specifically Tretyakov's 'bio-interview', *Den Shi-hua*. For Lukács, this book was neither journalistic reportage, which would use facts in all their concrete reality, nor a properly conceived novel because it relied on facts, not the imagination. Therefore it fell between the two stools of the particularity of journalism and the overview of reality which the novel provided. Lukács also attacked Tretyakov's idea of the 'biography of the thing', arguing that 'the infinite richness of life must inevitably be lost when no expression is given to the complex interweaving of the ways and byways by which individual men and women consciously or unconsciously, intentionally or unintentionally, realize the universal'.[184] Tretyakov's ideas, he wrote, were 'crassly fetishistic', and he fulminated against the very principal of montage: 'Born of the nihilist theory and practice of the various Dada trends, the theory of *montage* "consolidated" itself ... and became a deliberate surrogate for art: a special creative originality was supposed to manifest itself in the sticking together of disconnected facts'. He concluded with the assertion that 'the "cult of facts"' was 'a miserable surrogate' for the intimacy with people's historical lives which the great nineteenth century novelists possessed. 'And for this surrogate to dress itself up in *belles lettres* and to pass off a smooth or mannered prose as epic art only aggravates the situation'.[185]

Mass: Harvard University Press, 2005, p. 780.
184   Völker, Klaus, *op. cit.*, p. 249.
185   Lukács, Georg, *The Historical Novel*, Harmondsworth: Penguin, 1981, pp. 302, 303.

'It is the content of the story that matters', Lukács proclaimed. Tretyakov's response was already clear. In 1928, in *New LEF*, he had laid out his fundamental position:

> We say that ideology does not lie in the material which art makes uses of. Ideology lies in the devices through which that material is worked up; ideology lies in the form. Only expediently formed material can become a thing with direct social function.[186]

Of course, Lukács' position finally condemns all innovation or experimentation in the arts, and on one level Benjamin used Tretyakov's operativism as a counter to Lukács' case. For Benjamin, simply declaring solidarity with the proletariat was meaningless unless it had been experienced, as Tretyakov had experienced it at the Communist Lighthouse *kolkhoz*. It was thus more than the mere *content* of the work which mattered.

Tretyakov's closest comrade-in-arms in these literary conflicts was Bertolt Brecht, probably Europe's greatest twentieth century dramatist. When he heard about Brecht's latest documentary film, *Kuhle Wampe*, written in collaboration with Ernst Ottwald and directed by Slatan Dudow, he arranged for the premiere to take place in Moscow. In May 1932 therefore Brecht and Dudow arrived by train, coincidentally the same train as Sergei Eisenstein was on after his long trip to America and Mexico. They were met at the station by Tretyakov at the head of something of a welcoming party, including long-time Brecht associates like Bernhard Reich, the Austrian-German theatre director of Jewish origins, his wife Anna 'Asja' Lācis, from Latvia, and also a notable theatre director, as well as Erwin Piscator, all of whom were currently domiciled in Moscow. The Nazis had not yet achieved power, but the uncertainties of life in Germany had driven them all eastwards. Now they were keen to support Brecht and the new film which, despite Tretyakov's energetic efforts to promote it, was somewhat poorly received by the Muscovites when it was shown.

---

186   Lawton, Anna (ed.), *Russian Futurism Through its Manifestoes, 1912-1928*, Ithaca: Cornell University Press, 1988, p. 265.

However, Tretyakov drove Brecht round the city in a car. They visited a printing works, the Komsomol Club and Lenin's mausoleum on Red Square, and Tretyakov seemed proud of everything he saw. After some hours, Tretyakov's enthusiasm wore Brecht down: 'In the end I did get a bit tired', he told Walter Benjamin ruefully. 'I could not admire everything, nor did I want to. It's like this: they are his soldiers, his trucks. But, unfortunately, not mine'.[187] Tretyakov also took Brecht to the Vakhtangov Theatre to see the legendary production of Gozzi's *Princess Turandot*, which stuck in his memory so that in the end he made his own adaptation of it. Most importantly, they resumed their discussions. Brecht read *I Want a Baby* in a translation by Ernst Hube. He was enthusiastic about the play, and wanted to set up a production of it in Germany, though this never materialized, not least because of Hitler's acquisition of power. Meanwhile, Tretyakov began translating some of Brecht's plays. And Brecht outlined his idea for staging historical trials: 'The theatre would be built like a law court. Two trials every evening. For instance, the trial of Socrates. A witchcraft trial. The trial of George Grosz, who was charged with blasphemy because of his picture of Christ in a gas mask, saying: "Hold your mouth and obey orders!"'[188] And they discussed anti-Fascism, revolutionary realism and dramatic form, not always agreeing, but always passionately engaged with their subjects.

They did not meet again until 1935, and in 1933 Brecht left Germany to escape the Hitler regime. Nevertheless they kept in touch, and in 1934 Brecht, in exile, told an interviewer that 'in Russia there's one man who's working along the right lines, Tretyakov; a play like *Roar, China!* shows him to have found quite new means of expression. He has the ability, and he's working steadily on'.[189] In the autumn of 1933, Helene Weigel, Brecht's wife, came to Moscow, ostensibly to give some sort of recitals or performances. Actually, she was suffering with an ectopic pregnancy, that is when the fertilized egg is not growing in the womb but is elsewhere, probably in one of the fallopian tubes. The condition is dangerous and requires an abortion, which Tretyakov arranged for her. She stayed at the

---

187   Benjamin, Walter, *Reflections*, New York: Schocken Books, 1978, p. 206.
188   Witt, Hubert (ed), *op. cit.*, p. 74.
189   Willett, John (ed), *Brecht on Theatre*, London: Eyre Methuen, 1973, p. 65.

Tretyakovs' flat while she recuperated, and all three members of the family found her a warm and welcome guest.

When Brecht left Germany to go into exile, he entrusted a draft of his play, *Roundheads and Peakheads*, to Hans Richter, who was coming to Moscow, to pass on to Tretyakov. The latter was busy translating his work into Russian, both poems and plays, and trying to arrange a production in Moscow. Their letters are full of references to this. First it was going to be *St Joan of the Stockyards*, and Brecht writes in July 1933:

> How is *St Joan* coming along? And, incidentally, have you any news of Carola Neher, who hasn't been in Germany for the past six months and is thought to be in Russia? ... She would be a wonderful Joan. If the part is already taken, perhaps she could understudy it.[190]

On 15 July Tretyakov reassured him that *St Joan of the Stockyards* would begin rehearsals in September, and a few days later he wrote that he was setting up a meeting with Nikolai Okhlopkov, Erwin Piscator and Carola Neher. Whatever the fate of this meeting, unfortunately no production materialized. As time went on, Tretyakov continued to try to get a commitment from Nikolai Okhlopkov, perhaps to stage *Roundheads and Peakheads* at his Realistic Theatre. But Okhlopkov proved elusive. In June 1935 he writes that the director was away from Moscow, and a few weeks later he was still away, though Tretyakov knew that he was 'looking for a new theatre piece now'. But nothing came of this attempt to get a Brecht play staged either. In 1934, however, Tretyakov's translations of three Brecht plays, *St Joan of the Stockyards*, *The Mother* and *The Measures Taken* were published, and they at least introduced Brecht to prospective Russian audiences.

That same year, Tretyakov was to express his friendship with Brecht publicly at the Writers' Congress:

> In my friendship with Brecht, I have experienced that feeling of comradely closeness which makes one strong. I translate his work; I accept much of it. I protest much of it, but I follow his every step with the utmost attention, if you will, with love.

---

190   Brecht, Bertolt, *Letters*, London: Methuen, 1990, p. 141.

> Just such a relationship, just such an exchange of letters, I wish for each of you.[191]

To Brecht he wrote privately immediately after the Congress:

> It will be especially important now to work through several theoretical questions. We are now at a turning-point: extended treatments may be losing ground to the intensive. Reportage seeks larger forms, lyrics force their way into epic. Clear-sighted intellectualism is undermined by emotionalism. Emotional complexity is demanded.

These somewhat gnomic *pensées* seem almost like an agenda for future meetings. Certainly there is no doubt the two men influenced each other, as is perhaps especially clear from Brecht's reference later to Tretyakov as his 'teacher', though it is likely that Tretyakov learned from Brecht, too. For example, Brecht's collaborative method of working, if messy when practiced by the German, was picked up by Tretyakov and produced the disciplined procedure so typical of him. Though Albert Parry's description of Tretyakov and his brigade at work in 1935 is undoubtedly exaggerated for comic effect, it is nevertheless revealing:

> This is how Tretyakov writes his books, poetry, plays, criticism: he dictates his lines to a stenographer. In the next room two girls type from the stenographer's notes. In still another, assistant researchers pore over books and newspapers preparing Data of Fact for the Master ... The ideal of wide collectivism is introduced by Tretyakov into authorship. He revels in the mechanics of office and factory, and loves to show readers and playgoers the inner springs of his books and plays. The machine is the new god of his country; and he is one of the most sincere and energetic worshippers.[192]

---

191 Eaton, Katherine Bliss, *The Theatre of Meyerhold and Brecht*, London: Greenwood Press, 1985, p. 20.
192 See Reischl, Katherine M.H., '"Where Have I Been With My Camera": Sergei Tret'iakov and Developing Operativity', *Russian Literature*, Vol. 103-105, 2019, p. 120.

Can we see here an echo of the boy who had organised his siblings in the construction of the labyrinth on Riga beach all those years ago?

More significantly, Brecht and Tretyakov also shared certain themes, such as motherhood, which Tretyakov explored, tangentially in *The World Upside Down* and *Roar, China!*, more directly in *I Want a Baby* and *Eliso*, and Brecht addressed in a number of works, including *The Mother*, *Mother Courage and her Children*, *The Good Person of Szechuan*, and *The Caucasian Chalk Circle*. In *I Want a Baby*, when Yakov discovers that Milda is pregnant, he fantasises the child in the pram:

> Please, comrade baby, get your toes out of your mouth. Look, comrade baby, a jackdaw on the telegraph wire. Let's go. Keep to the pavement. Er, excuse me, citizen, move aside. Careful now, we're crossing a new little citizen here. Old woman, save yourself, any way you can. A citizen is on the move. Stand aside! Cars, give way! Don't cry, comrade son, we'll get across the road. Policeman, clear a way through. Hold up your truncheon! Bus, stop! Motorbike, stop! My little citizen, we're on our way![193]

In *The Good Person of Szechuan*, when Shen Te finds herself pregnant, she fantasises similarly:

> Oh joy! A new human being is coming to life in my body ... Come, my son, inspect your world. Here, that is a tree. Bow politely, greet him. (*She performs a bow.*) There, now you know one another ... Ah, the policeman! I think we will avoid him ... Here's the road. Now gently, walk slowly so we don't attract attention, as if nothing whatever had happened. (*She sings as she walks along with the (imaginary) child*).[194]

While the 'borrowing' here is clear, Brecht's 'borrowing' of the term '*Verfremdungseffekt*', probably from Tretyakov, or from Viktor

---

193   Tretyakov, Sergei, *I Want a Baby and Other Plays*, Glagoslav Publications, 2019, pp. 357-8.
194   Brecht, Bertolt, *The Good Person of Szechuan*, London: Eyre Methuen, 1977, pp. 73-4.

Shklovsky via Tretyakov, is more problematic. Usually translated as 'alienation effect', the German term is a not entirely accurate translation of Shklovsky's concept of *'ostraneniye'*, 'estrangement', which refers to Shklovsky's idea that poetry enables the reader to see afresh, to understand, for example, the 'stoniness' of a stone. Brecht's concept is more active than Shklovsky's and it may have been Tretyakov's operativism which has intervened here.

Brecht's use of 'open' endings, which Lukács so deplored, may also derive, at least in part, from Tretyakov's plays, most of which end, as it were, at a new beginning. Thus, *The World Upside Down* ends with the young taking the place of the old, *Are You Listening, Moscow?!* ends with the revolution just beginning, and *Roar, China!* concludes with the Stoker promising that even if the imperialists shoot him, 'ten will rise in my place'. In Brecht's later, great plays there are similar open endings. In *Life of Galileo*, Andrea's final line is: 'There are a lot of things we don't know yet, Giuseppe. We're really just at the beginning',[195] while, in a different key, *The Good Person of Szechuan* ends with Shen Te's appeal to the audience to find a suitable ending.

There are other, less specific, similarities, too: the peasants in *The Caucasian Chalk Circle* are like the Caucasian peasants in *Eliso*, for example, and the meeting which opens *The Caucasian Chalk Circle* seems to echo the meetings Tretyakov attended in the Caucasian Communist Lighthouse *kolkhoz*. The heroine of *The Caucasian Chalk Circle* is called Grusha Vachnadze, the same name as the actress in *Eliso*, Nata Vachnadze. More precisely, Tretyakov's summary of Brecht's dramatic practice in the 1930s might also be an accurate description of his own work in the previous decade:

> The essence of a play is not to send away the spectator after bathing him in catharsis, according to Aristotle's rules; the spectator should be changed, or rather the seeds of change should have been planted in him, seeds which must come to flower outside the limits of the performance. It should not be a circular performance in which everything is completed, in which the heroes and the villains are balanced; it should

---

195   Brecht, Bertolt, *Life of Galileo*, London: Eyre Methuen, 1980, p. 113.

rather be a spiral performance, a tilted circle rising to another horizon, and a spectator who is thrown out of balance.[196]

It is striking that the trajectory of Brecht's career is uncannily similar to Tretyakov's as a dramatist. Both began with plays which were almost anarchic in their form and content (*A Wise Man, Baal*). These were followed by much sharper and shorter polemical – or propagandistic – plays, *Are You Listening, Moscow?!* and *Gas Masks* in Tretyakov's case, the *Lehrstücke* in Brecht's. In the second half of the 1920s, Tretyakov moved from this to the open-ended, montage-based epic form of *Roar, China!* and *I Want a Baby*. But it was only after long and intense conversations with Tretyakov that Brecht followed suit and developed (to a higher form) the modernist epic – *Mother Courage and Her Children, Life of Galileo, The Caucasian Chalk Circle*, the plays upon which his reputation finally rests. Of course it is not suggested that Tretyakov 'taught' Brecht this, but it is probable that his influence was material at this juncture of Brecht's career. It is not to be forgotten that Brecht was to refer to Tretyakov in 1939 as 'my teacher'.

Tretyakov's written portrait of Bertolt Brecht, which forms the second chapter of *People Who Shared a Bonfire*, is shrewd and amusing, and has been widely quoted by critics and biographers of Brecht. But other portraits in this book are equally astute. The first chapter is devoted to John Heartfield, and after Brecht, we are presented with Erwin Piscator, Hanns Eisler, Friedrich Wolf, Gregor Gog, Oskar Maria Graf, Theodore Plievier, Johannes Becher and Martin Anderson Nexø. Each sketch is preceded by a photograph of its subject taken by Tretyakov himself, and each is a sort of mini-bio-interview, as Tretyakov strives to uncover 'how individual lives, buffeted by the forces of history, discharge into the same stream in different quantities over years and decades, in order to finally unite and to become a brigade of uniform revolutionary acts'.

This is not, therefore, literary criticism, though Tretyakov often articulates sharp insights into the work of his subjects. Nor is it precisely biography. It is perhaps an attempt to indicate how life and art interpenetrate. Tretyakov separates revolutionary innovation from the self-indulgent or formalistic experimentations of modernism: the

---

196   Witt, Hubert (ed), *op. cit.*, p. 78.

crux of each portrait is his personal encounter with his subject, as with his accompanying Brecht to the cemetery, or watching Friedrich Wolf doing his exercises. The special quality of each subject is pinpointed, and each forms part of the movement towards revolutionary awareness and preparedness. Each is an individual, but each is also part of something bigger – the movement of history, Germany's pain, but also its restive potential. Thus, the portrait of Johannes Becher revolves around Tretyakov's meeting with him, after he had sent a poem to translate into Russian to Tretyakov about Klara Zetkin, the Communist activist and fighter for women's rights, who died in June 1933. Tretyakov remembers his own meeting with the charismatic Zetkin, but also traces Becher's development as a poet from expressionism through anarchism to communism. These reflections are presented as part of Tretyakov's struggle to translate the poem adequately, which echoes Becher's own struggle. Finally, he is ready. The portrait ends: 'I have begun the translation of your poem about Klara, comrade Johannes'.[197]

---

[197] Tret'yakov, S.M., *Lyudi odnogo kostra*, Moscow: Khudozhestvennaya literatura, 1936, p. 247.

CHAPTER 12.
1935

1935 was not a good year for the Soviet Union. It really began on 1 December 1934 when Sergei Kirov, the First Secretary of the Leningrad Party, was shot dead. Eighty-three people were executed in response, one of whom was the presumed murderer, though why the other 82 were shot was not obvious. Soon however the State apparatus let it be known that significant Party members, most obviously Zinoviev and Kamenev, two of Lenin's closest and earliest comrades, were implicated in the murder. They were arrested in early 1935 and sentenced to five years' imprisonment, which was soon increased to ten. It was the preliminary move leading to their show trial, along with fourteen other high-ranking Communists, which condemned them to death in August 1936. The arrest of these prominent figures was the trigger for an accelerating frenzy of arrests of others, very many of them long-serving Party members, which engulfed the Soviet Union through that year.

Tretyakov must have known what was happening. He was a seasoned and perceptive observer of the political scene, and he had a subtle and discriminating ability to analyse events. But how to make sense of what was happening now? In April 1935 a law was introduced decreeing that children aged twelve and older who were found guilty of crimes such as theft would be subject to punishment on the same scale as adults, including the death penalty. In September Stalin introduced in the Red Army the titles which had been abolished by the October Revolution. As for the collectivization of agriculture, to which Tretyakov had devoted hours, days and weeks since 1928, in 1934 the *kolkhozes*' output had at last begun to rise appreciably: why then in 1935 were the peasants allowed to own private plots of land again?

Tretyakov still believed that the revolution needed to be defended, and that its ultimate victory was assured. Did he still believe in the Soviet Union? Perhaps his piano playing was a sign of his disquiet. His daughter recalled how his playing became increasingly stormy. She would watch his back stretching, swaying, crouching over the keyboard as he gave vent to the passions of Skryabin, Schumann, Liszt and others. His health, too, was beginning to deteriorate. He suffered from headaches, was frequently tired and began to feel 'very old'. Moreover, he took on probably too many disparate projects, a majority of which were never completed. Whether this was simply because he was unable to resist a challenge, and therefore became involved with so many different literary ventures; or because Party policy in so many areas was constantly shifting, and he needed to avoid political misdirection or 'counterrevolutionary sympathies', which probably meant abandoning a work or seeing it censored; or whether he was still scarred by the *I Want a Baby* disaster, is unclear. There is a sense in the mid-1930s, however, of Tretyakov flailing, seeking too many escape routes. And around him, the storm gathering.

People no longer felt safe. The most terrifying aspect of the gathering storm for ordinary Russians, especially for those with less than a totally clear conscience, was waiting for the police to arrive at their home. These intrusions usually took place at night. Yevgenia Ginzburg, a long-time, enthusiastic Communist Party member, remembered: 'The nights were bad. Our bedroom windows faced the street, and so many cars drove past! How we listened to each and shivered when it seemed to be pulling up in front of our house'.[198] A thirteen year old girl recorded in her diary what happened when the police did arrive:

> It was half past eleven. I was enjoying myself, telling Mum about school. We were laughing and joking together. Suddenly there was a sharp, loud knock at the door. Betka the poodle started barking furiously and I quickly leapt to my feet with a nervous start, the way you do sometimes when you hear a

---

198 Ginzburg, Evgenia S., *Into the Whirlwind*, London: Collins/Harvill, 1967, p. 40.

sudden noise. 'Who's there?' I asked, going up to the door and holding Betka by the scruff of her neck with one hand.

A coarse male voice shouted: 'The janitor.' I realized what was happening, but there was still a vague hope left somewhere in my heart and, letting go of Betka, I opened the door a little warily. The light wasn't on in the corridor, and it was dark on the stairs, too, so all I could make out was the vague outline of a man's figure in a threadbare jacket, with a peaked cap and a big moustache. Perhaps, just for a second, I hesitated, thinking: Yes or no? – but then I stepped aside to let in the janitor, two military men and two Red Army officers.[199]

Th procedure was always the same, implacable, impersonal. Here is the raid on Sasha's flat, from Anatoly Rybakov's novel, *Children of the Arbat*:

He was abruptly woken by the shrill ringing of the doorbell in the corridor. It was two in the morning and he had barely dropped off. The bell rang again, insistently and firmly. He went out into the corridor dressed only in his underwear and took off the chain.
'Who is it?'
'House management'.
Sasha recognized Vasili Petrovich's voice and unlocked the door. The janitor was standing in the doorway. Behind him was a stranger, a young man in an overcoat and soft hat, and two Red Army men in greatcoats with crimson tabs. The young man entered the apartment; one of the Red Army men remained at the door and the other one followed Vasili Petrovich through to the kitchen and took up his post at the back door.
'Pankratov?'
'Yes'.
'Alexander Pavlovich Pankratov?'
'Yes'.
Watching Sasha guardedly, he handed him a warrant for the

---

[199] Lugovskaya, Nina, *I Want to Live*, London: Doubleday, 2006, p. 14.

search and arrest of Citizen Pankratov, Alexander Pavlovich, a resident of the Arbat.[200]

After the arrest, and sometimes before it, came the forced confessions, and the need for repentance. Yevgenia Ginzburg's typist told her:

> 'You should admit you're guilty and say you're sorry'.
> 'But I'm not guilty of anything. Why should I lie at a party meeting?'
> 'You'll get a reprimand anyway. A political reprimand is a very bad thing. And by not saying you're sorry you make it worse.'[201]

The arrest usually made the suspect an 'enemy of the people', a term probably first introduced in 1935, and it was likely that such an enemy would simply disappear. Their loved ones, family, friends were left knowing nothing of their whereabouts or their fate. It is estimated that up to two million people were arrested at this time, a large fraction of whom were executed, the rest sentenced to hard labour. Their relatives were usually ostracized, the spouses of many of them sought and obtained a divorce. No-one dared to question what was going on. There was a riddle current at the time: Why do Soviet doctors remove tonsils through the backside? The answer: because no-one dare open their mouths.

To cheer people up, or to deflect their torment, there were publicised adventures and heroes of the Soviet Union, though not all of these acquired the kind of status afforded to the heroes of the Chelyuskin adventure which Tretyakov's work helped to cement. Not so admirable were the daring adventurers who ascended 22 kilometres above the earth in a 'stratosphere balloon'; horribly, the balloon crashed on its descent, killing the three heroic balloonists. Similarly, the 'biggest aeroplane in the world', the eight-engined *Maxim Gorky*, crashed over Moscow in May 1935, killing its hero pilot.

The greatest hero of all, however, one who never failed, was Joseph Stalin, and it was now that what was later called 'the cult of personality'

---

200 Rybakov, Anatoli, *Children of the Arbat*, London: Arrow Books, 1989, p. 121.
201 Ginzburg, Evgenia S., *op. cit.*, p. 16.

roared into top gear. The poet Alexander Avdiyenko proclaimed at the 1935 Congress of Soviets:

> Thank you, Stalin. Thank you because I am joyful. Thank you because I am well. No matter how old I become, I shall never forget ... Centuries will pass, and the generations still to come will regard us as the happiest of mortals, as the most fortunate of men, because we lived in the century of centuries, because we were privileged to see Stalin, our inspired leader.[202]

Children were exhorted to 'thank Stalin' for their happy childhood in a gesture in which fiction and life merged in a new way. Did Tretyakov share this euphoria? Not everyone did. Yevgenia Ginzburg, for instance, though she said that if she had been ordered to die for the party, not once but three times, she would have obeyed 'without a moment's hesitation', could not bring herself 'to deify Stalin'.[203]

Stalin was, among other things, of course, the supreme arbiter of the arts. Few films were released until Stalin had viewed them in his private cinema in the Kremlin, and it was clear what he disliked. Eisenstein's near total silence at this time is indicative. The poet Osip Mandelstam's flat was raided and he was arrested after a short poem he had recited privately which lampooned Stalin had been reported to the authorities. It prompted the apolitical Boris Pasternak to remark: 'Strange and terrible things are happening now: they've begun to pick people up. I'm afraid walls have ears'.[204] Writers soon learned the art of self-censorship. Galakhov, the novelist in Alexander Solzhenitsyn's *The First Circle*, imagines how his work may be received, and the more he thinks, the more he fears: 'in paragraph after paragraph' he finds himself 'watering the book down until it was as bland and insipid as all the rest'.[205] And if the year 1935 began in December 1934, perhaps it ended in January 1936 when Shostakovich's opera, *Lady Macbeth of Mtsensk*, which had premiered in 1934 and had been extremely

---

202 Cited from McSmith, Andy, *Fear and the Muse Kept Watch*, New York: The New Press, p. 169.
203 Ginzburg, Evgenia S., *op. cit.*, p. 11.
204 Ivinskaya, Olga, *A Captive of Time: My Years with Pasternak*, London: Fontana, 1979, p. 65.
205 Solzhenitsyn, Alexander, *The First Circle*, London: Collins, 1969, p. 440.

popular throughout 1935, came to a halt after Stalin had watched it. On 28 January 1936, an anonymous article – usually credited to Stalin himself – appeared in *Pravda* under the headline, 'Muddle Not Music'. It was the beginning of the bullying of Russia's greatest twentieth century composer.

Tretyakov must have observed all this, but there is no record of his response to any of it. At the end of 1934, it seemed to many that he was riding high in the esteem of those who counted. Yet a closer reading of the speeches at the 1934 Writers' Congress might have detected warning signs. Karl Radek, for instance, besides noting that literature was a weapon in the class struggle, condemned the use of photography: 'We do not photograph life. In the totality of phenomena we seek out the main phenomenon. Giving everything without discrimination is not realism. That would be the most vulgar kind of naturalism'. He also attacked John Heartfield's 'very dangerous speech' in which he had praised James Joyce. He (Radek) had suggested that 'Joyce photographs a heap of dung with a cinema apparatus through a microscope', to which Heartfield had objected, 'No, he does not photograph a heap of dung – he photographs his inside'. But Radek ridiculed this. 'The content of Joyce is a reflection of that which is most reactionary in the petty *bourgeoisie*', he declared, and, echoing Lukács, he asserted 'Balzac (and) Tolstoy are enough for us'.[206] Photography as an art form allied to writing, and the work of James Joyce, were both associated with Tretyakov more than any other Soviet intellectual or writer. Moreover, he was now preparing a monograph on the work of John Heartfield, Radek's target here.

Tretyakov was a patriot but he was also an internationalist. How did this sit with Stalin's aim of 'socialism in one country'? He was the editor of *International Literature* in which he had published no fewer than ten sections from Joyce's *Ulysses*. It seems his answer was to throw himself into work with more vigour than ever, even as his health deteriorated. Perhaps a sign of this was a certain lack of focus in his work, as if his energy was becoming dissipated, scattered over too many different projects. Engaging with too many projects at the

---

206   Gorky, Maxim, Radek, Karl, Bukharin, Nikolai, Zhdanov, Andrei *et al.*, *Soviet Writers' Congress 1934*, London: Lawrence and Wishart, 1977, pp. 178, 179, 180, 181.

same time had perhaps always been his weak point. Now it seemed this tendency was becoming more pronounced than ever. And it was not necessarily productive.

Thus, if Tretyakov's contacts with Brecht were almost entirely positive, his attempts at collaboration with others from Brecht's circle were less fruitful. At the time of the making of the film *A Song About Heroes*, he had agreed to write an opera with Hanns Eisler about Magnitogorsk, the premiere of which was announced for the Bolshoi Theatre. But in July 1933 he wrote to Brecht that 'Nothing has come of the opera: Eisler won't reply', adding that 'I've already wanted to drop him twice and look for another composer, but it wouldn't work. And for this reason alone I remain loyal to him. But for how long I don't know'. In 1935, he recorded that he had spoken to Eisler again, 'but it goes no further than talk'. Sadly, the opera was never written. He had also hoped to collaborate with Ernst Ottwald and Slatan Dudow, but nothing seems to have come of these, either, though he made a promising start to a 'bio-interview' with Dudow by researching his background and work, and recorded the beginnings of a book co-written with Ottwald, to be called *The Director*. 'It is a double bio-interview, half of which is written in the Soviet Union and the other half in Germany. The heroes (Tretyakov and Ottwald) are the same age and the similarity of their social status serves to underline starkly the different nature and polar contrast of the socio-economic systems under which they each live'.

Undeterred, he reported to Brecht in May 1935 that he was 'working like hell on books'. He described Olga as his time-keeper: she kept his deadlines before him, and ensured he divided his time between his various projects appropriately. He was deputy to the Chairman of the Overseas Committee of the Soviet Writers' Union, Mikhail Koltsov, a writer himself as well as a Party *apparatchik*, and this semi-official position took up time. He was also the editor of the Moscow-based *International Literature*, as well as being on the editorial board of the slightly different German language edition of this journal. It was in his capacity as editor of *International Literature* that he was responsible for publishing the first Russian versions of several modernist European classics, including Ernst Toller's *Requiem for the Shot Brothers* and the excerpts from James Joyce's *Ulysses*. Now, in 1935, he was unexpectedly relieved of his editorship, though he

Mei Lan-fang.

remained on the board of the German edition. It was a mixed, but perhaps ominous, sign.

Whatever the signs, 1935 was a full and exhausting year for Tretyakov, beginning with the visit to Moscow in January of the black American singer and political activist, Paul Robeson, and his wife, Essie. They stayed at the Tretyakov flat, and Robeson declared that in Moscow 'I am not a Negro but a human being for the first time in my life ... I walk in full human dignity'.[207] Tanya by this time was studying aeronautics at the Moscow Institute. Since she knew English, she translated for Robeson at home, as she did for other English-speaking guests, though when she found this difficult or was less than accurate in her translations, Tretyakov was apt to become impatient. One afternoon she returned home early from her studies, and found Robeson alone in the flat. After a little confusion, and some embarrassed laughter, he suggested he sing to her. She sat at one end of the room, while he stood at the other end and sang his best songs in full voice, just for her. She never forgot that afternoon for the rest of her life.

After a plenary meeting of the Soviet Writers' Union in Minsk in February, the next months for Tretyakov himself were filled with increasing international commitments, as his international reputation grew and his circle of international contacts widened. He was a significant mediator between the arts and culture of the Soviet Union and that of the outside world. Thus when Erwin Piscator and Bernhard Reich, both now resident in U.S.S.R., established the International Association of Revolutionary Theatres (MORT), they immediately involved Tretyakov in their plans. They set up an international conference in Moscow in April, to which theatre artists and writers from across the world came: Edward Gordon Craig, André Malraux, Harold Clurman, Joseph Losey, Lee Strasberg, Teo Otto, Alexander Granach, and more.

Among those attending was Bertolt Brecht, with his collaborator and lover, Margarete Steffin. Tretyakov took it upon himself to expand Brecht's knowledge of Russian theatre, introducing him to Nikolai Okhlopkov, whom he was still hoping would stage a Brecht play, and

---

207 Sheldon, Philip, and Foner, Henry, *Paul Robeson Speaks*, New York: Citadel Press, 1978, p. 94.

Mei Lan-fang with Tretyakov and Eisenstein.

taking him to productions at Okhlopkov's Realistic Theatre, including *The Running Start* by V.P.Stavsky about collectivization, and *Aristocrats* by Nikolai Pogodin about the building of the White Sea Canal. Both productions used highly imaginative settings, perhaps derived from El Lissitzky's original designs for *I Want a Baby*, and both featured anti-naturalistic acting as befitted a production by one of Meyerhold's star ex-students. He also took Brecht to the Jewish State Theatre to see Solomon Mikhoels in *King Lear*, regarded as one of the finest examples of Russian acting in this decade.

There was also much intense discussion, often at Tretyakov's flat (though Brecht and Steffin were staying at the Novaya Moskovskaya Hotel). Brecht had brought with him a draft of his significant text, 'Theatre for Pleasure or Theatre for Instruction' which contains his most trenchant exposition of 'epic theatre'. How far Tretyakov contributed to this essay, which was not published in Brecht's lifetime, cannot now be ascertained, but the fact that they were together as this essay was being put together seems telling. Ivan Martovitsky of the Communist Lighthouse *kolkhoz*, recorded one evening at the flat on Malaya Bronnaya when Brecht and Steffin were present, and Tretyakov was enthusing about the *kolkhoz*. Brecht sat leaning forward with his elbows on the table, like an eager school pupil, while Steffin quizzed him animatedly. 'It's a story without end', Tretyakov insisted fervently. Steffin voiced her desire to visit the *kolkhoz*, but there was no time, and in any case she was ill. She could go 'if the doctor says you're well enough', the attentive Tretyakov answered. But she was not well enough.

On 21 April, Tretyakov organized a 'Brecht evening', which he introduced with a speech outlining the political and artistic value of Brecht's plays and poetry, noting particularly the importance of epic theatre. Other speakers were Asja Lācis on Brecht as a theatre director, and Semyon Kirsanov, who read his translation into Russian of Brecht's famous 'Legend of the Dead Soldier'. The Kamerny Theatre presented excerpts from their production of *The Threepenny Opera*, Hanne Rosenberg sang two songs from *The Mother*, and the evening climaxed with Carola Neher singing songs from *The Threepenny Opera* and *Happy End*, including a rousing performance of 'Surabaya Johnny'. Among those attending were Wilhelm Pieck, the German communist who was to become President of the East German Democratic Republic after the Second World War, Vilhelm Knorin, a Latvian Party member who headed the Belarus Party, and Béla Kun, the prominent Hungarian communist who was to be executed in 1938. At the end of the evening, Brecht declared Moscow to be the theatre capital of the world.

Although he was still 'very nice', as Brecht reported to his wife,[208] Tretyakov was also extremely busy managing the appearance of the Chinese Opera, and in particular its star whom he had admired in China a decade before, Mei Lan-fang. Mei was of course the leading performer of female parts at the Opera. The company had sailed from China to Vladivostok, and journeyed by train from there to Moscow, where they were met by Tretyakov and a Party official by the name of Cherlyansky. Before any public performances, on the afternoon of 19 March at the Chinese Embassy, Mei presented a solo performance, dressed in casual clothes rather than the traditional ornate costume, for an exclusive Moscow audience which included not only international theatre figures but Party grandees like Maxim Litvinov, the Commissar for Foreign Affairs. Mei's performances as the princess who stabs her husband to death in *Killing the Tiger General* and the Snake-Maiden in *The Golden Mountain Monastery* were greeted with as much awe as admiration. In the latter, 'the actor playing the role of the Snake-Maiden dances with a pair of long swords in a series of rhythmic posturings and graceful movements which are accompanied by the soft notes of a bamboo flute'.[209] There followed a three week season in which the company performed at the Bolshoi Theatre in Moscow as well as in Leningrad (St Petersburg). Particularly appreciated by Russian audiences was *The Fisherman's Revenge* in which a fisherman and his daughter (played by Mei Lan-fang) overthrow the despotic ruler, though whether this signifies a proletarian revolution may be doubted.

Leaders of the theatrical profession as well as ordinary Russian theatregoers voiced their intense admiration for the Chinese theatre and particularly for the art of Mei's performance. Some of the most prominent specialists in Moscow at the time sought to understand his mastery. For Brecht, it was the distancing effect he achieved, the

---

208   Brecht, Bertolt, *Letters*, London: Methuen, 1990, p. 202.
209   Scott, A.C., *Mei Lan-fang: The Life and Times of a Peking Actor*, Hong Kong: Hong Kong University Press, 1971, p. 117.

rejection of naturalism, the fact that 'he limits himself from the start to simply quoting the character played': Mei observed himself and expressed his 'awareness of being watched'.[210] Meyerhold, who was also present, applauded Mei's ability to lead the theatre 'away from the blind alley of naturalism'. He was especially struck by Mei's expressive hands and suggested that no Russian actress was as 'feminine' as Mei Lan-fang.[211] It was another audience member, Sergei Eisenstein, however, who hit upon perhaps the key contradiction which made the performance so powerful for his watchers, the dialectical co-existence of realism and non-realism:

> The realistic depiction of woman is not part of the Chinese actor's art. Instead the audience is treated to an idealized, generalized image. Here we come upon the principal aspect of the Chinese stage. Realistic in its own specific sense, capable of touching upon familiar episodes of history and legend, as well as upon social and everyday problems of life, the Chinese theatre, nevertheless, is conventionalized in its form, from its treatment of character to the minutest detail of stage effect.[212]

It is important to notice that this unique meeting of the greatest theatre artists of the age from Asia and Europe was engineered by Sergei Tretyakov. We might also note that a short time after this, Bertolt Brecht began work on his most noteworthy 'Chinese' play, *The Good Person of Szechuan*, the protagonist of which is a strange blending of male and female.

In the summer, Ernst Busch, the Brechtian actor, singer and active communist, had arrived in Moscow at the invitation of MORT and Tretyakov, and he immediately set Olga off searching for a copy of *Princess Turandot* for Brecht, who had seen the famous production at the Vakhtangov Theatre. But it was a summer of 'African heat', and Tretyakov was tired and in need of a holiday. In June he suggested that

---

210   Willett, John (ed), *Brecht on Theatre*, London: Eyre Methuen, 1973, pp. 92, 94.
211   *VOKS*, 14 April 1935.
212   Mei Lan-Fang, *My Life on the Stage, to which is added* The Enchanter from the Pear Garden *by S.M.Eisenstein*, Dell'équipe italiana dell'International School of Theatre Anthropology, 1986, p. 47.

he and Olga might go to Narzan Spa at Kislovodsk in the Stavropol region – 'one can cure a tired heart there' – and in July he complained that he was finding work difficult and was always being distracted by 'trivialities'. Tanya had gone to the Black Sea with her Komsomol group, and Olga was well, but he was dissatisfied with what he was doing. 'Unfortunately I'm not getting any writing done', he complained to Brecht in one letter. He and Olga decided to go to Kislovodsk at the end of July.

Though he intended to use the peace of the holiday to focus on his writing, it appears he did little work. But he did take advantage of the fresh air and the open surroundings to indulge in various physical activities. The countryside in his beloved Caucasus region was wild – ravines and mountains – and he and Olga explored their surroundings in several trips out. He participated in a wild boar hunt, which he said was 'great', and he also climbed Mount Elbrus, the highest mountain in Europe at over 18,000 feet. It is not clear whether he reached the summit. He went with a large group of local mountaineers, and was impressed by their mutual support. 'Whenever someone felt weak', he reported, 'the others took him on their shoulders and carried him. And whenever someone started to slip, grips were thrown under the feet of those slipping, in order to stop them'. He even wrote a poem about the climb, which was, he said, the first poem he had written for over eight years.

The holiday obviously refreshed him, but on 25 August he wrote, perhaps regretfully:

> Our stay in the spa is coming to an end. In ten days time we will be travelling back to Moscow. I promised myself that I would work from 10 August, but as yet I haven't written a single line. Isn't that laziness? Olga tells me to be good and not to work until the end of the month and then after that I will be able to write with double strength.

Back in Moscow in September, he told Brecht he was 'keeping in the shadows because I know that one stop and I'll be overloaded with secondary work'. Perhaps this referred to his official duties. If so, he was not long 'in the shadows' because in October, he went with a Soviet delegation to Czechoslovakia, accompanying Mikhail Koltsov and

Alexander Fadeyev, the writer who was to become chair of the Soviet Writers' Union. There he renewed his friendship with Oskar Maria Graf, and met Hanns Eisler's sister, Ruth Fischer, and her husband, Gustav Golke. Fischer had been a leader of the German Communist Party in the 1920s, but had been ousted by Ernst Thälmann with Stalin's backing. Though she remained on the far left politically, she had become determinedly opposed to Stalin. Whether this was significant for Tretyakov cannot be known. When he returned to Moscow, he lectured on Czechoslovakia and its problems, and his last published book, *A Country at the Crossroads*, was about that country which Hitler was already eying greedily.

And after the success of the 'Brecht evening' earlier in the year, he was now organizing further cultural evenings. An 'Ernst Busch evening' was held on 22 November, and another evening which probably gave him more pleasure than most was the 'Mayakovsky evening' which was held on 20 December. It was probably the first such celebration of his friend since Lilya Brik had written the previous month to Stalin complaining that officialdom was obscuring the poet's work and legacy. In response, Stalin announced that 'Mayakovsky was and remains the best and most talented poet of our epoch. Indifference to his memory is a crime'.[213] It was an extraordinary *volte-face* from the arbiter of the arts, though what it portended was not at all clear.

---

213   Jangfeldt, Bengt, *Mayakovsky: A Biography*, Chicago: University of Chicago Press, 2014, p. 574.

CHAPTER 13.
AT THE CROSSROADS

After 1935, Tretyakov continued to work, but he found it increasingly difficult to bring his writing to the point of publication. Growing tensions within the Soviet Union and his own deteriorating health were reasons for this, though perhaps not the only reasons. He felt more and more threatened personally. His only publications in 1936 were the comparatively brief monograph on John Heartfield, the German visual artist and stage designer, written in collaboration with Solomon Telingator, who was to publish a Stalin-approved life of Vladimir Lenin, and the photographic record of *U.S.S.R. in Construction*. This was the October edition of this publication whose first number, published in 1933, had been largely guided by him. In the October edition of photographs with accompanying text, Tretyakov's work appeared alongside that of such prominent *avant-garde* photographers as Yury Yeryomin and Georgy Petrusov, as well as the visual artist and original stage designer for *I Want a Baby*, El Lissitzky, and others.

In November 1936, the Jewish-German writer, Lion Feuchtwanger arrived in Moscow. This friend and erstwhile collaborator of Bertolt Brecht had fled Germany and settled in France when Hitler came to power in 1933. He had been fiercely left wing during the Weimar Republic's heyday in Germany, and now he was on the way to becoming a strong supporter of Stalin. He hoped that his visit would cement his pro-Stalinist views. In this, his hopes were fulfilled. Tretyakov had first read his work while at Kislovodsk in 1935, and he had been impressed. Now he welcomed Feuchtwanger, and indeed spoke warmly at a Feuchtwanger evening held at Moscow's Polytechnic

Museum on 5 January 1937. However, Feuchtwanger was to leave Moscow in February and the relationship was not able to develop.

Other work which was engaging Tretyakov at this time included a book of photographs of the Red Army to commemorate the twentieth anniversary of the Bolshevik revolution, which would fall in October 1937, and a book of memoirs of his time in China in the immediate post-revolution period. There was also his play about the Communist Lighthouse *kolkhoz*. He had begun writing both these works in 1935, perhaps earlier, but he had not found the writing of either easy. In the meantime his visit to Czechoslovakia in the autumn of 1935 gave him the material for his last substantial work, *A Country at the Crossroads: Five Weeks in Czechoslovakia*, which was published in the spring of 1937.

The book perhaps served as an introduction for Russian readers to this central European republic, but if such was the intention, Tretyakov's grasp of his material makes it a sophisticated introduction. It consists of a prologue and eighteen chapters with titles such as 'The Language', 'Prague', 'Architecture', 'A Skilled Craftsman', 'Feathers and Footlights', 'The Surrealists' and 'Tomorrows', indicating the range of his exploration. He tells a story of the people's suffering, exploitation and resistance, which had led to the establishment of this *bourgeois* republic. His experience as a journalist enabled him, even as a result of a short stay, to provide the reader with sharp glimpses of places, people and individuals. In this sense the book is at least 'objective' reporting, perhaps shading into operativism. It may be read as a series of interlinked *ocherks* on the model of the photo-series, which add up to a piercing insight into an unhappy but heroic society. He expatiates on the details of daily life and the way people behave towards one another, but always with an eye to possible futures.

The main body of the book focuses on the productive work of agriculture and industry, and explores both industrial relations and the use of technology. He describes the factories of the footwear company, Bata, with its seemingly model villages for workers, and how this actually undermines ideas of socialism, giving rise to what he sees as the sometimes glaring contradictions in Czech society, exemplified not least by the reliance on foreign capital. This has, he implies, the unintended effect of driving many of the people's thoughts towards closer ties with the Soviet Union. But he also gives detailed descriptions of skilled craftsmen at work, such as a potter and a Bohemian glassblower.

Some of the most interesting contents of the book are Tretyakov's reflections on the question of the languages of the country, and the distinctions between its spoken and written forms. He also writes with typical insight into the work of several prominent Czechoslovakian writers, all of whom were more or less sympathetic to the Soviet Union: the Surrealist poet and playwright, Vítězslav Nezval; Karel Čapek, author of such plays as *R.U.R.* and *The Insect Play*; the novelist Jaroslav Hašek, best known for *The Good Soldier Schweik*; Egon Erwin Kisch, journalist and communist who had been expelled from Nazi Germany; Ivan Olbracht, a novelist who had been expelled from the Communist Party but was still very much on the left of politics; and Emil Burian, best known as a communist stage director.

Czechoslovakia was the crossroads country, the meeting point of Germany, Austria, Hungary and Poland, and was territory coveted by each of these. The book is shot through with an underlying anxiety about the direction in which the country is heading: Hitler's takeover is foreshadowed, though by no means predicted. The argument for some kind of alliance with the Soviet Union is unspoken but felt throughout. It is, however, an excellent example of Tretyakov's reportage. It shows how, in the words of Viktor Pertsov, 'Tretyakov strove to avoid descriptiveness, and sought for a method which, flowing from its concrete materialist basis, communicated with an unexpected incandescence; it intervened in the process of presenting the world'.[214]

In the spring of 1937, he was removed from the editorial committee of the German edition of *International Literature*. No reason for this seems to have been given. But he was able to broadcast on May Day – for the last time. Meanwhile, the exiled Bertolt Brecht was considering the formation of a Diderot Society, along the lines of several existing scientific societies: members would publish the findings of their theatrical experiments in the society's journal. Diderot was the French writer of the Enlightenment whose major contribution to theatrical theory is his essay, 'The Paradox of Acting', which still stimulates and

---

214   Tret'yakov, Sergei, *Den Shi-hua*, Moscow: Sovetskii pisatel', 1962, p. 15.

provokes in equal measure today. Brecht intended that the society should involve the leading international theatre practitioners who were more or less in sympathy with his ideas, and the list of those he wished to invite to join was impressive. It included his own collaborators, Hanns Eisler, Slatan Dudow, Fritz Kortner, Erwin Piscator, the Czechoslovakian Emil Burian, three Britons, W.H.Auden, Christopher Isherwood and Rupert Doone, the Americans Mordecai Gorelik and Archibald MacLeish, and from Russia Nikolai Okhlopkov, Sergei Eisenstein and Sergei Tretyakov. 'We must do something to ensure that something comes of the *avant-garde*', Brecht explained. 'Otherwise it will become a *derrière-garde*'.[215] Tretyakov was fully in sympathy, but the Diderot Society never materialized.

In this it was like too many of Tretyakov's late projects. He seemed to be the same man, tall, thin – even skinny – with a completely bald head, long nose and watery grey eyes behind his steel-rimmed spectacles. He was still giving talks, especially about Czechoslovakia, but his writing, for the first time, seemed to be faltering. In particular, he was struggling with the two works already mentioned, both of which could have been significant. In June 1935 he had confided to Brecht: 'I think a lot about the collective farm play and will make it, but not immediately, because I have to finish the China book'. The 'China book' was the memoir about his time in the Far East both after the revolution and his period as Professor at Beijing University. In June 1936 he had written about 120 pages, but it was heavy going for him, partly because Soviet policy towards China was so inconsistent. The other work, a play based on his experiences at the Communist Lighthouse *kolkhoz* to be called *We Feed the Earth*, was also never completed, as far as is known. In May 1937 he wrote further to Brecht:

> I'm still working on my China book and thinking about returning to my play on collectivization. I had already written a lot a few years ago but then I stopped. Now I see it again, there is a lot of value in what I wrote. You were right – it's important to do a play about collectivization, and make it simple, but extensive and very real.

---

215   Parker, Stephen, *Bertolt Brecht: A Literary Life*, London: Bloomsbury, 2014, p. 354.

What is noticeable about these two works, the 'China book' of memoirs and the play *We Feed the Earth* about his time in the *kolkhoz*, is that both involved looking backwards at episodes in his life rather than forwards into the future. Did this indicate that for Tretyakov at least Futurism itself was over, that operativism was no longer viable as a form of socialist realism? Or was it a tacit admission that the revolution itself was now no longer oriented towards the future? Perhaps it was that his ill health was sapping his energy (a falling off in energy has been mentioned with regard to some of his stories of the mid-1930s), that it blurred the focus which had so single-mindedly motivated his writing heretofore.

Throughout 1936 he was often ill. His friend of many arguments, Bertolt Brecht, sent him a poem, 'Advice to Tretyakov to get well':

> The arguments of a sick man
> Will be laughed at.
>
> Eat an extra meal and eat it slowly
> Being mindful of your enemies
> Sleep late into the day:
> They will be sleepless.
>
> For the good of the soviet
> Drink a glass of milk in the morning
> So that your advice to us
> Will not be the advice of a sick man.
>
> Swim in the lake for pleasure. The water
> That could drown you
> Will bear you up.
> What you part as you swim, behind you
> It comes together again.[216]

---

216   Brecht, Bertolt, *Collected Poems*, trans. by Tom Kuhn and David Constantine, New York: Liveright, 2019, p. 389. (Note: although this poem is in the section 'Uncollected Poems 1927-1930' in this book, Brecht did not meet Tretyakov before December 1930, at which time Tretyakov was not suffering from ill health.)

But his sickness remained. In May of that year he told Oskar Maria Graf in a letter that he was suffering from a 'nervous disease', and that summer was very hot. Olga Viktorovna left Moscow to visit Europe on her own, meeting Karin Michaëlis in Denmark and Ada Chesterton in England, and also going to France, Italy and Czechoslovakia, and while she was away he found himself lonely and friendless. In June, Maxim Gorky died, which left him feeling 'isolated', as he confided to Graf: 'You know, I'm pretty lonely when it comes to friends', he wrote. 'Friends in the sense of real closeness, intimacy and mutual interests'.[217]

By the beginning of 1937 his nervous exhaustion and general debility was actually stopping him writing and giving lectures. He slept very badly and was afflicted with 'blinding headaches'. In March and April he spent two months in a sanatorium where he was given different diagnoses – nervous breakdown, according to one doctor, a kind of tropical malaria, according to another. The treatment he received for this latter (though how he could have contracted it was not made clear) helped. The headaches were much reduced, and he found again the ability to work. Yet it may be noticed that even here, Tretyakov could not resist his impulse towards fun, writing comic verses about his fellow patients. His daughter spoke about this more than fifty years later:

> When he went to the rest home, he was the centre of attention – well, he played the piano, and he made little songs about the people there, little verses about the people staying in the rest home. He was liked by the people.

Then came the invitation to join Brecht's Diderot Society, but before he could respond adequately to this, he had some sort of relapse and was taken into the Kremlin Hospital for observation and tests. He clearly had a serious nervous disorder which was affecting both his body and his brain.

Whether Tretyakov's breakdown was due to overwork, or perhaps to some constitutional or hereditary problem – his mother's health had always been precarious and she had died in her early fifties – was far

---

217   Hofmann, Tatjana, and Ditschek, Eduard Jan (eds), *Sergej M. Tret'jakow: Ich Will Ein Kind!*, Vol. 2, Berlin: Kulturverlag Kadmos, 2019, p. 288.

Mugshot of 'Tretyakov, S.M.'

from obvious. Perhaps it was caused, or at least exacerbated, by events. Tretyakov watched what was happening in his country with unspoken anguish and dismay.

His shock at the death of Gorky has already been noticed. In August 1936 had come the first show trials which concluded with the sentencing and execution of Kamenev, Zinoviev and others. The horror was greatly increased in September when it was revealed that one of the witnesses, who said a meeting of Trotskyites had taken place at the Hotel Bristol in Copenhagen, had lied. The Hotel Bristol in Copenhagen had been demolished in 1917. Popular dissatisfaction with the trial and sentence was also bubbling: chalked on some factory walls were inscriptions such as 'Down with the murderers of the leaders of our revolution'. Tretyakov, always sensitive to what was in the wind, must have been at least disconcerted.

Towards the end of the year a new Constitution for the U.S.S.R. was announced. Apparently democratic, it actually legitimized the centralized, bureaucratic state, and Stalin's personal dictatorship. While this new Constitution was acclaimed, and even read out in schools, Stalin declared that true socialism had been achieved. 1937 opened with the second egregious show trial, at which Georgy Pyatakov, Karl Radek, Grigory Sokolnikov and others were found guilty and shot, and in February Bukharin was arrested, obviously pointing to a third major show trial. Yevgenia Ginzburg recalled: 'The newspapers were red hot, the news clawed and stung. After each trial the screw was turned tighter'.[218] The response of Tretyakov, who only four years earlier had saluted the Soviet press for 'its truth, active truth', when he insisted it was 'stubbornly reconstructing the world', has to be imagined. By June, it was the army generals who were being executed. Alexander Orlov remembered:

> During the summer of that year sensational events had taken place in Moscow. Beginning with the month of May utterly incomprehensible arrests had been made among the most faithful supporters of Stalin, who had never taken part in any opposition. Each day in Moscow and in other cities the

---

218 Ginzburg, Evgenia S., *Into the Whirlwind*, London: Collins/Harvill, 1967, p. 26.

highest dignitaries of the land were disappearing without a trace: People's Commissars, Presidents of the Soviet Republics, secretaries of Party Committees and the leading commanders of the Red Army.[219]

One day in mid-July, as he lay in his bed in the Kremlin Hospital, Tretyakov himself became the victim of an 'utterly incomprehensible arrest'. Agents of the NKVD dragged him out of bed, threw him into their 'black raven' and drove off. He was one of the first writers to be arrested in 'The Great Purge', though many others followed – Isaak Babel, Boris Pilnyak, Nikolai Oleinikov, Adrian Piotrovsky, the Georgian poet, Titsian Tabidze and many more. But perhaps he was arrested because he was from Latvia. The NKVD's 'Latvian Operation' was just beginning, and was to sweep away the visual artist, Gustav Klutsis, despite the fact that his recent work had contributed significantly to the cult of Stalin, Vilhelm Knorin, the Latvian leader of the Belarus Communist Party, the actress Marija Leyko, the painter Alexander Drevin, the poet Alexander Eiduk, and others. The truth is that tyranny delights in unexpectedness, in lack of logic, in capriciousness. There was no reason for the arrest of any of these, just as there was certainly no reason for the arrest of Sergei Tretyakov.

He was taken to Butyrka Gaol, the notorious prison which had stood in central Moscow since the reign of Catherine the Great, though most of the red brick building had been constructed in the nineteenth century. In 1909 Tretyakov's friend, Vladimir Mayakovsky had been incarcerated here. There was a certain irony, too, in the fact that four years earlier, in one of his articles eulogising the Soviet press, Tretyakov had recorded:

> In Wood Street in Moscow, not very far from the Butyrka Gaol, stands a Caucasian fruit stall, with a sign written according to the old style.
> If you climb over the counter, go down to the cellar and go down the well that stands there, you will find, by groping, a square hole in the wall of the well. You crawl through this on

---

219 Orlov, Alexander, *The Secret History of Stalin's Crimes*, London: Jarrolds, 1954, p. 197.

your stomach and arrive in an empty space hollowed in the ground. A few red bricks from the foundations of the gaol show here and there. There is not even room to swing a cat. A little printing press stands here.
This little hole was the secret printing office of the Bolsheviks of the 1905 period. It was never discovered by the Tsarist police, now it has been restored to its former state and has become a museum.[220]

Now he was inside the gaol. He was a prisoner. His case was handled by NKVD Lieutenant M.I. Tchaikovsky, under the supervision of Deputy People's Commissar for Internal Affairs, M. Frinovsky. Assuming that his case followed the set pattern, he was searched thoroughly on arrival at Butyrka, and all his loose possessions – passport, keys, watch, purse, as well as items such as toothpaste, and belt or braces – were removed. Then he was photographed, and his fingerprints taken. Next a form had to be filled in for his personal file: birth date and place; profession; was he a Party member; his last place of work; education; nationality; service in any armed forces; and details of his family – father, mother, wife, children, brothers and sisters. It appears that Tretyakov himself filled in this form. Once these formalities were complete, he was taken to his cell.[221]

For those left behind, words were perhaps inadequate. His sister Nina wrote: 'Like a fiery tornado, a hurricane rolled across our world! It crushed many beneath it, and our Seryozha was one of them, the most crystal-clear and genuine non-party communist that ever walked the earth!' His adopted daughter, Tanya, said: 'The arrest of my father was a great shock to all of us. We couldn't believe that this wasn't a misunderstanding, and we were so naïve that we waited for his return'.

On 26 July, the Tretyakov home on Malaya Bronnaya Street was entered and Olga Viktorovna watched as agents Sazhin, Skobstova, Augustov and Dorbes carried out a search. The officers confiscated and took away with them 28 notebooks and one 'alphabet' book,

---

220   Tretyakov, S., 'Words Become Deeds', *International Literature*, No. 3, July 1933, p. 54.
221   See Shentalinsky, Vitaly, *The KGB's Literary Archive*, London: The Harvill Press, 1995, p. 5.

presumably an address book or similar, and they ordered to be taken for delivery to the Main Department of State Security twelve folders with correspondence, some foreign currency (6 US dollars and 36 Czech krona), as well as a Remington typewriter, a watering can, and manuscripts and books.

When they left, Olga Viktorovna immediately wrote to Tanya, who was with her Komsomol group near the Black Sea. 'Something's happened', she wrote. 'Come home at once'. She did not specify what the 'something' was, but Tanya understood without the need for explanation. She caught the next train back to Moscow.

Some days after his arrest Tretyakov was interrogated for the first time by officers Vladimirov and Sagin of the NKVD. We know nothing of the methods adopted by these two officers on this occasion, though Yevgenia Ginzburg's comments are worth bearing in mind. She was interrogated in February 1937. 'By June, he [her interrogator] would be treating prisoners to the choicest gutter oaths'.[222] The first interrogation attempted to extract a confession from the prisoner. In Tretyakov's case he was supposed to confess to spying for Japan. If the prisoner attempted to deny the charges, the interrogators might quote the prisoner's friends or acquaintances, who had, he was assured, incriminated him. If the prisoner continued to protest his innocence, torture was the next step. We do not know whether Tretyakov was tortured. Meyerhold was laid on the floor and his back and the soles of his feet viciously beaten with a rubber truncheon. Then was seated on a chair and his thighs were similarly beaten. These beatings continued over several days.

The record of the interrogation of course makes no mention of any of this, nor how long the examination lasted nor whether Tretyakov at any point resisted. It is simply a seven-page, typed document, which tells an extraordinary story. Cynically, one might regard it as a sort of bio-interview.

According to the record, as soon as the examination began, he admitted spying for Japan. He said that he had been recruited by one, Mori, in Harbin in China in 1924. He explained his hostility to the Soviet state by referring to his membership of the Right Social Revolutionary group in 1917, and his struggle against the Bolsheviks

---

222 Ginzburg, Evgenia S., *op. cit.*, p. 44.

and the new Soviet regime, including acts of sabotage and other counter-revolutionary activities. He went on to oppose the Reds in Samara province, he says, and then in Vladivostok.

> *Question*: What did you do when you arrived in Vladivostok?
> *Answer*: I plunged into the corrupting environment of the interventionists, White Guards and ordinary people … My life proceeded in this environment, surrounded by crooks and various suspicious elements.

He goes on:

> In one of the card games in the Golden Horn restaurant, I lost all my money … I was standing near the game site. Suddenly a Japanese man, Adzuma, appeared near me and learning about my loss, he kindly offered me a loan. I willingly agreed to take this, and received 195 yen from Adzuma, and issued him with a receipt for this amount.

He then moves on to 1922 when, he says, he stayed with his father-in-law, Gomolitsky, in Harbin. Gomolitsky is supposed to have introduced him to the shadowy Mori, to whom Tretyakov told the story of his debt to Adzuma. Two years later, back in Harbin, Tretyakov meets Mori again, and this time Mori has on him the IOU which Tretyakov gave to Adzuma. But he refuses to return this to Tretyakov and threatens him with a scandal unless Tretyakov agrees to co-operate with him and help his intelligence work by supplying him with 'necessary information'. 'So on the one hand, my past active counter-revolutionary activity and on the other, blackmail by the dexterous use by a Japanese spy of my debt receipt, led me to the ranks of Japanese intelligence in 1924'.

In answer to further questions, Tretyakov said that he started supplying documents to Mori. When he returned to Moscow, in order to maintain contact, he agreed to be at Filippov's café on Gorky Street between 4pm and 6pm every day, drinking a glass of tea. Mori, or his surrogate, could meet him there, and they would recognize one another by an agreed password. One may interject here that this is obviously a fiction. Anyone who knows what

Tretyakov was doing in the 1920s in Moscow would realize that he simply could not have wasted two hours every day sitting in a café in Gorky Street. The wonder is how he fitted into each day everything we know he did!

The questions then lead to him expanding on various contacts and actions he professes to have been involved with, each more absurd than the last, and now sometimes laced with Trotskyism. In an interesting emendation to the record, he says: 'I considered Trotsky a great innovator who wanted to lead the country out of that stagnant ('hopeless' – crossed out by S. Tretyakov) state in which it was in my opinion. I considered it wrong that Trotsky was clamped down on and not given freedom of action'. He then says he passed over to the Japanese information about collective farms, photographs of the famous motorized sleigh ride, and his contacts in Germany, though how this could help Japan is never discussed. The invention becomes more fantastical with every question:

> *Question*: To whom did you transfer the materials?
> *Answer*: As we had stipulated, a Japanese came to meet me at the Krasnaya Zvezda Hotel in Irkutsk with an agreed password, who called himself a consular official. After making sure he was from Kurod, I handed him 21 photographs of the objects listed above.
> …
> *Question*: In Moscow did you contact Kuroda?
> *Answer*: No, in 1932 he was not in Moscow. But one day a man called me at the apartment and, on the basis of my password with Mori, suggested I go to the Savoy Restaurant. Arriving on the specified date, I met a well-dressed Chinese man who spoke excellent English at the appointed place. The Chinese man told me he came from Mori.

And so on. At the end of the interrogation, Tretyakov names five people whom, he says, '*could* be used by the Japanese' (my italics) – Boris Pilnyak, Shenshev, Lilya Brik, Anatoly Kantorovich and the theatre critic, Febral.

On 18 August Tretyakov's 'Statement' extracted from the interrogations was forwarded to Nikolai Ivanovich Yezhov, the People's

Commissar for Internal Affairs, and as such, head of the NKVD. Though called a 'Statement', it is more like a confession, and might not be out of place in a document of the Inquisition. It begins:

> Sincerely repenting before my Soviet motherland for the unheard-of atrocities committed by me against her ... I now promise to give sincere testimonies about my espionage activities ...

Then the spy story is recounted in somewhat more staid fashion. Whether it was Tretyakov himself who made this tale up, or whether it emerged from the imagination of one of the agents, cannot be known. It should be remembered, however, that Tanya, Tretyakov's daughter, stated flatly that not a word of it was true, and that the invention of the gambling debt as the trigger for this farrago of balderdash was a desperate signal to any later readers that it could not be true. No-one was more strongly opposed to gambling than Tretyakov. He never played cards.

The confession gives his supposed Japanese alias – Taska – as well as names (which had been prompted by his interrogators) of his Japanese contacts. It gives details of secret passwords, subtle forgeries and potential blackmail. Then it spells out the 'assignments' Tretyakov is supposed to have fulfilled over thirteen years and explains how contacts were made, what materials he passed on (mostly photographs) and clandestine meetings in parks. Finally, in 1935, Mori, his Japanese handler, becomes annoyed that Tretyakov refuses categorically to engage in violence, and threatens him. 'We parted coldly', the document concludes. As Elizabeth Papazian has pointed out, the whole narrative is 'worthy of a spy novel, complete with colourful bad guys, gambling, clandestine meetings at fancy hotels, and secret passwords',[223] just the kind of fiction which Tretyakov so fervently wished to be replaced by factography.

On 10 September, he was brought before a 'closed judicial meeting' of the Military College of the Supreme Court of the U.S.S.R., presided over by Comrade Kandybin, assisted by Comrades Stelmakhovich

---

223   Papazian, Elizabeth Astrid, *Manufacturing Truth*, DeKalb: Northern Illinois University Press, 2009, p. 66.

and Zhdan, with Comrade Kudryavtsev acting as secretary. The court convened at twenty-five past two in the afternoon.

> The secretary reported that the defendant had been brought to court and that no witnesses had been called in the case.
>
> The presiding judge verified the defendant's identity and asked him if a copy of the indictment had been handed over to him.
>
> The defendant answered in the affirmative. His rights in the court were explained to him and the composition of the court was announced.
>
> The defendant did not file any motions or challenge the composition of the court. At the suggestion of the presiding secretary, the indictment was read.
>
> The presiding judge explained to the defendant the essence of the charges against him and asked if he pleaded guilty.
>
> The defendant pleaded guilty which the testimony given by him at the preliminary investigation fully confirmed.
>
> The defendant answered the question of the presiding judge: was he a spy? 'That is correct'. The defendant had nothing to supplement his testimony. The judicial investigation was complete, and the defendant was allowed to speak. He asked for leniency.
>
> The court retired from the court. Upon the return of the court, the presiding judge announced the verdict.
>
> The case closed at 2.45 p.m.

The hearing had lasted for twenty minutes, and the verdict, not given in this report, was that Tretyakov, Sergei Mikhailovich, was guilty and was sentenced to capital punishment by shooting and the confiscation of all his personal property.

According to Secret Document 91.46, 'The verdict on the execution of Tretyakov Sergei Mikhailovich was carried out in the mountains' on 10 September 1937, that is, the same day as the trial.

This has usually been accepted by later commentators. However, in 1991 Tanya Tretyakova, the daughter of the accused, learned what she believed to be the truth of her father's death. After the verdict, he was taken back to his cell. On this walk, 'one step to the right or left was considered an attempt to escape'.[224] But it appears that when they reached the fourth floor of the Butyrka prison, Tretyakov suddenly broke completely free from his guards and leapt over the handrail. He fell down the stairwell, landing at ground level. He had killed himself.

---

224   Shentalinsky, Vitaly, *op. cit.*, p. 3.

CHAPTER 14.
AND AFTERWARDS

During the night of 4-5 November 1937, there was a loud knock on the door of the flat on Malaya Bronnaya Street where Olga Viktorovna, Tretyakov's wife, and his daughter, Tatyana Sergeyevna, still lived. It was the NKVD. After a further chaotic search of the flat, and the seizure of more of the flat's contents, including probably Sergei's huge photographic archive, Olga was arrested. She was dragged out and down the stairs, her head banging on the stone steps as she was pulled away. She was put peremptorily into a black raven and driven away at speed. Tanya, running down the stairs after her, was left behind. She fell to her knees on the pavement, sobbing: 'Oh God, if there is a God, help me!'

Olga Viktorovna was sentenced to five years in a labour camp, a sentence which was increased by a further four and a half years during the Second World War. In 1946 she was released conditionally, but forced to live at least a hundred kilometres from Moscow. She found work in a polyclinic in the Yaroslavl province, and then delivering mail in Pereslavl-Zalessky, north of Moscow. But in 1951, as Stalinism found renewed vigour for its terrorism, she was re-arrested and sent to northern Kazakhstan. She was only finally freed in 1954, after Stalin's death.

Meanwhile her daughter, Tanya was expelled from the aeronautical engineering college where she had been a brilliant student. This was a terrible time for her. Those who had been friends of the family suddenly no longer wished to know her: they would cross the road to avoid speaking to her if they saw her coming. Few, very few, retained any familiarity or kindness towards her. Among these must be mentioned

Sergei Eisenstein, who did go out of his way to help her, still calling her affectionately 'Baby', his nickname for her from the early 1920s when he and her father had worked together so closely.

Tretyakov's father, too, suffered greatly from the disappearance of his beloved son. His health was ravaged. In the summer of 1939 his friends, the Sokolovs, invited him to spend the summer with them at their country *dacha* at Alabino to the south-west of Moscow, where he received some comfort and could breathe fresh air. But one evening, his daughter Nina returned from a concert to find a telegram awaiting her. 'Come quickly. Your papa is very ill'. She caught a train to Alabino, ran through the forest, and found Mikhail Konstantinovich prostrate in bed. He was surrounded by the Sokolov family, but was very ill with pneumonia and running a high temperature. He was taken to the local hospital, but little could be done to help him. 'When papa's fever abated, he always asked one, just one, question: "What about Seryozha?" Each time I told him that it was a misunderstanding and would be sorted out soon'.

Mikhail Konstantinovich's illness gradually worsened over ten days till he could only move his lips and mouth his question, 'Where is Seryozha?' Nina's heartbreaking account of his end demonstrates the affection between Tretyakov and his father:

> And so the last day began. The last evening came. They gave papa medicines. I sat near his bed. With unbelievable difficulty he took my hand in his. I wrapped the blanket round him. I stroked his head, and said something affectionate. And for the last time papa moved his lips and I heard: 'Seryozha …' I felt in my heart and soul, and with every atom of my being, that the end had come and that now papa was going for ever, and that I would never see him again. And I said, choking with tears, that Seryozha was alive, that he had already come home, ill, but he was waiting impatiently for you, my own daddy, my beloved. Everything had become clear – it was a misunderstanding. It would soon be put right, my dear, and you will be together again. Papa closed his eyes and barely, barely stroked my hand. His face became peaceful like a child's. It seemed to me that he believed me. I went to the little table to pour out his medicine, but when I came back, papa lay with his eyes open, aspiring to

somewhere above. I realized that papa was no more. I want to think that papa went, believing that Seryozha was alive, and that soon they would be together. I don't remember any more.

Once someone had been declared an 'enemy of the state', Stalinism was steely in its ruthless annihilation of their life and work. Tretyakov's books were removed from libraries, withdrawn from bookshops, and suppressed. The film *A Song About Heroes* was banned in Russia in late 1937 because it had two songs by Tretyakov in it. On 17 December 1937, *Pravda* launched a vicious attack on the theatre director Vsevolod Meyerhold, including one paragraph which read: 'For several years (he) stubbornly tried to stage the play, *I Want a Baby*, by the enemy of the people, Tretyakov, which was a hostile slur on the Soviet family'.[225] When Viktor Shklovsky published his memoir, *Mayakovsky and His Circle* in 1940, the name of Tretyakov was not mentioned once, though no-one had been a closer comrade-in-arms of Mayakovsky than Tretyakov over many years. And many of his old friends and colleagues began to speculate privately. On 2 December 1937, Alexander Rodchenko wrote in his diary: 'Sergei Tretyakov has disappeared, it has been more than six months. Where is he?'[226] Walter Benjamin noted in his diary for 1 July 1938: 'Very sceptical answers are elicited whenever I touch on conditions in Russia. When I inquired recently whether Ottwald was still in prison, the answer was, "If he's still alive, he's in prison". Yesterday, (Margarete) Steffin said she doubted whether Tretyakov were still alive'.[227] And in January 1939, Bertolt Brecht jotted down without capital letters: 'nobody knows anything about tretyakov, who is supposed to have been a "japanese spy"'.[228] When he knew that Tretyakov was dead, Brecht wrote his searing poem, 'Are the People Infallible?', which begins:

> My teacher,
> My great and friendly teacher,

---

225 Braun, Edward, *Meyerhold: A Revolution in Theatre*, London: Methuen, 1995, p. 288.
226 Rodchenko, Alexander, *Experiments for the Future*, New York: Museum of Modern Art, 2005, p. 316.
227 Benjamin, Walter, *Reflections*, New York: Schocken Books, 1978, p. 214.
228 Brecht, Bertolt, *Journals, 1934-1955*, London: Methuen, 1993, p. 20.

Has been shot dead, condemned by a people's court.
As a spy. His name is condemned.
His books are destroyed. Even to speak of him
Raises suspicion, people fall silent at the mention of his name.
But what if we suppose he is innocent?[229]

In at least one manuscript version in the Brecht archive, Tretyakov's name is written at the end of the first line.

Once she was released from her prison in Kazakhstan, Olga Tretyakova began to campaign for her husband's 'rehabilitation'. She gathered testimonies from many of those who knew and worked with him: Boris Agapov, the writer of *ocherki*, Grigory Alexandrov, the actor who had starred in *A Wise Man* as far back as 1923, the poet Nikolai Aseyev whose association with Tretyakov had begun in the heyday of Futurism, Lev Kassil, a former member of *LEF* and *New LEF* who had worked most closely with Tretyakov on the radio broadcasts on national holidays from Red Square, Viktor Pertsov, Tretyakov's friend and biographer of Mayakovsky, the novelist Marietta Shaginyan, and several others. In their testimonies, they all admitted their surprise that Tretyakov had been arrested. Kassil, in his statement, noted that 'in everyday life, he was humble, an opponent of all sorts of excesses and easy behaviour', adding 'I know that Tretyakov not only did not play cards, but also discouraged others from doing this. Also Tretyakov was not fond of drinking alcohol'. Aseyev asserted that 'over the entire period of my acquaintance with Tretyakov, I can characterize him as a politically seasoned, disciplined person'. On 11 January 1956, the USSR Military Prosecutor's Office in the person of Lieutenant Colonel Kopasov, concluded that 'there is no objective evidence of guilt in this case'. Tretyakov was 'rehabilitated'.

Yet, as Frank Westerman has noted, 'when the families of "wrongfully accused writers" received their certificates of rehabilitation in 1956, it had been a pivotal moment; it could not, however, bring back books boiled to a pulp'.[230] The next tasks for Olga Viktorovna,

---

229 Brecht, Bertolt, *Collected Poems*, New York: Liveright Publishing, 2019, p. 754.
230 Westerman, Frank, *Engineers of the Soul*, London: Vintage Books, 2011, p. 291.

therefore, were to try to recover copies of her husband's books in order to place them in the central Lenin Library in Moscow, and to have his works reissued. In 1962, on the seventieth anniversary of his birth, a 'Tretyakov evening' was held at the Moscow Writers' Club, when many who knew him – the actor Maxim Shtraukh, the writer Viktor Pertsov, Ivan Martovitsky of the Communist Lighthouse collective farm, and others – spoke of the importance of his work and the magnetism of his personality. And when the Communist Lighthouse celebrated its jubilee, Olga Viktorovna was welcomed as an honoured guest.

The same year, a collection of three of his prose works – *Den Shihua, People Who Shared a Bonfire* and *A Country at the Crossroads* – was published in a fat volume, introduced by Viktor Pertsov, and this was followed four years later by a much smaller volume in which appeared three of his plays – *Are You Listening, Moscow?!, Gas Masks* and *Roar, China!* – together with several memoirs by people who had known Tretyakov and a selection of photographs of the original productions of the plays. Meanwhile, from 1952, translations of his works had been published in the German Democratic Republic (East Germany), Czechoslovakia, Poland and other European countries. *Roar, China!*, directed by Horst Zankl, was presented at the Theatre am Neumarkt in Zurich in 1975, *I Want a Baby* was staged at the Badisches Staatstheater in Karlsruhe in the Federal Republic of Germany in 1980, and at the Berliner Ensemble in 1989, directed by Gunter Schmidt, and finally in Moscow at the Teatr u Nikitskikh Vorot in 1990. It had been published in Russia at last in 1988. And in 1989 an international conference was held at the University of Birmingham under the title, 'Tretyakov – Brecht's Teacher'.

His work, in other words, was never totally lost. And it continued to interest international scholars, especially perhaps German scholars in the 1960s, 70s and 80s. In East Germany, for instance, a good deal of significant work was done by Fritz Mierau. He translated and edited at least two of the plays and several of the prose works. He also wrote about Tretyakov's creative ideas and theories, in *Erfindung und Korrektur: Tretjakows Ästhetik der Operativität*, published in 1976, in which he emphasized Tretyakov's continual willingness to move forward from one theoretical position to the next. In West Germany, Heiner Boehncke addressed the problem of the continuing relevance of Tretyakov's ideas: 'We study Tretyakov because we believe that in his theoretical and literary works he represented an aesthetic and political position that can reveal the general and the essential contradictions underlying the struggle for the new art', he explained.[231]

In the twenty-first century, Tretyakov's thinking has seemed ever more relevant in a postmodern world. Thus, as well as particular studies of aspects of his work, learned journals have produced special issues devoted exclusively to Tretyakov, including the Fall 2006 issue of *October* and the 2019 issue 103-105 of *Russian Literature*. 2019 was indeed something of a bumper year for Tretyakov: it saw major publications in Germany (*Ich Will Ein Kind!* in two volumes, edited by Tatjana Hofmann and Eduard Jan Ditschek for Kulturverlag Kadmos, Berlin), and in Britain (*I Want a Baby and Other Plays*, edited and translated by Robert Leach and Stephen Holland and published by Glagoslav Publications).

What this biography of Tretyakov has aimed to show is that, despite the desperate cruelty of his end, his ideas are still alive and his works are still worth reading or staging. The relevance of a great writer like Tretyakov is never dead.

---

231   Stephan, Halina, *'LEF' and the Left Front of the Arts*, Munich: Verlag Otto Sagner, 1981, p. 196.

Robert Leach with Tanya Tretyakova, 1991.

EPILOGUE.
DUSTPRINTS BY ROBERT LEACH

Notes Towards the Presentation of an Affidavit

(First published as a pamphlet by Q.Q. Press, Rothesay, Isle of Bute, 2004.)

PREFACE

The witness in the poem is Tatyana Sergeyevna Gomolitskaya-Tretyakova, known as 'Tanya', daughter of the radical poet and playwright, Sergei Tretyakov, who, with his comrades, imagined the Bolshevik Revolution would change the world.

Tanya was just a young child when the Revolution happened; and one of her earliest memories was of being bound to Mayakovsky by a belt, and then suspended over the stage in Meyerhold's production of *Mystery Bouffe*, while the poet declaimed his visionary lines. Mayakovsky, together with Tanya's father, and Alexander Rodchenko, Sergei Eisenstein and others, went on to produce the radical magazine, *LEF*, 'the Left Front of Art'.

Later, during the Great Purges, Tretyakov was arrested and committed suicide in prison (though Tanya didn't know how he had died till after 1990); and her mother was then taken and incarcerated in a labour camp, and not released till after the death of Stalin. She died within ten years of her release, leaving Tanya alone, seeking a living in the increasingly desperate late days of Communism. When Yeltsin supplanted Gorbachev, and the Communists were ousted, Tanya was radiantly happy ...

R.L.

1. THE SUMMONS

It was very quiet that afternoon,
As if a ghost were packing its things away,
Or dust was settling.
It almost seemed I'd been

Summoned through Moscow's
Sun-dried, tram-lined *pere-uloks*,[232]
Past a tease of nervy hooded crows,
Exhausted billboard exhortations,

And grey grass-stubble dying
In the no-man's-land between road and pavement.
Trans-continental journeyer, too hot
In Moscow-designated overcoat,

Was I witness or juror?
My destination: a mellowed building,
Flatted, with wide worn stairs –
Enough to make Raskolnikov laugh.

Floor four: a knock, and the papery sound
Of the old lady shuffling to unlock.
Hard chairs, a faded table-top,
Tall cadaverous window:

We watched sun and crows and dust motes
Float. Her face was chamois yellow,
Her nose almost a hawk beak, her voice
Like a quill scratching parchment

Quietly. So. Where to begin?
Black bread, red jam
Wait on a worn oilcloth, while

---

232 A side street.

Her *papirossy*[233] flare and glower,

And like a knife-edge cleaving onions
Her words
Slice the twentieth century,
Summoning

Through the squirming shifty tendrils
Of brackish *papirossa* fumes
Whole decades
To history's dock.

2. THE EVIDENCE

(a) The Twenties

Act One,
        when life
                was a drama
And the drama
                was life.
                      Begin!

High in the flies
              above the boards –
We look down,
        wait
            to enter –
An entry
        never dreamed of
                before!

Belt buckled
        in the yellowy dark –
The two of us –

---

[233] *Papirossa*, a particularly noxious Russian cigarette.

        I, a girl
                in pigtails,
He,
    poet
        of the revolution –
Whisper,
        giggle
                like we were both kids –
While down below
                declamations bellow!

Like para jumpers
                we're launched.
The belt goes taut.
                We dangle –
Silhouettes
        in the shaft of light,
We want
        to brighten
                the world!

Volodya Mayakovsky's words
                        boom out –
A new kind
        of poetry –
                a fresh beginning –
A new broom –
        the tap of truth
                turned full on!
Act One!
    A new world,
        please!

In the People's House
    (where we live,
        a dozen families
             to a house),
The lino'd stairs

                    clunk and bang
                                under the boots
                                            of friends.

They're making
            a magazine
                        of a new kind.

'Sasha!'
        'Seryozha!'
                'A comma's missing,
Gone astray!'
            'Taken
                    by a mouse!'
'Soon
        there won't be
                    any mice!'
'The mice
        'll have their own
                        Revolution!'

Rodchenko,
            Mayakovsky
                        compare sketches.
Tretyakov's poems march.
                    Eisenstein's hair
                                is flying!

We eat air,
            drink life,
                    feast
On a fabulous
                fricassee
                        of hope!
'Volodya!'
            More boots
                    on the echoey stairs.
'Kolya!'

This way
> for a montage of attractions.

New words,
> new minted,
>> new printed.

* * *

My father, Tretyakov,
Kindly and tall,
Also plays the piano.
The notes shimmer,
And topple
In a *galop*
Which had delighted
Even Skryabin …
In the *rondo*,
The top notes touch
The farthest frontiers
Of the Milky Way.

(b) The Thirties

June 1937: Papa
Is in hospital, ill
With exhaustion. Mama
Works in the kitchen, while
Tanya holidays in the south
With the Komsomol.[234]

Swimming, table tennis, dormitories
Are arranged for the young citizen.
Then a letter, in Mama's

---

234 The Communist youth movement, somewhat comparable to the Boy Scouts or Girl Guides.

Writing: 'Something's arisen.
Come home, please,
Immediately'. No reason.

And for hundreds of kilometres
The brown train chuffs
And clanks. Flies buzz.
An old man sleeps, his mouth
Wide open. Tanya
Clutches her handkerchief.

Water clouds Mama's glasses
In the steamy kitchen.
It runs down the lenses
Like tears. 'They seized him –
Papa. He's arrested'.
No reason.

* * *

– Ready, mates!
Rifle butt on wrenched wood.
Dog whines
To be entering.
– Open up! Police!
What time is it?
– Now! Out the way!
Four in the morning.

Doors swing back,
Eyes swivel, look.
Rapid panting
Of a hunting dog.
– Be still.
– Don't move!
A strained voice
Through yellow teeth. A nod.

Heart cartwheels.
– It's a mistake,
An error,
My husband's been taken!
Her voice
Withers
To silence,
Words godforsaken.

Paper piles scattered,
Half a loaf kicked under a chair.
Dust tangles set dancing
By spurting dog piss.
– What's here?
– And that?
– Where?
– What's this?

So – a blow,
And a blob of blood, red.
Hair spread like a web.
Flesh squeezed.
Hound's tail morse-codes danger,
Whacking nervy leathered knees.
The woman's voice: Don't!
Don't, please!

They drag mama downstairs.
No time
Even for an overcoat.
On each cold step,
Her head bangs
A devil's drumroll.
Against yellow headlights, she is
A momentary silhouette.

Air frozen with icy stars.
Rasp of engine starter.

Exhaust tumbles out
Tendrils of terror.
Shadows – dog and guard,
And she –
Cram in. Doors slam,
And effortless as error,

The brakes ease, and the car
Snakes away into the night
On smooth rubber wheels.
I'm on the hard pavement on my knees:
– Oh, God, up there!
If you are up there,
Help me!
Please!

(c) The Forties

I'm ashamed to name my destination.

I huddle down, head low, one
Among the shapeless hordes of grey souls,
Heads down, destinations
Places of shame. We're each
As like as the backs
Of the devil's playing cards …
The train
Steals out of the backend of Moscow,
Embarrassed to carry us. Grey steam
Squirts out like spite,
Hovers in tree branches, dissolves,
Probably preferring
Non-existence.

Relentless beat of steel wheels –
Demented clank on steel track –
Lament – redeem – sleep …

Eyelids, shamed with life,
Slither and close,
The dead beat of the steel wheels
Still squeals,
Still reels …
But feels
Nothing.

Jabbed awake,
Bellies empty, eyelids
Crusted concrete,
We shift like litter

On the wind-raked platform,
Under Five Year slogans[235]
To free the dream.
But our dreams
Drift to despair,
Where bare nightmare
Stares: an old man, white hair
Astir like angry herons –
'Lazy good-for-nothings!
Why don't you walk?
Enemies of the people.
Enemies of me!
Whores! Wasters! Traitors!'

We push up stiff
Onto floorboards
Scabbed with dried earth.
The cart starts,
Black squelchy tyres
Knobble and buck
Over dun orange clods.

---

235   *Five Year slogans*, billboard slogans urging people to fulfil Stalin's Five Year Plan.

Grass – coarse yellow stalks,
Stiff, defiant; mud-washed sky snarling;
And a sheaf of crows
Beating away from the
Cold tree knuckles
Where there's no shelter.

Bones bang,
Joints scrape,
And tease the unforgiving aches.
A dry wind
Sands lips, alarms
Red, dry eyes,
Bruised arms.
And the white-haired cart driver
Whines like Charon.[236]

The sun slithers away into evening.

A little stream, dark, almost dry,
And barbed wire enclosures
– Hell's slums –
Where wasted humans
Hang like rags – forgotten washing
On an infernal line:
Here – drab dog eyes peer out
Under a pall of frown,
Seeking, seeking …
There – lips stretch mouth
To a howl, hair
As if ironed on the skull …
And another – forehead furrowed
Like railway lines …
Then – grey face, grey eyebrows,
Grey straws of hair blown out, about …
A woman, head atilt,

---

236   *Charon*, ferryman who, in Greek mythology, transported the damned to hell.

Like a child looking for friendliness …
A wrinkled mouth –
A spring flower unwatered …

And more,
And more …
Moaning from unendurable unending
Pain of here-hell,
Where another face
I hardly know
Gazes. Whisper:
'Mama?'
Her cell self,
Lips listless,
Eyes empty,
Scarecrow arms askance.

We greet
Through wire,
Try to smile,
Unable to pretend
All's well, knowing
This is hell.

(d) The Fifties

On the day Sergei Prokofiev[237] died
The orchestras of the Soviet Union were quiet.
Factory hooters never blew,
The feet of marching men were mute.

But not for Prokofiev, no crows croaked,
Clanky trams and circus clowns
Stood dumb as fog. Not for him,
All Russia, exhaled like a punctured tyre.

---

237 The Russian composer who died on the same day as Stalin.

Wind over *versts*[238] of steppe dropped,
Trans-Siberian engines died.
Party conclaves muffled whispers.
Russia: and silence sighed.

Koba[239] was gone.

But if you listened hard enough,
You might have caught that day
The squeak of a gulag gate
Opening ... very faint, very far away.

(e) The Seventies

Hit by hope
Like a stone from the sky;
Knowing now
Life keeps on
Even when hope is blizzarded;
Man being man
Even as animal, scavenging.

Father: suicided –
Fourth floor, Butyrka Prison.
Mother: broken
On the wheel of weariness.
Old aged at fifty.

But even alone,
Dinner's to be got.

The hunt begins.
No fanfared tantivvy
This rime-ridden dawning –

---

238 Russian measure of distance, approximately two-thirds of an English mile.
239 Stalin's nickname.

Thick gloves, boots,
A pair of scarves,
And a worn woollen coat
Heavy as history:
A tram ride to treasure.

Under trees where grass has gone to mud,
And mud to frozen bolls of stumble-block earth,
Two men –
Ear-flaps down, breath cumuli vanishing,
Swifting into nothingness,
And a smell of sad ammonia hanging.
But they have
Nothing left. No salt. No sprats.
No fungi, or fowl, or sweetbreads. Try
Flat twenty-three,
Behind Taganka.

Which has a door
Strapped in steel armour,
And a peep-hole
Where an eye like a stickleback swims.
Prey.

Inside – brown, heavy doors,
Huddles of people in drab wool coats,
Shapes against the window light.
A smell of frying, black tobacco smoke,
Throat-corroding alcohol.
And boxes.

There, elegantly bent,
A squirm of silver –
Sardine. Several sardines
In several boxes.
Some without heads,
Some blood-smeared,
Some with saliva-slippery scales,

Sold by a man with a mulberry face-stain,
With thin-rimmed specs
Not used for looking at you.

The hunt's end: sardines –
Three or four – miniatures –
Meat from a remote ocean,
Today's menu.

And, grasped tight through sullen streets,
Up wide, worn stairs to where,
Sizzled in lard,
They're laid on a plate
On the oilcloth table top,
Beside a slice of onion,
Black bread, red jam –
The silver centrepiece
Of a feast for one.

The window steams up.
Droplets form, insignificant as hope,
And slither down the panes
Like tears.

(f) The Nineties

On streets bloody as their banners,
The bad-tempered and blind, the fanatics and cranks
Grappled, grasped, vomited spite,
Till the Union sank.

Communists-turned-Fascist, democratic demagogues,
Comrades, tyrants, the bossy and the bossed
Had played out their Snakes-and-Ladders of greed:
Now they'd lost.

Bullets scatterpranced, people stumbled and screamed;
Terror blinded – how to flee? Where to go?
One man, white hair quiffed, silhouette on a tank,
Shouted: No!

And in her fourth floor hideaway,
Tanya, eighty-something, shuffled to the door,
Met me with a wet eye, her soft skin
Downed with warmth.

– He's a good man, she said.
– A liberator.
I've read his life. Now you'll see –
Things'll get better.

Arms akimbo, *matryoshka*-silhouette,[240]
She sucked her *papirossa*, ready to debate;
Then set out black bread, red jam,
And we ate.

3. THE SUMMING-UP

Waking from a dream,
There's an instant
When you seem to have a choice –
Stay in the dream, or
Emerge to reality.

Does the same pertain
In life? When the phone rang
Could I have done nothing,
Let the thing ring; or
Did I have to answer?

---

240 A jolly Russian peasant woman doll, which contains within itself a series of other, similar dolls, each smaller than the last.

Svetlana, Tanya's friend:
'It's Tanya', she says.
I draw a breath.
'Jumped from the window.
Fourth floor. Immediate death …'

And instantly my mind
Strips out a mackerel backbone
Of testament and judgment:
The smoke dissolves; the dream
Is not redeemed.

'Is that all?' In the no-reply,
A ghost could have packed its bags.
You could have heard the dust fall.
Or perhaps such silence is usual
In a trans-continental call.

INDEX

Agapov, Boris, 197, 201, 257
Aksyonov, Ivan, 72
Alexander III, tsar, 15-16
Alexandra, tsarina, 45
Alexandrov, Grigory, 87-88, 164, 257
Alpers, Boris, 108
Alymov, Sergei, 54
Andreyev, Leonid, 29, 55
Aristotle, 220
Arvatov, Boris, 66, 87, 91-92, 97, 179-180, 193, 194
Aseyev, Nikolai, 14, 42, 54, 55, 59, 60, 63, 65, 72, 73, 91, 97, 175, 178, 257
Aseyeva, Oksana, 55, 63, 65
Auden, W.H., 241
Augustus, emperor, 208
Avdiyenko, Alexander, 227
Avetov, Mikhail, 54

Babel, Isaac, 197, 246
Balieff, Nikita, 31
Balmont, Konstantin, 23, 31
Balzac, Honoré de, 214, 228
Barr, Alfred Hamilton, 163
Becher, Johannes, 206, 221, 222
Bely, Andrei, 31
Benjamin, Walter, 9, 213-214, 215, 216, 256
Benn, Gottfried, 213
Beresnev, Nikolai, 68
Biberman, Herbert, 131
Blok, Alexander, 23, 29, 31, 116
Blyum, Vladimir, 158
Bobrov, Sergei, 72
Bode, Rudolf, 84
Boehncke, Heiner, 258

Bolshakov, Konstantin, 34, 35
Brecht, Bertolt, 9, 150, 189, 206, 207, 208-209, 212fig., 215, 216-218, 219-221, 222, 229, 231, 233, 234, 235, 236, 237, 238, 240, 241, 242, 243, 256, 257, 258
Breshko-Breshkovskaya, Yekaterina, 46, 50
Brik, Lilya, 59, 184, 237, 250
Brik, Osip, 14, 84, 91, 95, 97, 98, 99, 109, 172, 175, 177, 178, 184
Bubnov, Andrei, 143
Bukharin, Nikolai, 96, 143, 182, 245
Burian, Emil, 240, 241
Burlyuk, David, 32, 34, 54, 55, 56, 59
Busch, Ernst, 235, 237

Čapek, Karel, 240
Caruso, Enrico, 189
Chalyapin, Fyodor, 31
Chekhov, Anton, 29, 88, 115
Chekhov, Mikhail, 201
Chernov, Viktor, 46, 48, 50
Cheshikhin, Vsevolod Yefgrafovich, 20
Chesterton, Ada, 207, 243
Chiang Kai-shek, 140, 141
Chiaureli, Mikhail, 163, 171
Chopin, Frédéric, 21
Chorny, Sasha, 25
Chukovsky, Kornei, 63
Churchill, Winston, 28
Chuzhak, Nikolai, 53-54, 59, 60, 63, 66, 91, 95, 97, 99, 188
Claudel, Paul, 72
Clurman, Harold, 231
Craig, Edward Gordon, 231
Crommelynck, Fernand, 69

Darwin, Charles, 150
Den Shi-hua, 119, 133fig., 135-139
Diderot, Denis, 240
Dikovsky, Sergei, 197, 198
Döblin, Alfred, 213
Doone, Rupert, 241
Dos Passos, John, 206
Dostoyevsky, Fyodor, 32, 210
Dreiser, Theodore, 206
Drevin, Alexander, 246
Dudow, Slatan, 215, 229, 241

Eiduk, Alexander, 246
Eisenstein, Mikhail Osipovich, 16
Eisenstein, Sergei, 9, 15, 16, 66, 68-70, 75, 83, 84, 86, 87-88, 89, 90, 91, 99, 101, 102, 105, 106, 108, 111, 117, 118, 126, 139, 140, 154, 157, 164, 168, 194, 209, 210, 215, 227, 235, 241, 255
Eisler, Hanns, 171, 172, 207, 221, 229, 232fig., 241
Erdman, Nikolai, 201

Fabergé, Peter Carl, 31
Fadeyev, Alexander, 205, 237
Feng Yu-xiang, 141
Ferdinandov, Boris, 111
Feuchtwanger, Lion, 238-239
Fevralsky, Alexander, 70, 72
Fischer, Ruth, 237
Flynn, Errol, 169
Fokin, Mikhail, 31
Foregger, Nikolai, 75, 111
Frinovsky, M., 247
Fyodorov, Vasily, 82, 126, 129, 130

Galin, Boris, 201
Gan, Alexei, 172
Garin, Erast, 70, 71
Gens, comrade, 158
Ginzburg, Yevgenia, 224, 226, 227, 245, 248
Gippius, Zinaida, 31
Glazunov, Alexander, 31
Glizedr, Judith, 101
Gnedov, Vasilisk, 32
Gog, Gregor, 208, 221
Gogol, Nikolai, 157
Goldberg, Boris, 160, 161

Goldberg, Mikhail, 197
Golke, Gustav, 237
Gomolitskaya-Tretyakova, Olga Viktorovna, 13, 54, 55-56, 57, 58, 59, 62, 63, 65, 113, 122, 123, 131, 141, 159fig., 162-163, 176, 184, 206, 207, 229, 235, 236, 243, 247, 248, 254, 257, 258
Gomolitskaya-Tretyakova, Tatyana Sergeyevna, 11, 13, 14, 45, 54, 55, 57, 58, 59, 62, 63, 65, 113, 122, 141, 144, 162-163, 184, 224, 231, 236, 243, 247, 248, 251, 253, 254, 260fig.
Gomolitsky, Viktor, 54, 57, 58, 59, 122, 249
Goncharova, Natalia, 33
Gorelik, Mordecai, 241
Gorky, Maxim, 25, 29, 170fig., 201, 202, 243, 245
Gorlov, Nikolai, 96
Gorodetsky, Sergei, 73, 76
Gozzi, Carlo, 216
Graf, Oscar Maria, 206, 221, 237, 243
Granach, Alexander, 231
Gromov, Boris, 182
Grosz, George, 216
Gvozdev, Alexei, 104

Hašek, Jaroslav, 240
Hawley, Edward C., 120
Heartfield, John, 206, 221, 228, 238
Hikmet, Nazim, 73, 75
Hitler, Adolf, 100, 207, 210, 216, 237, 238, 240
Hube, Ernst, 216
Hughes, Howard, 180

Ibsen, Henrik, 72
Ignatiev, Ivan, 33
Ihering, Herbert, 207
Ilf, Ilya, 197
Ilin, M., 205
Ilinsky, Igor, 69
Isherwood, Christopher, 241
Ivanov, Vyacheslav, 31
Ivens, Joris, 171
Ivnev, Rurik, 34

Joyce, James, 228, 229

Kalatozov, Mikhail, 163, 167, 169

Kamenev, Lev, 142, 187, 223, 245
Kameneva, Olga, 73
Kamensky, Vasily, 91
Kammerer, Paul, 150
Kandybin, comrade, 251
Kantorovich, Anatoly, 250
Karakhan, Lev, 113
Karsavina, Tamara, 31
Kassil, Lev, 183, 257
Katershinsky, 132
Kazantzakis, Nikos, 131
Kazbegi, Alexander, 167
Kerensky, Alexander, 46, 47, 48, 50
Kerzhentsev, Platon, 201
Kharms, Daniil, 201
Khenkin, comrade, 158
Khidzikata, Iosi, 131
Khlebnikov, Viktor, 32, 33
Khokhlova, Alexandra, 167
Khrisanf, *see* Zak, Lev
Kirov, Sergei, 223
Kirsanov, Semyon, 99, 175, 233
Kisch, Egon Erwin, 240
Kitayev, Zyama, 88
Klutsis, Gustav, 91, 92, 246
Knorin, Vilhelm, 234, 246
Kolchak, Alexander, 51-52, 53
Koltsov, Mikhail, 229, 236
Kopasov, lieutenant colonel, 257
Korolenko, Vladimir, 25
Kortner, Fritz, 241
Kracauer, Siegfried, 213
Krasnoshchyokov, Alexander, 59
Kropotkin, Pyotr, 46, 115
Kruchyonykh, Alexander, 32, 33, 34, 91, 95, 98, 156
Kruchyonykh, Alexei *see* Kruchyonykh, Alexander
Krupskaya, Nadezhda, 101
Kudryavtsev, comrade, 252
Kuleshov, Lev, 91, 167, 175
Kun, Béla, 234
Kushner, Boris, 91, 97
Kuzmin, Mikhail, 23, 29, 31

Lācis, Anna, 215, 233
Lania, Leo, 131
Larionov, Mikhail, 33
Lavinsky, Anton, 91

Lavrenov, Boris, 34
Lazo, Sergei, 56
Lenin, Vladimir, 48, 59, 62, 64, 95, 96, 97, 100, 101, 104, 111, 116, 164, 165, 185, 216, 223, 238
Lentulov, Aristarkh, 33
León, Maria Theresa, 206, 207
Leyda, Jay, 167, 171
Leyko, Marija, 246
Lissitzky, El, 154, 156, 160, 161, 233, 238
Liszt, Franz, 21, 224
Litvinov, Maxim, 234
Lodder, Christina, 117, 172
Lorre, Peter, 209
Losey, Joseph, 231
Lu Hsi-kuei, 117
Lu Xun, 116
Lukács, Georg, 181, 214-215, 220
Lunacharsky, Anatoly, 14, 48, 62, 76, 96, 98, 143, 170fig., 201, 210
Lvov, prince, 47, 48

Machavariani, V., 190
MacLeish, Archibald, 241
Malevich, Kasimir, 33
Malraux, André, 231
Malthus, Thomas, 150
Mamontov, Savva, 31
Mandelstam, Osip, 227
Mardzhanishvili, Konstantin, 167
Margolin, S., 104
Markov, Vladimir, 34, 36-37
Martinet, Marcel, 75, 77, 78
Martovitsky, Ivan, 163, 189, 233, 258
Marx, Karl, 137, 164
Mass, Vladimir, 201
Matyushin, Mikhail, 33
Mayakovsky, Vladimir, 9, 13-14, 32, 33, 35-36, 40, 42, 49, 58, 59, 60, 62, 65, 72, 84, 91, 95, 97, 99, 116, 152, 154, 163, 170fig., 175, 176, 178, 184, 188, 190, 191, 197, 201, 237, 246, 256, 257
Mei Lan-fang, 117, 230fig., 232fig., 234-235
Meller, Elfrida Emmanuilovna, *see* Tretyakova, Yelizaveta Emmanuilovna
Meller, Emma Emmanuilovna, 17
Meller-Zakomelsky, Baron A.N., 27
Merello, Rafael Alberti, 206
Merezhkovsky, Dmitry, 31

Meyerhold, Vsevolod, 9, 31-32, 49, 62, 65, 69-70, 71, 72, 73, 75, 76, 80, 82, 83, 84, 86, 91, 108, 129, 130, 144, 154, 156, 157, 158, 160, 161, 175, 207, 209, 233, 235, 248, 256
Michaëlis, Karin, 207, 243
Mierau, Fritz, 258
Mikhoels, Solomon, 233
Mirbeau, Octave, 72
Morozov, Savva, 68
Muchanov, Leonid, 197

Napier, William John, 129
Neher, Carola, 217, 233
Nekrasov, Nikolai, 182
Nemirovich-Danchenko, Vladimir, 31
Nexø, Martin Anderson, 208, 221
Neznamov, Pyotr, 54
Nezval, Vítězslav, 240
Nicholas II, tsar, 30, 45, 49
Nicholls, Simon, 44
Nijinsky, Vaslav, 31
Novitsky, comrade, 158

Ognyov, Nikolai, 205
Okhlopkov, Nikolai, 217, 231, 233, 241
Olbracht, Ivan, 240
Oleinikov, Nikolai, 246
Olesha, Yuri, 197
Orlov, Alexander, 245
Ostrovsky, Alexander, 75, 83, 86, 87, 154
Otto, Teo, 231
Ottwald, Ernst, 206, 215, 229, 256
Ovid, 23

Palmov, Viktor, 54, 55, 59, 60, 62, 63
Parry, Albert, 218
Pasternak, Boris, 14, 91, 95, 175, 227
Pavlova, Anna, 31
Pertsov, Viktor, 95, 178, 188, 201, 240, 257, 258
Petrov, comrade, 157
Petrov, Evgeny, 197
Petrusov, Georgy, 238
Pieck, Wilhelm, 233
Pikel, comrade, 161
Pilnyak, Boris, 59, 246, 250
Piotrovsky, Adrian, 246
Piscator, Erwin, 207, 215, 217, 221, 231, 241

Pletnev, Valery, 157
Plieksans, Janis, 16
Plievier, Theodore, 206, 221
Ploetz, Alfred, 150
Pogodin, Nikolai, 233
Polonsky, V.P., 145
Popova, Lyubov, 69, 80
Pound, Ezra, 210
Prishvin, Mikhail, 201
Pudovkin, Vsevolod, 165
Pushkin, Alexander, 32, 73, 151, 177
Pyatakov, Georgy, 245

Rachmaninov, Sergei, 31
Radek, Karl, 135, 203, 228, 245
Rafes, comrade, 157
Rainis, *see* Plieksans, Janis
Raskolnikov, Fyodor, 157, 158, 160, 161
Ravich, comrade, 157
Reed, John, 48, 49
Reich, Bernhard, 215, 231
Reissner, Larissa, 157
Richter, Hans, 207, 217
Robeson, Essie, 231
Robeson, Paul, 231
Rodchenko, Alexander, 14, 91, 93fig., 95, 99, 172, 173, 175, 178, 198, 256
Room, Abram, 158
Rosenberg, Hanne, 233
Rostotsky, B., 55, 88
Rozer-Nirova, N.A., 155, 158
Rozovsky, Mark, 11, 108
Rybakov, Anatoli, 197, 225

Schiller, Leon, 131
Schmidt, Gunter, 258
Schumann, Robert, 224
Severyanin, Igor, 23, 32
Seyfullina, Lidia, 205
Shaginyan, Marietta, 201, 257
Shakespeare, William, 71
Shelley, Percy Bysshe, 35
Shengelaya, Nikolai, 163, 167
Shershenevich, Vadim, 32, 34-35, 40, 42
Shklovsky, Viktor, 14, 33, 35, 43, 91, 95, 167, 175, 177, 178, 184, 220, 256
Shostakovich, Dmitri, 191, 227-228
Shtempel, Boris, 54
Shtempel, Vera, 54

Shtraukh, Maxim, 86, 258
Shub, Esther, 165, 166, 167
Skryabin, Alexander, 21, 31, 43-44, 224
Smirnov, Ivan, 188
Smyshlyayev, Valentin, 68
Socrates, 216
Sokolnikov, Grigory, 245
Sokolov, Mr, 17
Sologub, Fyodor, 31
Solzhenitsyn, Alexander, 227
Stalin, Joseph, 9, 43, 53, 59, 130, 140, 141, 142, 165, 167, 168, 187, 188, 196, 199, 223, 226, 227, 228, 237, 238, 245, 246, 254
Stanislavsky, Konstantin, 18, 30, 31, 68, 201
Stavsky, V.P., 233
Steffin, Margareta, 231, 233, 256
Stelmakhovich, comrade, 251
Stepanova, Varvara, 91, 95
Sternberg, Fritz, 209
Stetsky, Alexei, 202, 203
Steyerl, Hito, 180
Strasberg, Lee, 231
Stucka, Peteris, 16, 21
Sukhovo-Kobylin, Alexander, 69
Sun Yat-sen, 116, 118, 119, 121, 132, 135

Tabidze, Titsian, 246
Tatlin, Vladimir, 33
Tchaikovsky, M.I., 247
Telingator, Solomon, 238
Terentiev, Igor, 156, 157, 158, 160-161
Tess, Tatyana, 197
Thälmann, Ernst, 100, 237
Tigel, Shie, 131
Toller, Ernst, 206, 229
Tolstoy, Alexei, 25
Tolstoy, Leo, 32, 115, 168, 177, 202, 214, 228
Tretyakov, Lev Mikhailovich, 18, 24fig., 63, 65
Tretyakov, Mikhail Konstantinovich, 17-18, 20, 23, 27, 40, 41fig., 63, 65, 163, 255
Tretyakov, Oleg Mikhailovich, 18, 25, 63
Tretyakov, Valery Mikhailovich, 18, 20, 63
Tretyakov, Vyacheslav Mikhailovich, 18, 26, 27, 63
Tretyakova, Natalia Milkailovna, 18, 27, 42, 43, 44-45
Tretyakova, Nina Mikhailovna, 11, 18, 20, 27, 43, 44, 65, 173, 183, 247, 255
Tretyakova, Olga Viktorovna *see* Gomolitskaya-Tretyakova, Olga Viktorovna
Tretyakova, Tatyana, *see* Gomolitskaya-Tretyakova, Tatyana Sergeyevna
Tretyakova, Yelizaveta Emmanuilovna, 17-18, 20, 25, 26, 40, 43, 44, 45, 63
Tretyakova, Yevgenia Mikhailovna, 18, 20, 65
Trotsky, Leon, 51, 73, 75, 76, 80, 82-83, 92, 96, 97, 100, 101, 140, 142, 143, 155, 182, 185, 191, 250
Turgenev, Ivan, 210

Vachnadze, Nata, 220
Varminsky, Janos, 131
Velizhev, Alexander, 76
Vertinsky, Alexander, 44-45
Vertov, Dziga, 91, 92, 166
Vishnevsky, Vsevolod, 163
Vvedensky, Alexander, 201

Wagner, Richard, 20
Weigel, Helene, 209, 216
Whitehorn, lieutenant, 120-121
Wolf, Friedrich, 204fig., 207, 208, 221, 222

Yablonovsky, Sergei, 33
Yeryomin, Yury, 238
Yevreinov, Nikolai, 31
Yezhov, Nikolai, 250
Yuan Shihh-kai, 118

Zaichikov, Boris, 69
Zak, Lev, 34
Zankl, Horst, 258
Zetkin, Klara, 222
Zhdan, comrade, 252
Zhdanov, Andrei, 202, 203
Zinoviev, Grigory, 187, 223, 245

I Want a Baby and Other Plays
by Sergei Tretyakov

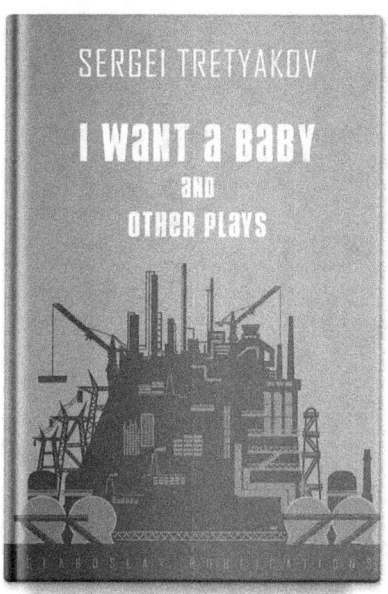

When Sergei Tretyakov's ground-breaking play, *I Want a Baby*, was banned by Stalin's censor in 1927, it was a signal that the radical and innovative theatre of the early Soviet years was to be brought to an end. A glittering, unblinking exploration of the realities of post-revolutionary Soviet life, *I Want a Baby* marks a high point in modernist experimental drama.

Tretyakov's plays are notable for their formal originality and their revolutionary content. *The World Upside Down*, which was staged by Vsevolod Meyerhold in 1923, concerns a failed agrarian revolution. *A Wise Man*, originally directed by the great film director and Tretyakov's friend, Sergei Eisenstein, is a clown show set in the Paris of the émigré White Russians. *Are You Listening, Moscow?!* and *Gas Masks* are 'agit-melodramas', fierce, fast-moving and edgy...

Buy it > www.glagoslav.com

MEBET

by Alexander Grigorenko

Mebet concerns a man of the taiga, a hunter, in a moving narrative that blends ethnographic detail, indigenous mythology, and the snowy landscapes of the Arctic. The protagonist is a Nenets, a member of one of the peoples who call far northern Russia home. Dubbed "The Gods' Favorite" for his seeming imperviousness to harm or grief, Mebet earns the envy and derision of his fellow tribesmen. He lives that carefree and blessed life until his old age, when one day a supernatural messenger arrives to lead him to where the realms of the living and the dead meet. Now the Gods' Favorite must confront the price to be paid for his elevated position, and a series of dread trials that lie in store.

Called a dark and terrifying fantasy and the Nenets *Lord of the Rings* by Russian writer and journalist Sergey Kuznetsov, Grigorenko's *Mebet* is a powerful story about humanity, personal fate, and responsibility. Leading Russian literary critic Galina Yuzefovich welcomed *Mebet* as a true epic for the Nenets, a book that is profound, thrilling and vibrant. Whether the book will earn that lofty place within Nenets culture remains to be seen, but the very publication of the book marks a watershed event.

Buy it > www.glagoslav.com

ORCHESTRA
by Vladimir Gonik

This novel by Russian novelist and screenwriter Vladimir Gonik is set in eleven countries around the world.

Orchestra is based on documentary materials: the author has delved into the archives and met eyewitnesses, and now he recounts secret operations that took place across the globe in the second half of the twentieth century.

The novel tells of certain little-known and mysterious events, some of which the author was personally involved in, and it is a story of extraordinary human lives, and of course, love…

Buy it > www.glagoslav.com

A Brown Man in Russia
Lessons Learned on the Trans-Siberian
by Vijay Menon

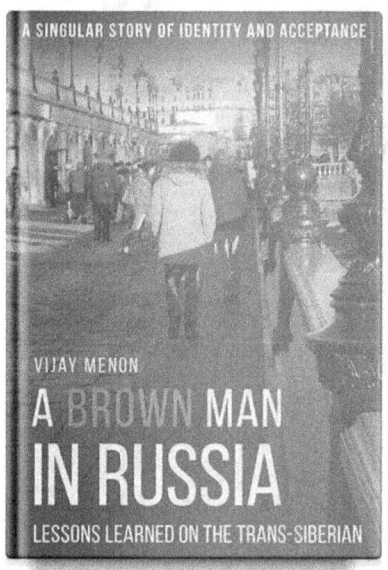

A Brown Man in Russia describes the fantastical travels of a young, colored American traveler as he backpacks across Russia in the middle of winter via the Trans-Siberian. The book is a hybrid between the curmudgeonly travelogues of Paul Theroux and the philosophical works of Robert Pirsig. Styled in the vein of Hofstadter, the author lays out a series of absurd, but true stories followed by a deeper rumination on what they mean and why they matter. Each chapter presents a vivid anecdote from the perspective of the fumbling traveler and concludes with a deeper lesson to be gleaned. For those who recognize the discordant nature of our world in a time ripe for demagoguery and for those who want to make it better, the book is an all too welcome antidote. It explores the current global climate of despair over differences and outputs a very different message – one of hope and shared understanding. At times surreal, at times inappropriate, at times hilarious, and at times deeply human, *A Brown Man in Russia* is a reminder to those who feel marginalized, hopeless, or endlessly divided that harmony is achievable even in the most unlikely of places.

Buy it > www.glagoslav.com

Leo Tolstoy – Flight from Paradise
by Pavel Basinsky

Over a hundred years ago, something truly outrageous occurred at Yasnaya Polyana. Count Leo Tolstoy, a famous author aged eighty-two at the time, took off, destination unknown. Since then, the circumstances surrounding the writer's whereabouts during his final days and his eventual death have given rise to many myths and legends. In this book, popular Russian writer and reporter Pavel Basinsky delves into the archives and presents his interpretation of the situation prior to Leo Tolstoy's mysterious disappearance. Basinsky follows Leo Tolstoy throughout his life, right up to his final moments. Reconstructing the story from historical documents, he creates a visionary account of the events that led to the Tolstoys' family drama.

Flight from Paradise will be of particular interest to international researchers studying Leo Tolstoy's life and works, and is highly recommended to a broader audience worldwide.

Buy it > www.glagoslav.com

Glagoslav Publications Catalogue

- *The Time of Women* by Elena Chizhova
- *Andrei Tarkovsky: A Life on the Cross* by Lyudmila Boyadzhieva
- *Sin* by Zakhar Prilepin
- *Hardly Ever Otherwise* by Maria Matios
- *Khatyn* by Ales Adamovich
- *The Lost Button* by Irene Rozdobudko
- *Christened with Crosses* by Eduard Kochergin
- *The Vital Needs of the Dead* by Igor Sakhnovsky
- *The Sarabande of Sara's Band* by Larysa Denysenko
- *A Poet and Bin Laden* by Hamid Ismailov
- *Zo Gaat Dat in Rusland* (Dutch Edition) by Maria Konjoekova
- *Kobzar* by Taras Shevchenko
- *The Stone Bridge* by Alexander Terekhov
- *Moryak* by Lee Mandel
- *King Stakh's Wild Hunt* by Uladzimir Karatkevich
- *The Hawks of Peace* by Dmitry Rogozin
- *Harlequin's Costume* by Leonid Yuzefovich
- *Depeche Mode* by Serhii Zhadan
- *Groot Slem en Andere Verhalen* (Dutch Edition) by Leonid Andrejev
- *METRO 2033* (Dutch Edition) by Dmitry Glukhovsky
- *METRO 2034* (Dutch Edition) by Dmitry Glukhovsky
- *A Russian Story* by Eugenia Kononenko
- *Herstories, An Anthology of New Ukrainian Women Prose Writers*
- *The Battle of the Sexes Russian Style* by Nadezhda Ptushkina
- *A Book Without Photographs* by Sergey Shargunov
- *Down Among The Fishes* by Natalka Babina
- *disUNITY* by Anatoly Kudryavitsky
- *Sankya* by Zakhar Prilepin
- *Wolf Messing* by Tatiana Lungin
- *Good Stalin* by Victor Erofeyev
- *Solar Plexus* by Rustam Ibragimbekov
- *Don't Call me a Victim!* by Dina Yafasova
- *Poetin* (Dutch Edition) by Chris Hutchins and Alexander Korobko

- *A History of Belarus* by Lubov Bazan
- *Children's Fashion of the Russian Empire* by Alexander Vasiliev
- *Empire of Corruption: The Russian National Pastime* by Vladimir Soloviev
- *Heroes of the 90s: People and Money. The Modern History of Russian Capitalism* by Alexander Solovev, Vladislav Dorofeev and Valeria Bashkirova
- *Fifty Highlights from the Russian Literature* (Dutch Edition) by Maarten Tengbergen
- *Bajesvolk* (Dutch Edition) by Michail Chodorkovsky
- *Dagboek van Keizerin Alexandra* (Dutch Edition)
- *Myths about Russia* by Vladimir Medinskiy
- *Boris Yeltsin: The Decade that Shook the World* by Boris Minaev
- *A Man Of Change: A study of the political life of Boris Yeltsin*
- *Sberbank: The Rebirth of Russia's Financial Giant* by Evgeny Karasyuk
- *To Get Ukraine* by Oleksandr Shyshko
- *Asystole* by Oleg Pavlov
- *Gnedich* by Maria Rybakova
- *Marina Tsvetaeva: The Essential Poetry*
- *Multiple Personalities* by Tatyana Shcherbina
- *The Investigator* by Margarita Khemlin
- *The Exile* by Zinaida Tulub
- *Leo Tolstoy: Flight from Paradise* by Pavel Basinsky
- *Moscow in the 1930* by Natalia Gromova
- *Laurus* (Dutch edition) by Evgenij Vodolazkin
- *Prisoner* by Anna Nemzer
- *The Crime of Chernobyl: The Nuclear Goulag* by Wladimir Tchertkoff
- *Alpine Ballad* by Vasil Bykau
- *The Complete Correspondence of Hryhory Skovoroda*
- *The Tale of Aypi* by Ak Welsapar
- *Selected Poems* by Lydia Grigorieva
- *The Fantastic Worlds of Yuri Vynnychuk*
- *The Garden of Divine Songs and Collected Poetry of Hryhory Skovoroda*
- *Adventures in the Slavic Kitchen: A Book of Essays with Recipes* by Igor Klekh
- *Seven Signs of the Lion* by Michael M. Naydan

- *Forefathers' Eve* by Adam Mickiewicz
- *One-Two* by Igor Eliseev
- *Girls, be Good* by Bojan Babić
- *Time of the Octopus* by Anatoly Kucherena
- *The Grand Harmony* by Bohdan Ihor Antonych
- *The Selected Lyric Poetry Of Maksym Rylsky*
- *The Shining Light* by Galymkair Mutanov
- *The Frontier: 28 Contemporary Ukrainian Poets - An Anthology*
- *Acropolis: The Wawel Plays* by Stanisław Wyspiański
- *Contours of the City* by Attyla Mohylny
- *Conversations Before Silence: The Selected Poetry of Oles Ilchenko*
- *The Secret History of my Sojourn in Russia* by Jaroslav Hašek
- *Mirror Sand: An Anthology of Russian Short Poems*
- *Maybe We're Leaving* by Jan Balaban
- *Death of the Snake Catcher* by Ak Welsapar
- *A Brown Man in Russia* by Vijay Menon
- *Hard Times* by Ostap Vyshnia
- *The Flying Dutchman* by Anatoly Kudryavitsky
- *Nikolai Gumilev's Africa* by Nikolai Gumilev
- *Combustions* by Srđan Srdić
- *The Sonnets* by Adam Mickiewicz
- *Dramatic Works* by Zygmunt Krasiński
- *Four Plays* by Juliusz Słowacki
- *Little Zinnobers* by Elena Chizhova
- *We Are Building Capitalism! Moscow in Transition 1992-1997* by Robert Stephenson
- *The Nuremberg Trials* by Alexander Zvyagintsev
- *The Hemingway Game* by Evgeni Grishkovets
- *A Flame Out at Sea* by Dmitry Novikov
- *Jesus' Cat* by Grig
- *Want a Baby and Other Plays* by Sergei Tretyakov
- *Mikhail Bulgakov: The Life and Times* by Marietta Chudakova
- *Leonardo's Handwriting* by Dina Rubina
- *A Burglar of the Better Sort* by Tytus Czyżewski
- *The Mouseiad and other Mock Epics* by Ignacy Krasicki
- *Ravens before Noah* by Susanna Harutyunyan

- *An English Queen and Stalingrad* by Natalia Kulishenko
- *Point Zero* by Narek Malian
- *Absolute Zero* by Artem Chekh
- *Olanda* by Rafał Wojasiński
- *Robinsons* by Aram Pachyan
- *The Monastery* by Zakhar Prilepin
- *The Selected Poetry of Bohdan Rubchak: Songs of Love, Songs of Death, Songs of the Moon*
- *Mebet* by Alexander Grigorenko
- *The Orchestra* by Vladimir Gonik
- *Everyday Stories* by Mima Mihajlović
- *Slavdom* by Ľudovít Štúr
- *The Code of Civilization* by Vyacheslav Nikonov
- *Where Was the Angel Going?* by Jan Balaban
- *De Zwarte Kip* (Dutch Edition) by Antoni Pogorelski
- *Głosy / Voices* by Jan Polkowski
- *Sergei Tretyakov: A Revolutionary Writer in Stalin's Russia* by Robert Leach
- *Opstand* (Dutch Edition) by Władysław Reymont
- *Dramatic Works* by Cyprian Kamil Norwid
- *Children's First Book of Chess* by Natalie Shevando and Matthew McMillion
- *Precursor* by Vasyl Shevchuk
- *The Vow: A Requiem for the Fifties* by Jiří Kratochvil
- *De Bibliothecaris* (Dutch edition) by Mikhail Jelizarov
- *Subterranean Fire* by Natalka Bilotserkivets
- *Vladimir Vysotsky: Selected Works*
- *Behind the Silk Curtain* by Gulistan Khamzayeva
- *The Village Teacher and Other Stories* by Theodore Odrach
- *Duel* by Borys Antonenko-Davydovych
- *War Poems* by Alexander Korotko
- *Ballads and Romances* by Adam Mickiewicz
- *The Revolt of the Animals* by Wladyslaw Reymont
- *Liza's Waterfall: The hidden story of a Russian feminist* by Pavel Basinsky
- *Biography of Sergei Prokofiev* by Igor Vishnevetsky

More coming . . .

GLAGOSLAV PUBLICATIONS
www.glagoslav.com

www.ingramcontent.com/pod-product-compliance
Lightning Source LLC
Chambersburg PA
CBHW071726080526
44588CB00013B/1917